CHURCH AS

CHURCH AS A SAFE PLACE

A Handbook

Confronting, Resolving and Minimizing Abuse in the Church

"It's not finding a safe place,
but being safe people, like Jesus."

Peter R. Holmes
Susan B. Williams

Authentic

MILTON KEYNES ● COLORADO SPRINGS ● HYDERABAD

First published 2007 by Authentic Media
9 Holdom Avenue, Bletchley, Milton Keynes, Bucks, MK1 1QR, UK
1820 Jet Stream Drive, Colorado Springs, CO 80921, USA
OM Authentic Media, Medchal Road, Jeedimetla Village,
Secunderabad 500 055, A.P., India
www.authenticmedia.co.uk
Authentic Media is a division of IBS-STL U.K., limited by
guarantee, with its Registered Office at Kingstown Broadway,
Carlisle, Cumbria CA3 0HA. Registered in England & Wales No.
1216232. Registered charity 270162

British Library Cataloguing in Publication Data

A catalogue record for this book is available from the
British Library
ISBN-13: 978-1-86024-603-6

Cover Design by fourninezero design.
Print Management by Adare Carwin
Printed and bound in Great Britain by J.H. Haynes & Co.,
Sparkford

Contents

Our Thanks!

As with anything in life, we cannot do it alone, but this is particularly true of this book. So we would like to say a huge thank you for the support of a range of people, both sides of the Atlantic, who have brought life to these pages.

The question of who had the idea first is now part of the mythology of this book's origins. We do, though, need to thank Malcolm Down of Authentic for encouraging the idea in the early stages. If he had not done so, this book would not now exist. His support is seconded by Annie Frazer-Simpson, a key member of our community, who met with, drew out of folk, and then edited a number of the stories that we are using in this volume. She has been a true professional.

When we had completed a first draft of the book, it was then read by several brave souls in our own church, Christ Church Deal (CCD). Among these were Simon Clarke, Jane Dryden, Nicola Carnall, Kate Riseley, Patrick Davidson and, being a glutton for punishment, Annie! This has helped us enormously as we have sought to give an honest reflection of some of our experiences together, as well as giving credence to our own observations and suggestions. We have included some of their comments in the final text.

But this is also a "mid-Atlantic" book. So we have to thank Dr. Jules Glanzer, Prof. Mary Kate Morse, the Rev. Derry Long and Norma Davidson, all from the USA, who did an outstanding job in talking through with us their impressions and concerns. We would also like to thank the Rev. Mike Gammill, who spent over an hour on the telephone from Houston giving us very helpful and positive feedback, and Carolyn Glaser, who made a number of encouraging comments.

The single biggest thanks must go to the dozens of anonymous contributors who shared their painful and traumatic stories, which now form the core of this book. The stories alone do great credit to the book, and we are very grateful to all those who walked the road with us, allowing us to listen to them, share their pain and record their stories.

A final thanks (Peter) must go to my wife Mary and my son Christopher, who did not flinch at the idea of such a book when I first mentioned it, and have been nothing but encouraging ever since.

I (Susan) want to thank the women of Christ Church Deal, who have accepted me as I am, and who have supported me through the ups and downs of giving birth to this book.

Peter R. Holmes
Susan B. Williams
Deal, Kent, UK

A HEALTH WARNING

*If you have been abused in or by the Church
you may find this book challenging.
It is written in a way that will help you think through the issues,
though you will need to be willing to confront them
and learn how to give what happened to Christ.*

Introduction

In essence, our message in this book is simple. Human nature is the same the world over, despite the veneer of language and culture. We are all looking for relationships and environments that are safe, that give us life. But the nature of abuse and the failure to create a safe place are also the same from one situation to the next. Only the expression, means, and impact of abuse are different, depending on people and circumstances. Unless we proactively choose to find ways of making churches safer places, they will naturally take on the character of the surrounding environment.

We offer this handbook as a small step in a dialogue on the subject. We hope that others will enter the discussions and develop a range of more detailed comment so that we may make Tomorrow's Church a safer place for both members and newcomers.

No one is really qualified to write this book because at one time or another all of us have behaved in ways that have made others feel less safe. We—Susan and Peter—have been aware of this for many years, but even so we were shocked as we learned how many people have been hurt in churches. In fact, we have been very shocked. Let us tell you what happened.

We had heard from Malcolm Down, the manager of Authentic Media, UK, that they needed a progress report on a book we were writing for them. It was to be called *Abuse in the Church*. What we did not admit to him at the time was that the book was off to a slow start. We had an outline, lots of illustrations and ideas, but had made little further progress. So we decided to call a focus group of folk in our church—Christ

Church Deal (CCD)—to help explore the subject. We invited some long-in-the-church Christians, and a few self-confessed former Christians. About twenty-five of us met here in Waterfront, my wife Mary's and my (Peter's) home, and spent two and a half hours talking about the experience of being abused in and by the Church.[1] Some of the stories were shocking, others just sad. But everyone in the meeting, one way or another, at some time in their pasts, had been a victim of abuse in the Church. There were no exceptions even though we had chosen each of the contributors on a relatively random basis.

At the end of the meeting, after everyone had left, we—Mary, Susan and Peter—continued sitting in our lounge, stunned by the history of toxic pain, damage, trauma and its abuse that folk were still carrying from their pasts. But we were also very shocked about something else. We realized that in our initial idea of calling a meeting, we had unconsciously made the assumption that anyone who has been part of congregational life for any length of time must have been abused. To our dismay, this assumption turned out to be true of this group that we had brought together. In our dazed state we began to ask: What does this say for the wider Church? Is this true for *everyone* who is or has been a Christian? We had already admitted this was true for the three of us, but . . .

So we decided to put our shocking observation to the test, and over the next month or two, wherever we met Christians on our international travels and workshops, we told them we were writing a book on abuse in the Church and asked if they had any experiences they would like to write up for us. One declined because he was too scared to write about what had happened to him. Another told us the conflict was ongoing, having followed the couple to their new church. The rest said they were willing to write something so we agreed to drop them a line or have our narrator, Annie, meet with them.

During that couple of months we did not find one person who had been in the Church for any length of time who had not been abused in some way. We even had a nine-year-old girl, who knew nothing of the book, casually start telling us about how she didn't feel she was welcome at her previous Sunday school and how upset that made her feel! Admittedly, some of the abuse was "minor," but at the other end of the spectrum some folk would now class themselves as "former Christians" because the abuse had been so bad. It may not be true that everyone has felt abused in church. But it does seem to apply to many.

Something else just as shocking also emerged as we talked to people. We have held thousands of pastoral counseling sessions over many years, and worked with hundreds who have been abused (many of them in business and in their personal lives, not just in the Church!), but we had never really noticed before that for many this was the first time they were admitting to the fact of the abuse. A large number had never acknowledged that what had been happening to them had actually been abusive. Instead, many had resigned themselves to accepting that this was normal. Some needed permission to call abuse abusive.

Then we went through another stage in the evolution of this book. We had originally been writing a book on "abuse in the Church." But the more we thought and wrote, the more we realized that this was not what we wanted to say, and it wasn't what the publisher wanted, either. As specialists in congregational formation and the theology, psychology, and relational social processes that help people become *ekklesia*, we realized that we wanted to talk about how congregational life could be safer. Rather than yet another book on abuse in the Church, we wanted to write a more positive book, a book about creating a "social Place"[2] that would be safe for those committed to it. We wanted to talk about a place where the culture and environment of the Body of Christ would be a catalyst to "meeting Jesus" on a journey of experiential redemption. We wanted to be able to help Christians learn from the numerous mistakes we had made ourselves, and were hearing about, so that churches would be places where Love[3] prevails.

For many of us, abuse has become synonymous with church life. We are unable any longer to distinguish easily between what is normal and what is abusive. We have become anesthetized to it all, losing sight of God's perspective, where Love and honor should be the norm. So enlisting the help of Mary and our able story editor, Annie, we began putting pen to

paper. Please join us on this journey and share in our prayer
that together we may all help to make Tomorrow's Church
safer.

It was while we were writing this book that our publisher
was approached by several former members of our community. They made a number of outrageous accusations against
our congregation. They said that we were a cult, that I (Susan)
was a witch, and I (Peter) was leading this deceit. The accusations focused around the suggestion that we were a secret,
devil-worshiping coven masquerading as a Christian faith
community. None of these accusations had any evidence in
fact. But as we go to press the accusations continue, so, as if we
were needing further qualification for writing such a book,
they have ungraciously given it to us. Sadly, they have conducted the whole matter in a vindictive and malicious manner,
with no regard to Christian conduct, for example, our duty to
love our enemies, as commanded by our Lord.[4]

The Biblical Framework for This Book

From earliest Scripture we find the theme of safety: "But you
will cross the Jordan and settle in the land the LORD your God
is giving you as an inheritance, and he will give you rest from
all your enemies around you so that you will live in safety"
(Deut. 12:10). This theme is followed through in numerous
other verses (1 Kgs. 4:25; Ps. 4:8; Prov. 3:23, etc.). But the Old
Testament predicts a shift from a physical place where safety is
enforced by military power to a person who will be safe for
Israel: "In his days Judah will be saved and Israel will live in
safety. This is the name by which he will be called: The LORD
Our Righteous Savior" (Jer. 23:6). Through this initiative of
Messiah coming, Israel will find safety (Jer. 32:37–41; 33:16),
and Christ Himself claims to be this safe place: "While I was
with them, I protected them and kept them safe by that name
you gave me . . ." (Jn. 17:12). Through His finished work, the
atonement, He becomes, Savior, Redeemer, Protector, and Lord.

So we invite you to come on a Biblical journey with us to
meet a person who is Christ. From Him, we will suggest, we

all need to continue growing to increase our capacity to be like Him so that we, like Christ, may become safe people. These themes will be expanded in Chapter 2.

Introducing Ourselves and Christ Church Deal

No one in our faith community here in Deal, in east Kent, UK, would say that we are yet the safe place that we are talking about in this book. We work hard to make our community safe but we ourselves are still some distance from this goal. As imperfect beings, we are not ideal material for such high goals! But since 1998 we have grown together and written a history that, despite mistakes, has been pleasing to us. In nearly a decade we have grown from a couple of dozen people to over 150 plus kids. We are enjoying the journey of learning to be who Christ would have us be, both individually and as a congregation.

Deal is a small coastal town with a long history. Its primary way of life used to be the navy, fishing, and smuggling! It is a lovely place to live. We are not on a main road to anywhere important so the only people who arrive to add to the 24,000 of us who already live here are those who have a reason to come.

Within a year or so of beginning to meet as a local church, we realized that we were not just a congregation, but were also becoming a therapeutic community (TC).[5] I (Peter) have written elsewhere about how this happened and described the characteristics of a TC.[6] In essence, it is a group of people who, within a health-care context, and through the talking cure method, seek mutually to ease one another's pain and toxic history. By being a church as well as a TC, we are also able to invite God's Love into this process so as to help people grow into wholeness in Christ.

On this journey of helping to run such a therapeutic faith community, we have learned a lot about what is safe and what is not safe. But we have done this while working with highly sensitive, damaged, and abused people. It has sometimes been very hard to get it right. For instance, a number of times we struggled to find a balance between the needs of the individual and what was best for the community. We have also sometimes had to follow professional best practice with some members, when what we wanted to do was far more unconventional and higher risk. This cauldron of pained learning has led us to numerous observations of what is more safe, and what is not.

In this book we could have been more specific about the mistakes we have made together at CCD and the numerous ways that we have sought to resolve them. We would not have been short of material! We have talked a lot about our faith community in other books, however,[7] and after some thought we decided that this was not so relevant for you, as the reader of this book. So here, taking a less confessional approach, we will be drawing on all our experience over the last few decades of what safe and unsafe is for damaged people.

In this process we have been greatly helped by our own research. My (Peter's) studies have focused on both the theology and psychology of the idea of therapeutic faith community, with a foray into the sociology of spirituality. I (Susan) have specialized in social psychology and the social processes facilitating change-enabling, developing a synergistic model for human well-being in community. Much of what we will be exploring in this book is the distillation and application of these learning journeys, integrated with the personal experiences of many other people. What applies in our own personal setting, we have come to realize, could be helpful in the wider Church.

Introductory Comments on Our Approach

Our intention for this handbook is that it should be a broad landscape on the subject of how to make the Church a safer place. To help us, we have used our own experience and other people's stories. The diversity of stories, spread across the denominations and international mission, has drawn us to the sad conclusion that the abuse we speak of occurs throughout the Church, as it occurs in wider society. Though the book talks a lot about "abuse in the Church," we do not in any way want to judge the Church. Instead, it is our desire to suggest that for some people the Church is not much safer than society as a whole. We will be presenting evidence suggesting that unless it makes positive efforts to change, the Church will reflect the culture it is in. So we will be making numerous suggestions on how faith community might become safer.

Connected to this is our decision to talk in generalizations. Since the problems seem to stretch across the whole Church, we did not feel that it was appropriate to place the book in one tradition or to be specific about individual churches or whole denominations. We are both of a European Evangelical background, but our stories are not just from Evangelical Church members. Instead, we will speak in general terms about the "Western Church," focusing on the European and North American parts of the communion of faith. Please accept our generalizations, and our apologies ahead of time if you struggle with this.

We could have written an academic tome. I (Peter) have already written such text books, and I (Susan) am just completing mine! But instead we decided to make the book available to a wider readership, with only a modest bibliography. Virtually every paragraph could have been supported with academic data or evidence, but we have felt this to be unnecessary to make our points. Some of what we are saying others have already said in a more academic context. Other things we believe we may be saying for the first time. Even though short, the bibliography will lead you into a wealth of interesting further reading.

The other key decision we made at an early stage was to write a *handbook*. This means that the text is written in a series of short chapters, each with a specific theme, its own case studies and a concluding range of questions that allow you, the reader, to think more about the matters we are covering. You can dip and dive in and out of the text as you please. You do not necessarily have to read the whole book. By making this a handbook, we have also had in mind its use for small groups, congregations and pastoral training. We hope it will be used in these ways. For instance, individual stories could become case studies for group discussion. It is intended to be a resource book that you can refer to as and when you wish.

Throughout the text we have made a range of positive comments or "guidelines." Although these are not intended to form a comprehensive plan, they do begin to outline what can be done to avoid such abuses happening again. We have imagined a church, "Tomorrow's Church," but more in a practical than an idealistic sense. This is a make-believe congregation that we would all probably want to be members of, a church that is successfully becoming a safe place for its members. We have imagined this future congregation, and commented on what its members might expect from each other and their leadership. On occasions we speak in a "prophetic" sense that we believe will resonate with most readers.

At the end of each chapter you will find a list of questions for you to think about or use in a group or congregational setting. They are not intended to be exhaustive, but to open up some of the key themes we are focusing on. You may also want to write your own questions, but those provided are, we hope, a useful starting point.

You will see that throughout the book we have avoided a dogmatic definition of abuse. We know that this is going to frustrate some readers so we apologize in advance. The reason is simple. Like beauty, abuse is in the eye of the beholder. It is the individual who feels hurt who subjectively decides that there has been abuse. For anyone else to then tell them they haven't been abused would feel like abuse! In our own ministry, if someone comes to us saying they have been hurt or abused, we will first help them express how they feel, then indicate how they can give the pain to the Lord. In our support of them we do not judge whether what occurred was abusive. We just seek to help them find healing. So we see abuse as any hurt that might be interpreted as abusive by the person concerned. This creates a safe place for them. Also, if the person is committed to finding healing from that "abuse," then defining whether it was abusive or not becomes largely irrelevant.

Connected closely to this, a number of times we say that a person can deal with abuse *therapeutically*. But we do not refer to this in detail. Footnotes lead to further reading, teaching, and training that will help those suffering abuse. In our wider ministry we offer a range of resources in the form of books, tapes, and workshops supporting those who feel they need help in letting go of personal historic damage.[8] I, Peter, have on occasions touched into the profound pain of abuse. I have also sensed how the Lord must feel because of the abuse of the Bride by the Bride: abuse such as rejection, isolation, fragmentation, arrogance, and self-righteousness, to name but a few examples.

Some Comments on the Use of the Stories

(Do feel free to move on to the next section, "Our Personal Comments," if you are not so interested in the methodology behind this book . . .)

In looking at the subject of abuse and the need to make the Church safer, we have made some basic assumptions about the stories we are using. To begin with, we have assumed that the Church is a victim of behavior patterns within our wider culture. Abuse is part of modern society, and sadly the Church is not exempt. But because of the "God factor," the Church has added its own brand of abuse, making the Church still more unsafe. This book both illustrates and expands on aspects of abuse unique to the Church, and considers how it might now respond.

But we have gone further. We felt that such a book needed to be well illustrated. So we invited people to write their personal experiences of how they have been abused. Many found it difficult even to think about this abuse so we recruited a member of our community, Annie, as our story editor. Digital recorder in hand, she met with a number of people and very ably "talked" the stories out of them. She then transcribed these, and gave them back to each person to check that the stories were a true reflection of what they remembered. Only then did we use them.

Other stories came to us typed or emailed. We condensed some, and divided others into shorter specific subjects or incidents. We then returned our drafts to be checked. Other stories are reminiscences of our own personal experience. In all cases, the names and locations have been changed. But in every case, though sometimes unbelievable, each of the stories is authentic—as genuine, that is, as human memory can make them.

The issue of memory is very complex, and is hotly debated in areas such as jurisprudence. Every one of us subconsciously rewrites our history over time, and in doing so often makes changes. Some research has suggested that within ten months of an event our memories may only be 25 per cent accurate.[9] Had we taken a more academic approach to this subject, we would have needed to make a whole range of qualifications to support our methodology and use of memory. Instead, following a narrative therapy tradition, we have accepted what people have recalled. If you are a social psychologist, therapist or counselor unfamiliar with this approach, and have reservations, we apologize. What we are saying is that people sought safety in the Church and did not find it. From their perspective they were hurt by these events, and this is how they now remember them.

Using a narrative tradition, we therefore chose not to attempt to verify the stories independently. In deciding this, we were very aware that we were getting only one side of the story. The other side may well help explain some of the events, and maybe even change the details of what happened. Our reason for not doing this is simple: we do not need to. This book is written from the perspective of those who found the Church unsafe so does not need a response from the "abuser." Where reconciliation and restoration of relationship could happen, we have encouraged and noted this. But we are taking the stories at face value. Since some details have been changed, no repercussions are expected.

At the end of many of the stories there is a short postscript: a brief account of subsequent events or a comment on how the person has dealt with the abuse. Often we (Peter and Susan) are familiar with the outcomes because we have been involved therapeutically with the person, and although space does not permit extended notes, we have felt it helpful to "finish" the story.

A Personal Comment from Peter

Committing myself to writing this book, felt like walking through a minefield. How can you write a book that talks about abuse in churches, illustrated by dozens of stories from a range of Church backgrounds, and still remain friends with the wider Church? I began to feel a "them and us" type of discomfort.

So after agreeing to the book, I panicked. I had accepted that I would be speaking on behalf of all those I had talked to or ministered to over the years who had been hurt by the Church. But how would this make others feel as they read it? Especially, how would other church leaders respond? What would they think of me? Would they perceive me as judging them? I realized that I did not want to be ostracized by the wider Church simply because I had sought to articulate what abuse is and isn't. I found myself in a deep quandary as I thought through the consequences of writing such a book.

I decided that the first thing I needed to do was to go through a personal period of retrospection and examine where I really stood on the abuse done to me over the years. Sadly, this has been extensive. In this sense, I am well qualified to write this book. I needed to satisfy myself that I was not still carrying any hurt, bitterness or desire for revenge for what had happened to me. This proved a difficult path, involving me in several "sorry" conversations with people, and a re-giving to the Lord of all that has happened in my eventful life. I began to accept that throughout our lives all of us have a similar need for times of reflection and repentance.

But I had a deeper problem. My own life has broken, damaged relationships in it. Even though I have tried very hard, I have not always been able to stay in relationship with everyone. Some people have just not wanted to know me after there has been hurt, misunderstanding, mistakes or tragedy. With others I have made serious mistakes. So although I have gone great distances in resolving difficulties, I have not always been successful. In some situations I still feel the accusing finger pointing at me, "You hypocrite!" I tend to agree. Some people have focused their anger on me, and in some instances this may have been just. Does that disqualify me from writing such a book? After much heart searching I came to the conclusion that it does not. It just means that I must remain mindful that I have been both abuser and abused, that I have been on both sides of the relationship.

No one is exempt from abuse or from being abusive. We may like to think that we have never been that bad, or done such things, but we probably have. One of the difficulties is that abuse means different things to different people in different situations. What is abusive for one will be normal or acceptable behavior to another. So writing a book like this would be a challenge for any person.

These thoughts have led me to the conclusion that none of us gets it right all the time. I am personally ashamed of this. For instance, I have a letter in front of me written by a man who has left our congregation. He documents a list of things that happened to him while he was a member of CCD. In addition, he cites a range of changes that need to be made in the community. I agree with him on a number of counts. I hope to stay in open relationship with him, but he may not want this. I have to accept it.

Likewise, in *Rapha* (our workshops in which we learn together to hear, interpret, and apply the healing word of God) and in our Life Giving Trust workshop and training ministry, we have not always been wise with those attending workshops or in our presentation of material. For instance, a friend, who is an international Christian leader, listened to some of my tapes and expressed concern that the teaching could give the impression that we think we are a better type of church than any other. Along similar lines, when we started Christ Church, some more traditional congregations found it hard to understand us, and on our side we were less than wise, making little effort to remain in open relationship with them. What I am saying is that at times neither our community nor I have responded in mature ways. Where I have been able to, I have said sorry.

So in seeking to prepare myself to write this book, I have had to do a great deal of soul searching, and some issues remain unresolved. But I decided that these things did not actually disqualify me from writing; they could even enrich the material if I wrote in full awareness of my own humanity. I leave you, the reader, to come to your own conclusion.

A Personal Comment from Susan

As I was preparing to make my own contribution to this book, I had a terrible shock. I had known of mistakes I had made in my ministry. I could recall times when I had spoken without love, times when I had said something unwise or had miscommunicated. I was also aware of times when something I had done had felt hurtful to others. But I guess I felt somewhat removed from most of it. I would not really have called it abusive. I was not ready for what was about to happen.

Over a period of several months I discovered that there were some in our own congregation who were feeling deeply hurt by things I had said and done or had omitted to say and do. They felt I had abused them. In addition, there were some who were feeling deeply hurt by others in the community, and had expected me to do something about it. I had not. So they also were feeling hurt by me, abandoned in their pain.

In the past I would have excused myself. I would have assumed that they were over-reacting. I would have reminded myself why I had acted the way I had and gone over the facts that they weren't aware of. I would have cognitively protected myself from their feelings. Perhaps I'd have said sorry, sorry that they felt hurt. But that would have been as far as it went. But this time those defense mechanisms felt shallow and unacceptable. These were people who were hurting, and they felt I had added to their hurt. My self-justification felt shallow, arrogant, even pharisaical.

I guess this book has been the Lord's opportunity to teach me something I wish I'd learned many years ago—that when someone feels hurt by me I must allow myself to meet them in their pain. I need to listen deeply. Even if I don't agree rationally with what they are saying, they need me to weep with them (sometimes literally) and say a heartfelt sorry to both them and the Lord. So over these last few months I have had much weeping, honest words, and openness. I have discovered that if I let it, my heart can break for people who I've hurt. I've had to learn that it is partly my response that makes it safe for others to admit their hurt and let it go.

It hasn't just been me, of course. The Lord has been asking many of us to face the reality of the pain we have brought into one another's lives. Often it has been entirely unwitting and almost always without intention. But a lack of intent doesn't change the reality of the pain that the other person feels.

But there is a problem. There are those who aren't ready to let go of their hurt. Do I rush to weep with them, too, even though it feels premature? Is my "sorry" a way of trying to manipulate them into responding in the way I need them to? Each situation needs its own unique wisdom. Sometimes I feel compelled to ring someone who I know is feeling hurt by me. At other times Love seems to suggest it is kinder to wait. What of those who aren't able to forgive? Do I avoid them, judge them, fear them? How best to Love? Have I taken on board too much blame, too much responsibility for failure and wrongdoing that I may be blamed for but was not mine? These are complex questions. But I have to confess that I'd rather live engaging the pain now than claim a righteousness that the Lord doesn't agree with.

Of course, there are so many times over the years when I myself have been deeply hurt by fellow church members and leaders. Some of the abuse has been extreme and I wish I'd had a book like this to help me through the trauma. It may have given me courage to honor myself in situations where I was being deeply dishonored, and to seek out a supportive friend.

Most of all, I need the opportunity to learn more about how to live in a way that offers Christ's safety in a hurting world. How can we offer the Love of Christ to one another in times of deep pain? If the anguish in this book helps us on this journey, then perhaps together we can all contribute something to making Church a safer place.

In Summary

In writing this book we are both pleading with you as the reader not to act in a way that judges us. Please bear in mind our own tarnished humanity as authors, and our desire to live at peace with everyone as much as we are able! Read the book and only then decide if we have made a good case.

As Christians we have a duty to ensure that all misconduct is kept away from the doors of the Church so that we can make it a safer place for all of us. This is complicated by the fact that some past Church traditions and practices may no longer be considered "safe" by postmodern people. Contemporary people will not tolerate what some of us have thought of as normal. Good though many of our traditions and values were in their time, they may no longer be appropriate. We will be illustrating this point at various places in the book. To welcome the unchurched we may need to make some changes.[10] They sometimes step inside a traditional church only to be upset by what they find. They quickly leave.

Although conceding that we are seeking to respond to contemporary values, we would not want to associate ourselves with those who would dismiss Confessional or traditional Christianity. We both love the Church as the Bride of Christ, and believe in her future. We accept the importance of historic Christianity but, along with many others, feel the need to find new ways of living faith community without condemning our history. In this spirit we commend this book to you . . .

Peter R. Holmes
Susan B. Williams
Christ Church Deal, Kent, UK

Notes

[1] Throughout the text, we will put "Church" when speaking of the universal Church, in both its Catholic and Protestant forms, from institutional to independent local and emerging congregations; and "church" when referring to a local congregation or faith community.

[2] This is a phrase I (Susan) am developing in my research. I use it to describe the relational network of shared identity that members of a group carry when they feel they belong, and are part of something greater than themselves (see Chapter 19).

[3] Our reasons for capitalizing this word will be explained in Chapter 4.

[4] For recent developments, please go to the Christ Church Deal website on <www.christchurchdeal.com>. In response to these accusations, the leadership team took the opportunity to teach what Christ requires of us in such situations. This material is available through this site.

5 For more background on our faith community, and our involvement as a TC, together with our membership of the Community of Communities project within the Royal College of Psychiatrists, see our website <www.christchurchdeal.org>.

6 For an academic introduction to these themes, see P.R. Holmes, *Becoming More Human: Exploring the interface of spirituality, discipleship and therapeutic faith community* (Milton Keynes: Paternoster, 2005), 163ff. For details of our other books, see the Bibliography.

7 The best introduction to our work is from the stories of members of the church (and others) in P.R. Holmes and S.B. Williams, *Changed Lives: Extraordinary stories of ordinary people* (Milton Keynes: Authentic Media, 2005). For an introduction to the life of the church, see P.R. Holmes, *Trinity in Human Community: Exploring congregational life in the image of the social Trinity* (Milton Keynes: Paternoster, 2006). My (Susan's) own journey of healing is described in S.B. Williams and P.R. Holmes, *Letting God Heal: From emotional illness to wholeness* (Milton Keynes, Authentic Media, 2004).

8 See our website <www.LifeGivingTrust.org> and details of our books in the Bibliography.

9 P. Martin, *The Sickening Mind: Brain, behaviour, immunity disease* (London: Flamingo, 1998), 38.

10 For an outline of some of these new values, see T. Hunter, *Beyond Foundationalism: Shaping theology in a postmodern context* (Louisville, Ky.: Westminster John Knox Press, 2000), or M. Yaconelli (ed.), *Stories of Emergence: Moving from absolute to authentic* (Grand Rapids: Zondervan, 2003), or the writings of Brian McLaren: B. McLaren, *A New Kind of Christian: A tale of two friends on a spiritual journey* (San Francisco: Jossey-Bass, 2001), and B. McLaren, *The Story We Find Ourselves In: Further adventures of a new kind of Christian* (San Francisco: Jossey-Bass, 2003). For a recent critique of the emerging Church, see D. Carson, *Becoming Conversant with the Emerging Church* (Grand Rapids: Zondervan, 2005).

Part 1

The Need for a Safe Place

In this first part of the book we are going to explore some of the huge challenges facing the Church if we are to offer a safer place for people in a world ravaged by violence and abuse. This may be a bigger challenge than any of us realize.

1

Life in an Unsafe World

In this chapter we take an overview of our society and conclude that abuse is more common than we might imagine or admit. Many people feel unsafe today. Which begs the question: Where abuse is concerned, is the Church an exception or is it like other institutions? We end the chapter by suggesting that society is continuing to fragment, with more and more people living alone or in broken, damaged relationships.

Nelson Mandela, writing the Foreword to the World Health Organization's *World Report on Violence and Health*, suggests that the twentieth century will be remembered as a century marked by violence and abuse. There has been more abuse,[1] violence, death, and even genocide than ever before. The statistics speak for themselves. More recently, Mandela's views have been endorsed by Niall Ferguson in his exhaustive work *The War of the World*, in which he asks why the twentieth century has been the bloodiest century yet.[2]

As authors, we have been directly engaged in this violence, not only in our pastoral counseling, but specifically in our efforts to develop a model of dealing with the post traumatic stress suffered by victims of the genocide in Rwanda.[3] This has proven a huge challenge. Most Western people have little awareness of the difficulties facing the people of Rwanda. With physical and sexual abuse, torture, murder, and loss, come a range of dehumanizing feelings that make us less able to be human and more able to hurt because we have been hurt.

Mandela observes that one of the tragedies of this legacy is the way that abuse reproduces itself. Instead of developing an aversion to abuse, victims learn abuse from victimizers and, perhaps unintentionally, begin to perpetuate it. He believes that our only hope for breaking these cycles is our willingness to expose such abuse through the democratic process. "Safety and security don't just happen," he says, "they are the result of collective consensus and public investment."[4] Collective consensus in this field is focused on the area of human rights, be they the right of the mentally ill to be treated with dignity, the right of children to be protected or of a divorced mother to have the same standard of living as her professional ex-husband. Outside the Church the contemporary human rights agenda is moving fast and furious.

So what is the response of the Church to these twentieth-century developments? In our local congregations, how can we respond to the pain, betrayal, fear, and loss being experienced in the culture around us? Also, how effective are we at engaging in public debate on these issues? The answer we are proposing in this book is that the Church needs to intentionally become a "safe place," where those who are hurting can find comfort and healing in restorative relationships, and where people with no Church background can feel that their personal rights are being respected. But achieving this is a daunting task. Let us look at some of the reasons why.

Abuse is Normal

Mandela points out that those who live with violence and its abuse day in and day out begin to assume that it is an intrinsic part of the human condition. People not only resign themselves to it, they accept it as normal. So abuse becomes deeply rooted in the social, cultural, and economic fabric of human life. Today, whether through personal experience, the eye of television and other news media, or by means of video games and films, assault by one individual against another is part of our daily experience. Most video games, for instance, are violent. They are not programs teaching us ethical love. And once abuse and violence become "normal," it is very hard to change.

But it is not only individuals who learn to abuse. Institutions do, too. It is particularly disturbing when the systems and organizations that are intended to stand against such abuse themselves become the abusers. As Mandela knew well, governments can be abusive. During the last century, whole countries, even, practiced democide—the eradication of entire ethnic groups—under leaders such as Stalin, Hitler, and Idi Amin. Such crime is now a major concern to modern society.[5] We have seen it repeated over and over in recent history, from Hiroshima through to Mao, the genocide of Rwanda, the abuse of the Kurds in Turkey and Iraq, and the stateless Palestinians. Modern Europe is not exempt. Note the second-class citizenship of the Turkish and Algerian *gastarbeiters* (guest workers) or the illegal white Russian, Eastern European, Vietnamese, and Thai sex-slave victims being imported into our countries for our gratification. Likewise, consider the treatment of the native Indian, the damage from the Vietnam War, and human rights abuses by the military in Iraq. Some would even point to the retaliatory imperialism of the American government. All of these, along with numerous other forms of abuse, are allowed freedom to exist here, in and on behalf of our "civilized" society.

Behind such extreme abuse lies the issue of power, which, like that of abuse, is a vast and complex subject.[6] When given power, some people sometimes change for the worse. Power by people over people becomes the power to abuse. What is becoming evident from "power" research is that when people have the power or opportunity to abuse, some always will. This will become a key theme of this book.

But the world of dictators is not the only arena in which power is abusively used. Here in the UK, the Macpherson report, published following an enquiry into the murder of a black teenager, Stephen Lawrence, documented institutional racism in the London Metropolitan Police Force. It distinguishes between abuse by individual policemen and an organizational structure that allows racism to exist.[7] Societal abuse is widespread. Even the most mundane access to power creates the opportunity for misuse and abuse. There will always be some who abuse simply because they have the opportunity.

Whether it is driving above the speed limit, using the "black economy" to avoid paying tax, pilfering pens and paper from an employer or fudging one's tax returns, abuse of power is endemic in our Western society. At one time or another we have all misused the power we have.

Whenever someone sets a standard or lays down the law, some of us will have a tendency to lean against it, pushing out the boundaries a bit farther. Toddlers do it: "I wish you were dead!" Teenagers do it: "I hate him!" It is rife in many supposedly adult environments, too: "I'd love to teach her a thing or two!" Many of us perceive the "institution," political leaders and even our bosses as the enemy so we deviously challenge or disobey their wishes. We wouldn't think that we were being abusive, of course. We merely take a few "liberties" from time to time.

Feeling Unsafe

The misuse of power is so prevalent in our society that it raises the question of whether anyone can ever feel safe. Have we all been abused? Are we all abusers? Do we all feel unsafe at one time or another? The huge growth in security systems, personal alarms, tinted windows on cars, expensive locks, and closed circuit TV in both public places and homes is clear testimony that many of us do not feel safe and are afraid of abuse.

Most of us have had the experience of feeling unsafe, vulnerable, and many of us will be able to recite a range of times when we have been abused or have not felt safe. Our examples may include standing in a bus queue, traveling with someone who is not a "safe" driver or no longer being able to trust someone we once relied on. When we say that we live in an abusive society, we are saying that most of us, at one time or another, have felt the lingering aftertaste of hurt or abuse.

The reaction of some of you reading this book may be that feeling unsafe is not your own personal experience. Perhaps you cannot recall ever having been abused by others. Nor do you feel that you are at risk of being abused. If this is the case, then we are pleased for you. But think of those you know, friends and family, who do feel unsafe. Most of those close to you will at one time or another have felt vulnerable or abused, though many have coping mechanisms that help repress or deny the harm.

Having met many hundreds of people, Christian and non-Christian, in a pastoral capacity, we have noticed an interesting trend. Many people are becoming aware that something is not "right," but they are unable to identify what that something is. What they will then often come to realize is that they have been or are being abused. Or perhaps they are abusing themselves. Maybe the word "abuse" seems a bit too strong, but they realize they are feeling hurt. For instance, many people are in abusive personal relationships or have bosses who are abusing them. Or they have been abused in the past, but have been denying how deeply it has hurt them.

Some of these people may be seeking Christ in a deeper way or trying to live more responsible lives, but their circumstances and history are standing against this. Good is not something that happens to us unless we are able to imagine it. Likewise, until we admit the truth, it is hard to change. So in our ministry we frequently find ourselves asking, "Do you realize that is abusive?" Or, "Why are you allowing them to do this to you?" Until a solution is found, human nature will often be reluctant to admit how bad bad really is. To admit to abuse, or to be honest about what took place, is only possible when one knows that others can help resolve it. This understandable reluctance to own up to abuse, or to feelings of being unsafe, is sadly very common.

Is the Church a Safe Place?

If abuse and not feeling safe is part of modern society, how do we feel about our churches? Is being part of a local church a safe experience for us or are churches also places that are not safe? Maybe the fellowship or support group is not safe? Or the youth work we help with? Or are we part of the choir and feel unsafe? Again, the same principle seems to apply. Some of us will be in abusive or unsafe situations in our congregations, but will not be willing to admit this unless someone else gives us permission. It is often not until we are with a safe friend, pastor or counselor that we begin to admit that we do not have a way of dealing with this. They may be able to help us but only if we are honest with ourselves and them.

We are not suggesting that every church is unsafe. Neither are we giving everyone permission to accuse others unjustly. But our congregations are part of our Western society, and can be as abusive as the society they are part of. One consequence is that when congregations become abusive or hurtful environments, it is all too easy for the organization and its members to develop a tolerance to it. It becomes normal. Whether the abuse starts with a leader or a powerful person or group, it will often spread until even the victims become abusive, either to themselves or to someone else. Numerous incidents of abuse that result in situations where we have been hurt or feel unsafe are never addressed. We either deny them or pretend they are not as bad as they really are. Or perhaps we try to raise the problem but no one listens so we give up or quietly leave.

The Church has an historic problem to contend with. Many of us have grown up in congregations with traditions that for centuries have been helpful in establishing the uniqueness of the Church. Yet today the unchurched would consider them a breach of human rights—that is, abusive. Teaching that seems safe or "normal" to us because of its familiarity might be considered unsafe by newcomers, outsiders or those who are postmodern in their ideas. Perhaps we think it is normal to be told we are sinners. Or to be told we must forgive seventy times seven as the leader in his sermon mocks us publicly yet again. Cruciform theology (dying to self) is sound Biblical teaching but can be interpreted in ways that postmodern people (and perhaps even God) find unacceptable. For instance, being "dead to self" can mean we no longer have any rights. We agree with such teaching, but to the unchurched it can all sound too (self-) abusive.

From 1850 to 1900 Evangelicalism ruled in Europe. The Church had enormous influence and prestige, establishing values and ideals for itself and society as a whole. This was not dissimilar to the growth of the Wesleyan movement in North America.[8] Many of these cultural values survive today and are part of the warp and weft of church life.[9] In this book we will be suggesting that not all these beliefs, values, and associated practices are of benefit in the way they may have been in the past. For instance, in North America, when the topic of abuse in the Church is raised, people tend to think immediately of the scandals and cover-up of sexual abuse in the Catholic Church. We will be making reference to this. And we will also be suggesting that the Protestant Church is not immune. In this book we will be suggesting that in reviewing what is safe or harmful, we must consider more carefully the perspective of the unchurched newcomer. In our work with many unchurched we have learned that this is one of the main reasons why they never want to go near a church. Or, along similar lines, it is why some Christians leave the Church, becoming post-Evangelical.[10]

For many of us, of course, local church life is an enjoyable and safe experience. But you may be in a congregation where it could improve. In this book we will be suggesting that a great deal of "soft" abuse goes on un-checked in local church life, for instance, the subtle control of others in influencing who we should be friends with or a theology that penalizes those who are suffering—"You're sick because you lack faith." There can also be an exclusivity that makes an outsider feel unwelcome or pressure to attend more meetings than are healthy for family life or a family feeling judged because the parents are not married. This book draws on over a hundred experiences and illustrations of such harm and abuse in church settings, which we hope we can all learn from.

What we will be noting is that much of this damage never surfaces, both because of cover-ups by leadership and denial by members. It is often so much easier to walk away than confront an issue. Newcomers will also leave because they concede that congregational life will not change to accommodate their needs. Perhaps it is time for us to listen more carefully to those who are on the fringe or who are leaving?

As Christians, many of us have no illusions about the kind of society that we live in. We are pragmatic, and even cynical, while campaigning for human rights. Yet we are in danger of attributing messianic qualities to our church leaders. Sometimes we refuse to see that they struggle to handle power with integrity, and we are unable to accept that, because they are not safe people they cannot create a safe environment for us. We are often passionately loyal to our congregation and its leaders, and this can be a good thing. But sometimes it isn't.

In this book we are suggesting that it is unrealistic to think that people who make others feel unsafe in one setting, say, in business life, are somehow transformed into qualitatively different people when they are in a church environment, that they somehow become safe when they are being "Christian." Rather than clinging to the illusion that the Church is free from abuse, it is more helpful for us to assume that the harm prevalent in society as a whole is also present in the Church. Instead of thinking that the damage that we do hear about in our churches is an exception to the rule, it is more realistic to accept that unsafe behavior prevails in the Church, too, albeit in a variety of ways.

In his summary of the violence of the twentieth century, Mandela suggests that we should take national as well as corporate initiatives to stop such violence and abuse. Surely the Church should lead the way in creating structures and guidelines that minimize the potential for abuse and harm, and should be seen to be responding healthily when and where damage has been identified?

We are suggesting that making congregational life a safer place is a learning journey. While creating what is safe for people, we must retain the ability to speak the truth to one another. Holding this balance is a real challenge. The large number of abused people suggests we have a long way to go.

Preferring Isolation?

Returning to the broad picture, we cannot avoid the fact that social relations in our Western society are breaking down. Around 25 per cent of people in the UK now live alone, while a growing number "live together apart."[11] This phrase refers to two people who spend some time together, perhaps a few nights a week, while maintaining separate homes that they can retreat into.[12] Any property developer will tell you that one-bed units and bedsits are the biggest area of demand in the housing market. The "family home" is not the prized property it used to be, either side of the Atlantic.

This trend is part of a complex social change that is taking place in our society. It is driven by a number of factors, including greater economic wealth, social welfare support, and self-ism—a selfishness that puts "number one" at the center of our lives. But more disturbing is the fact that many of us feel safer when we are in control. So living alone is an obvious preference. We have learned over the years that other people are unsafe. We may need others, but are more guarded toward them than we would have been in the past, evoking echoes of Sartre's, "hell is other people." It is essential that the Church buck this trend if churches are to be authentic faith "communities." But in an age where being safe increasingly equates to being alone, offering people persuasive reasons for being together and staying together is a much stiffer challenge than it used to be.

Most people will say that a safe place is where they feel safe. For many men safety is their car when *they* are driving! Or their garage, workshop, greenhouse, garden shed or golf course. For some women this safe place will be their kitchen or (hopefully) their bedroom. For other women being safe is being with a man they love, being with their children and grandchildren or behind locked doors in their one-bed apartment. Is this what safety really means? Do we have to avoid other people and create highly controlled environments in order to feel secure and protected? In the next chapter we will explore God's idea of what is safe—something contrasting to the norm in our society today.

Questions to Ponder

1. What do you think about Mandela's statement that the twentieth century has been the most violent so far?

2. In what ways does our contemporary culture impact our congregations?
3. In what ways, if any, is the Church different from the world around it?
4. If there has been a time when you have been abused in the Church, how do you now feel about it?
5. If you know of a newcomer who has come to your church having been hurt, how can you help that person to feel safe?
6. How would you describe a "safe place?"

Notes

[1] E. Krug, et al., *World Report on Violence and Health* (Geneva: World Health Organization, 2002).

[2] N. Ferguson, *The War of the World* (London: Allen Lane, 2006).

[3] I (Peter) am currently writing a book with the Archbishop of Rwanda, His Grace Emmanuel Kolini, on the subject of violence and genocide. Hopefully, it will be published early 2008.

[4] Foreword—Krug, et al., *World Report*.

[5] S. Tombs and D. Whyte, *Unmasking the Crimes of the Powerful: Scrutinizing states and corporations* (Oxford: Pater Lang, 2003).

[6] K. Dowding, *Power* (Buckingham: Open University Press, 1996), 1ff.

[7] W. Macpherson, et al., *The Stephen Lawrence Enquiry* (London: The Stationery Office, 1999).

[8] R. Finke and R. Stark, "How the Upstart Sects Won America: 1776–1850," *Journal of the Scientific Study of Religion* 28 (1989), 1:27–44.

[9] D.W. Bebbington, *The Dominance of Evangelicalism: The age of Spurgeon and Moody* (Nottingham: Inter-Varsity Press, 2006).

[10] G. Lynch, *After Religion: "Generation X" and the search for meaning* (London: Darton, Longman & Todd, 2002).

[11] Martin noted in *Sickening Mind* that "if present trends continue over one third of British homes will be occupied by a solitary person by the year 2106."

[12] A. Milan and A. Peters, "Couples living apart," *Canadian Social Trends* (Summer 2003), Office for National Statistics, "First estimates of the number of people 'Living Apart Together' in Britain" (2005, online). Available from <www.statistics.gov.uk/pdfdir/poptrends1205.pdf> (accessed 10 June 2006.

2

The Church as a Safe Place

We begin this chapter by looking in Scripture to see God's perspective on what is a safe place. We then note that God requires that people, as well as places, be safe, and consider four key principles or ideas which, if followed, help people be safe for themselves and others. We introduce our own faith community, which is also a therapeutic community. But anyone who knows us will admit that we are not there yet! We finish with the suggestion that Christ is the safest person in the world, and that together we need to emulate Him. Becoming more like Christ will make us all safer people, and create safer places.

In our unsafe world, a worrying proportion of harm comes from those we know, those we trust and even those in our immediate families. We are all more likely to be abused by those we know than by a stranger. So perhaps it is inevitable that isolation is the closest many people get to being in a safe place. In our private world, the only time we can relax is when we are behind closed doors. The message of this book, however, is that God's version of a safe place is rather different. Those congregations that take up safety from God's perspective have a radical alternative to offer those in need and those who have been harmed or feel unsafe. We, as a faith community, can be the safe place that people are intuitively searching for. Surely the Creator is the One most able to meet human need—after all, humanity at its best is in His image.

God's Idea of Safety

The concept of a safe place is not a modern, but a Biblical, idea. Eden was the first safe place that God created in our material world. It was a place where two people could live and love, with God "dropping in" in the evenings (Gen. 2:15–25; 3:8–9). Even though this did not last, God continued leading His people to create safe places. For instance, the Old Testament cities of refuge were safe places for those who were wrongly accused of murder (Num. 35:6–15). They were places of protection, free from danger. Such safe places were God's idea.

The Old Testament idea of "sanctuary" defines in some ways what a safe place is. Yahweh Himself was sanctuary for Israel (Ex. 25:8). He resided among them, in the Most Holy Place, symbolically sharing Himself with them as they shared their life with Him. Sadly, Israel also defiled the sanctuary by seeking other gods beside Yahweh (Lev. 20:3). They gave up the safe place that God offered them. Throughout the Old Testament we see the ebb and flow of Israel's commitment to Yahweh. The people bought into covenant with Yahweh, then bowed out when it suited them. When committed to Him, they sought to put things right (2 Kgs. 19:14–19; 23:1ff.), but when they went away from the Lord the community was no longer a safe place (2 Kgs. 24:1–7).

The principle of the Church as a safe place is based on the protection, care, and comfort that are in God's nature. Scripture illustrates how He favors those who are oppressed, invites His people to call on Him for protection and rescues those who are abandoned. For instance, we see Him providing safety for Israel as they journey through the wilderness: the pillar of fire and of cloud, the daily provision of manna, and the rituals that remind Israel that they have a God who loves them. Even foreigners are invited to become part of God's chosen race and benefit from His grace (Mt. 25:35; Heb. 13:2). In New Testament times Christ Himself becomes *the* sanctuary, replacing what was still built in stone (Jn. 2:19–21; Heb. 9:1–14ff.). This new sanctuary is the safe place to be (Heb. 9:28). In English, the word "sanctuary" and "sanctify," have the same root: to be holy to God, separate and safe for His use. Safety is at the heart of holiness.

For those Christians who believe that God does not let bad things happen, it is a shock to be confronted with God's idea of safety. It is not one that allows us to abdicate responsibility. He does not remove us from "the valley of the shadow of death." Instead, He walks with us through it. He doesn't take away the battles, but provides wisdom on how to fight them. For instance, when Jesus sent His disciples into the storm on the Sea of Galilee (Mk. 6:45–52), He knew what He was doing. Was He waiting for them to invite Him into the situation to calm it? He became the answer to the storm that He saw coming.

A further Biblical principle is that God is a social Trinity, a divine community.[1] He is safe with and within Himself. We read of no "falling out" between the persons of the Trinity, no divisions or conflict, no disharmony (Jn. 7:16; 5:19–20,30). In fact, there is a continual giving and receiving within the Godhead as they co-mingle within one another. Such teaching suggests that being "in God," part of this divine community, is the safest place to be. God as social Trinity is also Love. This is one of God's names (1 Jn. 4:7–8). The social Trinity is the cosmic womb of true or authentic Love, and we are invited to join Him in this Love (Jn. 3:16; 14:20–22).

The interesting thing to note, therefore, is that nowhere does God speak of safety in terms of being alone. Safety, from God's perspective, always involves relationships, love, belonging, giving, and receiving. This is life, this is *imago Dei*, the image of God in us. So God brings at least two essential qualities to the idea of a safe place: His desire and capacity to share His love with us, and His example as community living in divine harmony. God's standard of safety is Himself, His own character. His Kingdom should reflect this. This means that it is the duty of all Christians to be safe in the way that He is safe. Damaged human nature will fail in its efforts to achieve this, but God's nature is to be safe, and He would have us seek to live this safety with as much maturity as we can.

Four Biblical Ideas for Becoming a Safe Person

It is impossible to consider what is meant by a safe place, without also considering the people who make a place safe. For we are only safe for others as we begin to be safe for ourselves. We have a God who offers us safety, but discovering *imago Dei* in us, becoming more Christ-like, and therefore more safe, can be a real challenge. The challenge we face may be expressed in terms of four principles.

First, *because of the darkness in all of us* (Gen. 6:5,11; 8:21, etc.), at one time or another *we will all be unsafe for others*. Christ saw this gravity, this downward pull, toward darkness in all humanity (Jn. 8:43–47). It suggests that we live in death far more naturally than in abundant life. We see darkness more often than light, find it easier to do wrong than to do right. In a sense, we are incessantly drawn to the vices of our fallen, damaged, sinful natures (Rom. 3:9–20; 7:7–11). Sin entangles us with itself (Heb. 12:1) and we are easily naturally lured into its ways. In this fallen, damaged world we are all damaged. We even tend to see the power of evil as greater than the power of good. So we all start from a place of being unsafe people.

The second principle, following on from this, is that because none of us is naturally safe from time to time, especially when we see ourselves in our "unsanctified" raw state, *we all need to change*. For us to be safe for others, we need to mature, to grow up a little. Positive change in our lives is something we should seek and welcome so that we may become more like Christ, who is the safest person in the world to know. In our ministry we call this a discipleship journey toward Christ-likeness. It brings an increased love for ourselves, for other people, and for God. Such discipleship change is a journey to which we are all called.

Third, because God is divine Trinity community, *He is an example to us of how we should live in relationship with ourselves and with others*, a quality we call in our ministry an "honoring" of ourselves and others. Most of us have a love-hate relationship with ourselves. We have a tendency to project ourselves in a positive way in all our relationships, while inwardly feeling very different, perhaps even carrying a secret loathing or despising of ourselves. Outwardly, we all have a tendency to think more highly of ourselves than we should, while inwardly we tend to dwell on the dark side of our natures. With the help of the Lord, we need to see this fragmentation of ourselves, and to realize that we are loved by God. We need also to see that we have a God-given good in us that will help us to love ourselves. After all, God thought we were worth dying for (Jn. 15:9–13). Discovering God in us, *imago Dei*, enables us to feel safe within ourselves. This will help us to be safe with other people.

Finally, *we have to become Christ-like in our capacity to love others*. To be safe we all need to develop a natural, spontaneous love for people. What we are describing here is more than just a polite, smiley kind of love. Christ suggests that we are all capable of loving one another as an act of human will, hence His command to love (Lk. 10:27). But love can be faked very easily. It is all too easy to gloss over the "warts and all" that we might have in our lives, or that we see in others. But loving one another while turning a blind eye to our own and others' baggage, sin, and weaknesses is not how God wants us to live. Instead, we are called to love our enemies and to live in Truth. Christ "knew what was in their heart" and yet loved us all. Mother Teresa knew the personal dangers but chose to love intimately all those who came to her. This radical form of safe love is God's call on all our lives.

What we are suggesting is that none of us naturally loves others or is a safe place for others. We can fake it for a while but usually end up burning out. We all have to learn from Christ to be safe for ourselves and others. We need to become at ease and safe with ourselves, carrying a maturity and capacity that we can offer to others. Mutual honor should be naturally and spontaneously lived, without our needing to repress or deny our baggage, or pretend that it is gone. In much psychotherapy, the goal is learning to manage and live with our baggage. But Christ-likeness is being free of it. Few of us start off with this capacity. None of us is naturally Christ-like. This is a journey that we must all walk.

In this suggestion we are going beyond what Nelson Mandela expects from us. It is not enough merely to educate people. Some of the most educated people are also some of the most abusive (take, for example, the perpetrators of the Holocaust). Instead, we are suggesting the need for deep positive personal change in our lives, the need to set out on a journey to become more like Christ so that we can be the people others need us to be. For we become safe as people as we become more like Christ. Such a journey develops our Christ-like capacity to be the person we are created to be. Only as we become that person will we be able to require such positive Christ-like change from others, helping them also to build a greater capacity to be a safe place. In our local faith community this is something we have been struggling to achieve for the last decade.

Christ Church Deal and "Tomorrow's Church"

It is because of the Biblical teaching that God protects us that in modern times people have sought refuge in church buildings or the priest's home, expecting them to be safe places. The idea of a safe place is used extensively to describe Church. Google has over 33 million references in a search for "church/safe place!" Many of these revolve around two key themes. One is related to issues of sexual abuse and the failure of the Church. The other is our claim as congregations and even denominations to be safe places for hurting, broken people. In contemporary thought, a safe place is a congregation where someone like Rahab, the prostitute of Jericho who harbored the Israelite spies, would be welcomed (Jos. 6:17; Heb. 11:31). It is where someone can come who is emotionally damaged or suffering addictive disorders, someone who needs to learn to change but will find it hard to do so in the early stages and will have numerous relapses.

The measure of what makes a place safe is inevitably subjective rather than objective; we all know when we *feel* safe. This simple fact creates problems for organizations since safety cannot be created solely by policies and structures, but is dependent on the quality of relationships, on how people feel. Even the best-run company will become unsafe if an abusive individual has power that is used unrighteously over others. Nonetheless, some work has already been done on defining some of the qualities of a safe place.[2] A number of churches and denominations now have "safe place" policies, for instance, the Anglican Diocese of Adelaide, Australia, the Diocese of

Western Massachusetts, and the Fountain City United Methodist Church, the latter two both in the USA.[3]

In our own congregation of Christ Church Deal, this has been a tough journey. When you have a growing congregation of needy people, as we did when we started in 1998, there aren't enough "healed" people to go round. We all needed someone to listen to us, someone to love us. We were in danger of having too few givers and far too many takers. So we all had to give to one another, each knowing that the next day others would be giving to us. Relationships were an investment and a risk. As one of our readers said, "Yes! Although this should have felt unsafe, it was actually the reverse. Maybe because we all understood what was happening?" (Jane Dryden).

Such a situation can be tough. But as healing was possessed by a number of us, we grew in Christ, letting go of the bitterness, pain, and abuse of our pasts. We began to experience new energy and capacity, and a desire to move into our futures. Central to this process was an increasing ability to give love, rather than to continue being only takers.[4] This journey allowed us to begin enjoying relationships in a way we had not done before.

One of our goals from the birth of the congregation was to be a safe place for hurting people. We didn't stop to ask what that meant. We just all knew it was what we wanted for ourselves and others. It was an important shared goal that in the early days seemed to grow intuitively amongst us. More recently, partly because of numerical growth, we have been through a time when most of us would agree that we haven't been a safe place for one another. Though sad, this has added to our learning of what a safe place is and isn't. But we are now moving forward together into a new capacity for love, discovering a new form of safe place for a more diverse local church.

This book benefits from the experience of CCD, but we are not using our faith community as a focus. Although we are drawing on its example and experience, we are not talking a great deal about our own faith family. It is still a young congregation. It has some unique features that are not mainstream— that it is a therapeutic community, for example—and it is still learning what safe really means. Instead, we are going to introduce a congregation that we call "Tomorrow's Church."[5] A number of the ideas in this book will take some years to evolve, and we would like to think that some congregations will want to learn more about how to change positively in order to become safer places for those seeking them.

My (Susan's) own academic research includes a sociological exploration of the dynamics of a safe place based both on our experience as a congregation and on literature from several different fields. A number of themes are emerging, some obvious and some surprising. The stories we will share suggest that the characteristics that create a safe place are not necessarily typical of much congregational life. We will be outlining some practical suggestions on how our churches can become safer.

Controversially, Christians may sometimes be heard to say that the God of the Bible (or the Old Testament) is an abusive God, that He speaks Truth regardless of the consequences for people, that He judges people and delights in suffering and killing. The implicit suggestion is that this somehow justifies the bad behavior of Christians toward one another. Although arguably we do see these sides to God's nature in the Old Testament, they have to be put into the context of the whole of Scripture. This problem of the apparent dissonance between God in the Old and God in the New Testament has already been adequately dealt with by theologians.[6] All we need to say is that we do not accept the idea that there are two different Gods or that we should relegate the Old Testament God in favor of Jesus. We need both Testaments, Old and New, as well as both views of God. Without them, we do not have the whole story and are unable to comprehend fully what God wants us to know about Him.

But in looking at the idea of abuse and a safe place, we also need to comment on the difficult relationship, as some see it, between the Father and Son. For some people, this is the most abusive relationship of all. The Father gave up the life of the Son, making him a living sacrifice. The Father let His Son die. Is this not abuse? Is this not a betrayal of all that God stands for? This act of "abuse" is starkly epitomized in the moment

Jesus experienced the feelings of being forsaken (Mt. 27:46). This is either an act of extreme abuse or it is an act of extreme Love. If you look at it as relational, a requirement of the Father, it could be seen as abuse. But if you look at it as the Son's free choice, it is an act of extreme Love.

Others have questioned whether it is helpful for a church to be described as a safe place. The idea is summed up in the comment, "The evangelical belief that the Church is safe while the world is not is the concept that I recoil from."[7] We would support the sentiment of this blog. To pretend that the Church is safe in an unsafe world is rose-tinted-glass theology. It could be seen as deceitful. But as we have now suggested, unless we take clear and decisive steps to make it so, the Church will be no safer than the culture it is in or the people who are in it. In this book we want to outline some of those steps—steps that could help make congregational life more safe, and our churches places where we can become as human as we dare to be but without being judged and hurt by others.

In Summary

We began the chapter by reminding ourselves that God has a radically different perspective on safety from that in contemporary society. He Himself is our safe place. As social Trinity, God seeks to extend the harmony of the divine community to us also. In this context we noted four Biblical values for our being safe people: that we all have a dark side that we must surrender to Christ; that we all need to change; that Christ's Trinity example is how we should live together; and our need to become more like Him, especially in our developing a greater capacity to love ourselves and others. God Himself is our safe place. One of our readers comments: "He Himself being our safe place is not something most Christians seem to believe in. But the possibility of this, the thought that it is not just a dream, that it could happen for me, is like a diamond, so beautiful it's worth fighting for. It's treasure" (Nicola Carnall).

By living such a journey of personal positive change, we begin to possess a greater level of relational maturity, Christ-likeness, and a capacity to meet all that life and the Enemy might throw at us. We must move from death to life in Christ. His atonement is sufficient for us all. We may roll under the pressure, but we bounce back to continue to be the people others need us to be. In working alongside other people who are also doing this journey of seeking more of Christ in their lives, we will spontaneously, together, begin to create safe places for any newcomers. This process could be through marriage, through working alongside professional colleagues or in discipleship groups. Where we meet to do this journey together is not as important as the common purpose of Christ that we share.

What we are describing is the knitting together of ourselves into Christ, allowing us to "be one," mirroring the social harmony of the Divine Trinity. Ultimately, our goal has to be to recreate what we learn and know in God Himself. These are Trinity harmony relationships that put others first but also allow our own true selves to surface and mature. As we seek to live these principles, we become safer for others, and with others who are doing the same journey we create common purpose that builds trust and allows us to bring about a change-enabling culture. This would create Tomorrow's Church.

Let us now look at what abuse is in our culture today, and what happens as we begin to apply these simple principles.

Questions to Ponder

1. Describe one of your experiences of being in a "safe place."
2. Talk about some of the "safe places" described in the Bible.
3. How does Jesus describe a safe place?
4. What problems, if any, do you have with the idea that sin entangles our lives?
5. How does this sin make us unsafe?
6. In what ways do you think God might not be safe?
7. How can we be safer for others?
8. Outline some of the qualities of Christ-likeness.

Notes

1 See my (Peter's) book, Holmes, *Trinity*.
2 See <www.nationalcoalition,org/resourcesservices/place,html>.
3 For some theological ideas on the subject of what makes a safe place, see <www.brethren.org/abc/hps_theme/hps_00/Theology.htm>.
4 For an academic exploration, see Holmes, *Becoming More Human*. For something that goes into more depth and application, see Holmes, *Trinity and Human Community*.
5 See the Introduction for our background comments on the idea of Tomorrow's Church.
6 See E. Peels, *Shadow Sides: The Revelation of God in the Old Testament*, H. Lalleman (tr.) (Milton Keynes: Paternoster, 2003).
7 See <www.badchristian.com/2005/01/31/should_church_be_safe/>.

Part 2

Types of Abuse

In this part of the book we are going to take a long and careful look at how abuse might be defined. We will also look at the different forms of abuse that are occurring in both society and our churches. It is a bit shocking. But if we are to engage and solve some of these problems, we first need to acknowledge them. So we will start with the general context of abuse in society, then move on to a definition of abuse.

3

The Social Context of Abuse

In this chapter we return to the social context of abuse, and look at some of its features, such as selfism, relationship background, the persistence of abuse in our societies and abuse in business. We also look at "ordinary" abuse and at the research that is currently being undertaken in these areas, especially asking why more is not being done. We finish the chapter with a consideration of ways in which the Church might respond to this situation.

As Mandela has already illustrated for us, abuse is commonplace across all levels of society. This means that in order for the Church to become a safe place, it has to be a haven or environment that is able to resist the negative trends of the society that we all live in.

It is not just individual choices that can lead us into abusive situations, it is the social milieu as well. Natural momentum in any society will take it to the lowest point, unless resisted. For example, traditional institutions and organizations will always create hierarchies that in themselves can be abusive. They will have a tendency to act abusively in order to survive. Where there is power, there is vulnerability to abuse of power. The Church's greatest power to resist such hierarchical abuse comes from living Christ and His values by the Holy Spirit. That is, in all our relationships with one another we must creatively implement Christ-centered, love-centered mutuality, making it central to Body life.

It should be no surprise to us, then, that our congregations and Church denominations have become environments where some members experience abuse and others don't feel safe.

The good news is that the Church doesn't need to stay that way. We can adopt a counter-cultural way of life in our relationships together. But this will require a significant commitment to be different. First, we need to understand a little more about the type of society we live in with all its multicultural variations. As we look at our society, we will recognize a number of pervasive patterns.

In this section we will be exploring some general trends in society that create an environment that permits abuse. We will note, sadly, that such an environment can become as natural as the air we breathe. Just like the air, our environment can give us life or bring harm. We must choose what air to breathe. Will it be good for us or will it be harmful?

Selfism

It is now widely accepted that our modern Western society can be abusive. But this leaves us with the question of why this is. We cannot pretend in this book that we can even to begin to explain this complex question. But what we can say is that Western society is increasingly characterized by selfism—the practice of putting ourselves at the center of our world. Some link this attitude with several modern Enlightenment values, such as individualism and materialism. The explanation may not be that simple, but it is true that selfism, as a value system, has its roots in the idea of individuality. We are not opposed to personal uniqueness and personal development, which we will look at positively and in greater detail in Chapter 8, but we are going to suggest that this emphasis on individualism has a dark side to it.

Selfism can be seen in the contemporary media. All too often the focus is, "What do I get?" It may seem a little cynical or far-fetched to say that people are preoccupied with such a question—until, that is, one listens to the reasons they give for a range of actions such as ending relationships, changing friends or looking for a new job. "I'm just tired of him," they say; or, "This doesn't suit me any longer." So many of our decisions are about self. Modern advertising tells us we can have almost anything we wish, whether it be more leisure, owning grown-up toys, taking revenge through damage litigation, creating credit debt or choosing to live alone. The attitude is no longer, "What are we working towards?" or, "What do we want to do *together*?" Instead, it is more frequently, "What is important for *me*?" and, "What is best for *me*?"

To go through a period of asking, "What is best for me?" can be a positive step in the journey of someone who has been abused. But if people stay in this place, this question can turn into selfism. The culture we are living in increasingly encourages us to believe that we *can* have it all. There seems to be an underlying assumption among many of us that one can have it all if one wants it—the house, car, job, family, holidays, and disposable income. Some of us may remain grounded in reality, but more and more of us want all we can get regardless of the consequences to others. This attitude now extends to the Internet, where the "cyber violence" of hate mail, obscenities, and sexual harassment is now common.[1]

The culture of selfism breeds the belief that we have the right to it all. And since we have the buying power, why shouldn't we? Approaches that challenge this attitude, such as the traditional principles of giving back to society, doing what is best for the kids or supporting those we love, seem less and less important to some. For instance, twenty years ago I (Peter) could appeal to a Christian couple who were having a difficult time in their marriage to work harder at it "for the sake of the children and the Lord." Many would respond well to this appeal, and want to learn how to repair their lives together. That response is less likely today. More probably, the couple have already made up their minds about what is best for them. "Old-fashioned" values are disappearing from people's agendas. This observation is backed up by sociologists, who are now suggesting that the family is the most dangerous place on earth for many of us.[2] When abortion statistics are added, this conclusion becomes irrefutable. Selfism rules.

Behind the worst aspects of selfism is the old-fashioned idea of sin. We are keen on sin in our ministry! As someone once said to us, "You are seeking to restore sin to the Church." In the best sense we are! Although we often describe sin as "baggage," it remains sin. Selfism is sinfulness. Selfish sinfulness. Sin carries with it an unwillingness to change or repent. It is a lawless unrighteousness (1 Jn. 3:4; 5:17). Christ the Lamb of God takes away the sin of the world by His atoning sacrifice (Jn. 1:29; 8:46; 1 Jn. 2:2). This is needed, since sin and its selfism are destructive desires (Rom. 1:18–32). Enslavement to sin is broken by Christ (Rom. 6:1–23; 1 Cor. 15:3,17). But sin is also contagious and communal so all things in heaven and on earth need reconciling to Him (Col. 1:19–22). He is our Redeemer from selfism.

Relationship Breakdown

Consistent with a society in which selfism is endemic, as few as 10 per cent of all relationships in the USA today, it is now suggested, follow long term the "Waltons" family model.[3] Instead, many postmodern people are more likely to look cynically at *The Walton's* rather than view it as an ideal dream! Similarly, although the ceremony of marriage is now more popular than ever (note the proliferation of marriage consultants and wedding-gown shops), staying married is not. It is now common to have a "pre-nuptial agreement" relating to the separating of assets, should (or when) the couple break up. Lack of commitment is now so pervasive that sociologists have invented a new term to describe it—"serial monogamy." This refers to the exclusive committed relationship between a man and a woman that will last for maybe three to four years, before one or both of them tire and move on to the next partner.[4] Typically, the relationship ends when one partner says, "I'm not getting anything out of this any more—I'm out of here!" "A lawyer recently told me that a 'long-term marriage' is seven years or more!" (Jane Dryden).

In Western Europe and the United States today, around half of all children will live much of their childhood with one biological parent or even without any.[5] Some children end up having several fathers or mothers during their childhood. Society seems to have no idea how damaging this is going to be for the children concerned or what needs to be done to minimize the harm. The trend away from a long-term commitment to a relationship brings with it a rise in abuse: it becomes easier to abuse those we no longer value or want. Traditionally, the mother kept the kids after separation but this is often no longer the case. In our ministry we are now beginning to teach divorced fathers how to look after their children because when the mother finds a new partner, the new "couple" may decide they no longer want the kids from the previous relationship. Perhaps the new partner has no intention of feeding, housing, and clothing someone else's offspring. We have seen this in a number of instances.

The implications of such social mega-trends and their impact on personal commitment are huge. The insistence that one has the right to take what one wants when one wants, to demand in a selfish way without long-term commitment for better or worse, is a recent sociological phenomenon. With it comes a desensitizing of human emotion, especially and increasingly among the young.[6] The less we feel, the less we notice when we hurt, or when we hurt others.

Likewise, there is an insatiable need to possess things. But once we have possessed the people and the "toys" we want, we learn they are not as satisfying as we had hoped. The more we have, the more we want. For those who do not learn about the shallowness of possessing things, life becomes a relentless treadmill of ongoing emptiness. The desire to possess and control goes hand in hand with relational ineptitude and a selfish lack of commitment to relationships. Some are suggesting that such a search will always lead to abuse in one way or another. Much of this thinking, we are suggesting, emanates from contemporary selfism.

The "Background Noise" of Abuse

Is it true that we are more abusive today? Or do we merely get this impression because we are now more aware, through the media, of the abuse that has always been going on? There is currently little research on which to base any conclusions. But things are not looking good. In our ministry we take for granted the possibility that abuse will become greater in the future. Moreover, in addition to the quantitative increase in abuse, we also assume that the types of abuse perpetrated will radically change as society changes.

The media can be brutally, abusively, truthful. We are now seeing, in our living rooms and bedrooms, scenes on TV that many of us have never been exposed to before. It can be very stressful to see yet another suicide bomber or watch instant, uncensored footage of a drama unraveling in some part of the world, and the daily killings of men, women, and children in Iraq and Afghanistan. The visual images can be shocking, as though you are there. At one time or another, we have both felt assaulted by them. More disturbing, in some ways, is the fact that some people seem intoxicated by the unfolding events, hooked on them. Along similar lines, we should note the computer gaming culture, the steadily rising sophistication of the graphics of violent games and their addictive nature. Addiction to these games can be seen as a form of self-abuse. The first clinic for compulsive computer gamers opened recently in the Netherlands.[7]

Another area of concern stems from the observation that all forms of bad behavior, violence, and trauma beget violence in the next generation. Mandela refers to this and assumes it, based no doubt on his own experience. That there is a cycle in which the abused becomes abusers is an idea that is now widely accepted, being not only taken for granted in our culture, but also assumed in much therapeutic work.[8]

Not everyone agrees that such a chain of cause and effect actually exists. Some argue that such learned behavior is not as well evidenced as we might assume. Abuse can be learned, but is it always learned?[9] From our own pastoral clinical work, we would say that violence and abuse are frequently learned, and will be reproduced when and where they can. We have also observed that such behavior is in some ways both addictive and compulsive. If the abuse gives you pleasure, as it often will (why else would you take the risk?), then you will want to do it again. But maybe go further next time. Likewise, once someone has abused (and not been caught), the next time will often be easier.

Whatever the outcome of research, as a landscape to this book, we are assuming that we all have a "background noise"[10] in our natures that gives us a gravity toward inner darkness and harm, whether of others or ourselves. This was certainly the case in my life (Peter). I learned to be violent because I had a violent father who physically and verbally abused me. For me (Susan) the damage from bullying meant that I assumed that most group settings would be abusive so began hating myself and fearing others.[11] Much of our clinical experience also supports the principle that a capacity to harm is mostly learned behavior. The anger we feel at being abused makes us want to vent abuse on ourselves and others.

So, as Mandela suggests, damaged people may well be responding by damaging others and/or harming themselves. Processes like stress, pain, trauma, and fear and its anxiety, may well become both addictive and contagious. A lot of sexual misbehavior, for instance, seems to fall into this category, developing into addictions such as sexual deviance, multiple partners, voyeurism, pornography, and pedophilia. In the business and commercial world, as in government and society as a whole, this is both profoundly disturbing and little understood.

Abuse in Corporations and Business

Personal abuse and its selfism pale into insignificance alongside the abuse carried out by the world's "democratic" states, but even they are not the greatest culprits. Multinational corporations, some with turnovers larger than nations, have the economic, social, and geographical opportunities to perpetrate abuse on a terrible scale, and do so. In the UK, for instance, the impact of their misconduct is greater than all forms of traditional crime added together.[12]

States and corporations play key roles in defining law and guiding national policy. But this also means that they are more able to violate such legislation.[13] One of the key factors impacting the power of government and large corporations is their ability to operate beyond public scrutiny, without accountability. Some of the biggest crimes in history, for instance, the asset stripping of pension funds, the Exxon Valdez scandal, or, as some see it, the Enron Corporation scandal, have all been the result of the misuse of corporate power. The bigger the company, the more power and control it has, and therefore the greater the possible abuse. Other activities—this time within governments—such as espionage and counter-espionage, sometimes hide behind a scandalous veil of "state secrecy."

The workplace can be a place of abuse, whether in the private or public sectors. The institutional nature of many offices and departments can help ensure that such abuse and its perpetrators survive unchallenged. This is mirrored in UK corporate legislation, in which it is laid down that one of the duties of a director is the responsibility to keep a limited company alive, regardless of what that might mean to individual staff. The individual comes second to the company's survival. It is not only the directors of large corporations who have power to abuse. We have both suffered abuse in our business lives on more than one occasion. Staying within the law in order to act in a proper manner sometimes means that others suffer in the process, which has not always been easy. Let us illustrate from our own experience.

Commercial theft

With our own money and with investments, in both time and cash, from friends, we spent five years working on the development of an environmentally-friendly bio-technology to clean contaminated soil. The success of the company was assured when we received a commitment for our first commercial contract.

But some of our highly-qualified staff got greedy. They left work one Friday evening in the normal way, but did not turn up to work on Monday. They had started their own rival business. It was a well-planned move, with advertising coming out in the trade press the following week: they even used photos of our equipment, but with their logos. They stole the contract we were told we had, and sabotaged our computer systems.

Because of this betrayal, the company went into receivership and we all lost everything we had worked for. Most tragically, the ten other members of staff we had been able to employ, some previously long-term unemployed, also lost their jobs. We had no way of vindicating ourselves or the other investors, and had to walk away from the whole sad affair.

Redemption As a result, we had time on our hands so started *Rapha* workshops and helped plant Christ Church Deal. The rest is history!

"Ordinary" Abuse

What is most disturbing in all this is our own fragile, vulnerable humanity. We often talk about abusive hierarchies and institutions, and the resulting proliferation of powerlessness and exploitation. What we do not say is that we are all part of such establishments, one way or another, so potentially we all have the power to do something about it. As we have already noted, many of us carry an unhealthy fear that holds us back, together with an unwillingness to face up to the evidence of what is really happening. This fear and unwillingness to get involved turn us into a generation of observers rather than activists. Very few of us willingly engage in confrontation. In this sense, all of us become passive abusers.

Most abuse is not as brazen as sexual assault or corporate fraud. It is much more subtle, hidden, and subversive. Often it cloaks itself in a veil of the ordinary. In the business world it might take the form of paying below minimum wages to the illegal "wetbacks" who have no work permits; or the office bully getting away with it yet again; or the director "kicking arse" with junior staff; or smutty jokes, racist bravado and hollow camaraderie. As already noted, what becomes accepted then becomes the norm regardless of how bad it might be. Much of this behavior is contagious so others quickly learn it, thereby allowing the spread of abuse into other areas, such as the home and church.

Randall observes that there is a hidden epidemic of intentional aggression and resulting abuse in both the workplace and community.[14] The most straightforward response would be to see this as simple cause and effect, with blame being laid at the feet of those causing the abuse. Unfortunately, reality is rarely that simple, most abuse being the result of a cluster of complex interacting factors.[15] For instance, you confront some-one with what they have done, then later learn that they were being abused by the person claiming to be abused. Abusive cycles do exist.

Trying to define legally what has happened proves far more complex than one might at first imagine as there is little guid-ance and precedent in law.[16] This is not helped by the fact that we do not yet even have a range of terminology to describe what is unlawful, unethical, and abusive in either the market-place or in law. In areas such as sexual discrimination, unfair dismissal, and racism we are building legal protection, but with the dearth of established terminology and language, it is unlikely that there will be many successful prosecutions. This is seen frequently in rape prosecutions and the issue of con-sent. Women prosecuting a man who has raped them will often say that because of the way the "justice" process is set up, the court case felt like a second assault, leaving them even more deeply traumatized than before. Our society has a very long way to go before justice is also merciful for the abused.

Research into Abuse

What makes the subject of abuse an even more difficult area at a national level is the almost complete absence of textbooks or current independent research on the subject of abuse. There is very little vigorous sustained research on the ways we are being abused by anyone, be it government, business, individ-uals or the Church. This absence of support is especially true in the UK.[17] For example, in the UK there are virtually no undergraduate or research departments looking at the subject of government or corporate abuse. But why should this surprise anyone, given that increasingly academic research sponsorship comes from either the government or large corpo-rations (the "private" sector)? All this is serious, since to change a situation, it is first necessary to understand how it arose in the first place.

A recent initiative to correct this dearth of evidence was the Violence Research Programme (VRP). Commissioned in 1997 by the Economic and Social Research Council (ESRC), and comprising 20 UK-based research projects, it sought to begin outlining patterns of violence and abuse.[18] It reported that the statistics of violence and abuse in the UK far outweigh the knowledge currently available as to how and why it happens, but added that research knowledge is now increasing. It indicates that much has been hidden in our British culture and is only now beginning to surface. The report also calls for a more strategic coordinated approach, suggesting that in our research we tend to move toward victimized sub-groups rather than looking at the broader landscape or overview. Funding is needed to facilitate much more research.

Other initiatives are beginning at various levels. For instance, a literature is emerging regarding institutional abuse, while there is a growing recognition that though abuse is found in all levels of society, it appears to be more common in some social groups than in others. Is there a correlation with those less privileged economically, socially or ethnically? A further factor is that most modern societies are structured in a discriminatory way. In the UK and the USA, for instance, disadvantaged sub-groups would include minorities such as immigrants and the mentally ill.

This reality is often compounded by the contemporary proliferation of institutions, clubs, societies, and groups. Probably because of the increasingly impersonal nature of society where we can all be lonely in a crowd, people form sub-groups with distinctive characteristics, be it the quilting group, cricket club or real ale brigade. But not everyone can be a part of such groups. Individuals such as the mentally ill and those with learning disorders are particularly vulnerable to exclusion as they may not have either the capacity to do relationships well or the protection of peers. Such people, alongside other vulnerable groups—for instance, children and dependent women—will often have to "suffer in silence" because they have no one to talk to who is willing to listen to their perspective on life. Honoring such disempowered sub-groups is all too often not the experience of people in mainstream society.

What we are also observing is that none of us has a great deal of power unless others give it to us. At a social level, much power is actually taken away from us by our circumstances, leaving us little choice but to be vulnerable to abuse because of who we are, where we are or what we do. Violence and abuse seem to have the capacity to find the deepest soil, where they can occur without accountability.

The Church's Response

An increasing phenomenon in our society is the tendency to see religions as bad—a tendency no doubt fed by events such as abuse by priests, 9/11, the London bombings, and religious terrorism generally. Religion, traditional Christianity in particular, is often seen as controlling and irrelevant.[19] Some parts of the Church are seeking to respond, grappling with postmodernism. The so-called Ancient–Future church (loving the ancient history of the Church, for example, Acts 2, but seeking to become future Church) is one example.[20] This new and "emerging" Church is something we are proud to be part of, especially in its role of seeking ways to be relevant to postmodern people.

As in the wider society, very little rigorous research has been done on the problem of abuse in the Church. A body of academic research, especially in the UK, has been slow in coming. Comments Dr Peter Brierley, a church statistician, in personal correspondence, "[abuse in churches] is a topic that simply hasn't been researched very much at all . . . to the best of my knowledge."[21] It is not hard to see why. Even years later, many are unwilling to talk about the abuse they have suffered. They either (understandably) deny knowledge of it altogether or refuse to talk because of fear of litigation or of having to go through the pain or shame of reliving the events. When we were writing this book, it was in some cases only the relationship we had with individual people that gave them the confidence to share their stories. Another challenge is to find research methodologies that meet stringent academic criteria.

In contrast to the lack of vigorous academic research, a great deal of popular Christian writing is now being published about abuse in the Church. A simple search on one Stateside library network on the subject of "spiritual abuse" selected over 50 titles published in the last 12 years. If this sweep were to be widened to "abuse—church" that number would be much greater. Likewise, there are an increasing number of websites, such as SAFE (Love and support for those hurt by churches).[22] All these more popular resources are helpful and should be encouraged, but specific, in-depth academic research is still needed to increase our understanding of the full extent of the problem of abuse in the Church.

Traditional Christianity, based on the example of Christ, has had a leaning toward the sick, poor, and needy. So it is somewhat bewildering to us that as the issue of abuse has begun to raise its head in society, we see only modest evidence that any part of the Church has begun to take up these issues and to campaign for the abused.[23] If the Church were to do so, this would help it to be seen as seeking to become a safe place. What a radical statement this would be to a watching world! The abuser, as some contemporary people see the Church, becomes the champion of the abused. It would take very little for faith communities, and even whole denominations, to begin to learn more about abuse, and start campaigning to change society for the better. The agenda would not only be Biblical, but would also be social, putting people first. Such an agenda would seek out abusers, identify abusive organizations and institutions, and welcome information that could help the oppressed. We wait.

Questions to Ponder

1. What evidence is there that there is a rise in selfism?
2. What has recently occurred on the news that could be described as state or corporate abuse?
3. What do you think are the long-term dangers of broken families?
4. What do you think of the idea of "serial monogamy"?
5. Give some illustrations of the "background noise" of abuse in your life.

6. In what ways are your workplace and social groups not safe?

7. What initiatives do you see in your congregation that could help make it a safer place?

8. If you had the authority, what would you change in your congregation to make it a safer place?

Notes

1 D. Bondareff, "Numbers," *Time Magazine* (28 August 2006), 12.

2 S.W. Duck, *Human Relationships* (London: Sage, 1986/1998), 96.

3 Duck, *Human Relationships*. By the term "Waltons," we are referring to the now "old-fashioned" TV soap, broadcast for many years, portraying an extended family from the Midwest in an apparently idyllic rural setting.

4 N. Vanzetti and S.W. Duck (eds.), *A Lifetime of Relationships* (Pacific Grove, Calif.: Brooks/Cole, 1996).

5 A. Cherlin, *Marriage, Divorce and Remarriage* (Cambridge, Mass.: Harvard University Press, 1992).

6 J.P. Murray, "TV Violence and Brainmapping in Children," *Psychiatric Times* 18 (2001), 10.

7 See the BBC story at <http://news.bbc.co.uk/2/hi/technology/5191678.stm>.

8 P. Mollon, *The Fragile Self: The structure of narcissistic disturbances* (London: Whurr Publishers, 1993); P. Mollon, "Is human nature intrinsically abusive? Reflections on the psychodynamics of evil" in U. McCluskey and C.A. Hooper (eds.), *Psychodynamic Perspectives on Abuse: The cost of fear* (London: Jessica Kinsley, 2000), 67–78.

9 C.A. Hooper and U. McCluskey, "Introduction: Abuse, the individual and the social" in U. McCluskey and C.A. Hooper (eds.), *Psychodynamic Perspectives on Abuse: The cost of fear* (London: Jessica Kinsley, 2000), 7–24.

10 Mollon, "Human nature," 77.

11 Williams and Holmes, *Letting God Heal*.

12 S. Tombs, "Death and work in Britain," *The Sociological Review* 47 (1999), 2:345–67.

13 Tombs and Whyte, *Unmasking the Crimes*, 3ff.

[14] P. Randall, *Adult Bullying: Perpetrators and victims* (London: Routledge, 1997), vii.

[15] J. Brearley, "Working as an organizational consultant with abuse encountered in the workplace" in U. McCluskey and C.A. Hooper (eds.), *Psychodynamic Perspectives on Abuse: The cost of fear* (London: Jessica Kingsley, 2000), 223–39, 226.

[16] J. Brearley, "Working as an organizational consultant with abuse encountered in the workplace" in U. McCluskey and C.A. Hooper (eds.), *Pschodynamic Perspectives on Abuse: The cost of fear* (London: Jessica Kingsley, 2000), 224.

[17] Tombs and Whyte, *Unmasking the Crimes*, 3ff.

[18] B. Stanko, et al., *Taking Stock: What do we know about interpersonal violence?* (Egham, Surrey: ESRC Violence Research Programme, 2002).

[19] P. Young-Eisendrath and M.E. Miller, "Beyond enlightened self-interest: the psychology of mature spirituality in the 21st century" in P. Young-Eisendrath and M.E. Miller (eds.), *The Psychology of Mature Spirituality: Integrity, wisdom, transcendence* (London: Routledge, 2000), 1–7.

[20] R.E. Webber and P.C. Kenyon, "A Call to an Ancient Evangelical Future," *Christianity Today* 50 (2006), 9:57.

[21] By email, 5 August 2005.

[22] <www.safeinchurch.co.uk>

[23] We are not saying that nothing is being done. Note, for instance, the work of PASCH (Peace and Safety in the Christian Home).

4

The Complexities of Defining Abuse in a Church Context

In this chapter we will be looking at ways of defining and describing abuse. It is specifically tailored to a Church context and is based on Biblical teaching. Such an approach and the definitions are more far-reaching than legal or psychological definitions. We will deliberately be noting a range of behavior that makes a local church an unsafe environment, especially for the more vulnerable members of society.

The "background noise" of abuse is continuous in Western society. But abuse is a strong word. Surely it refers to those extreme situations where someone has been cruel and vindictive? We'd all like to believe that this "noise" hasn't permeated our churches. Surely such people aren't found in our churches, are they?

Thankfully, we would agree that it is not commonplace to find someone in a local church who is intentionally and repeatedly cruel to others. But, sadly, that doesn't mean that damage is not occurring regularly. This is because much abuse is unintentional: perhaps it is careless, accidental or circumstantial. But do such things really count as abuse?

The topic of abuse certainly provokes complex questions that need careful consideration if we are to understand how to make the Church a safer place. For the purpose of this book, our example, of course, has to be Christ. He set a high standard. His treatment of the Pharisees was direct and decisive when He saw them despising the sick and poor. People who many would have dismissed or ignored, Christ gave noticeable time to, and supported 1,000 per cent. Christ was also on the receiving end of abuse, especially from the religious leaders and His immediate family. Fancy telling the Son of God that He is mad (Mk. 3:20–21)! As already noted, the ultimate abuse, of course, was being murdered on the cross.

Our simple perspective in this book is that anything in the Church that is not safe, should be made safer! To use the language of those outside the Church, any abuse of human rights is not acceptable. But we must beware lest we use this as a way of asserting our own rights "unrighteously." Most of us still have much to learn about how to respond in a mature and gracious way when we are hurt and abused.

We have already noted that human nature has a gravity to darkness, and struggles to love God, others, and self. Both Scripture and our own experience make this point loud and clear. Put another way, if people have the power to abuse, some will always use that power in a way that hurts others. At one time or another we have all met people who change in a negative way after being given responsibility (power) or who, having been given a task, tenaciously follow the letter of the law in completing that task, regardless of the consequences to others. "Don't they see what they're doing? Someone needs to talk to them . . ."

Defining Abuse

Harm is labeled differently in different contexts[1] so seeking a comprehensive definition of what is abusive is difficult.[2] Every one of us has a different view and experience of abuse, and this will even vary with the same person in different relationships, at different times in their life, and in a range of situations. Abuse that may be tolerated in one situation (for instance, within marriage) may be a cause for litigation in another (in the office). In any definition of abuse, it is important not to slip into the language of personal human rights. The Bible and faith community are about relationality, with all its giving and receiving, not about the asserting of one's personal rights. Nonetheless, we must have a response to twenty-first-century society when it calls for justice for the individual.

There is also the complex issue of intent. Did the person intend to abuse the other? One often hears the abuser later plead, like a kid in the playground, that it was not intended— "I didn't mean to do it!" But in some instances, the deliberate nature of the act or attitude leads the observer to feel that the abuse was intentional. Conversely, someone hurt "unintentionally" often feels unjustified in calling their experience abuse. In this book we are adopting the view that intent is hard to establish and is complicated by its closeness to the idea of a blame culture (see Chapter 17). We therefore make no correlation between intent and abuse and instead focus on the abused person's perspective of what happened. But what we do want to note is that all types of harm and abuse have one thing in common: they are an offence against the person. Therefore abuse is a denial of human rights.

In the Introduction we noted our reluctance as authors to define abuse in a specific way. *The Oxford English Dictionary* has a range of ideas of what abuse can be: it is taking advantage of the person, resulting in insult or even injury; in its "milder" form, abuse can be verbal; in its more severe manifestation, it is physical or sexual assault, and can lead to permanent injury, mental and emotional breakdown, or even the death of the victim; it is the maltreatment or defilement of the person. From a dictionary definition, then, we can summarize abuse as "the violation of a person, whatever form that may take."

But as authors we do not feel that this is an adequate definition of abuse within a Church context since harm and abuse have numerous aspects that would not normally be considered "violation." For instance, violation often suggests a specific event and might exclude damage that accrues gradually over some time. Even a congregation where everyone's rights are respected may not be a safe place. Abuse may still be common. Let us explain.

When most of us think of violation, we have a tendency to overlook the more subtle damage done at an emotional or psychological level. He may claim to have never touched her, but he frequently raped her with his eyes or sexually abused her with his words. On the other hand, he may maintain that she came on to him, made herself available with her seductive looks, and he was merely responding. In such situations, one will struggle to find any evidence other than one person's word against another's. The long-term emotional damage can be difficult to quantify in law, yet it may fester and prove more harmful years later than the more obvious physical assault. For instance, he may become emotionally obsessed with her and women who look like her, while she may develop a distrust for people in positions of power that filters into every area of her life. Perhaps she may become incapable of trust and long-term relationships. Were they violated? Have they been abused? Certainly both have been harmed. Let us give you an example.

Feeling trapped

Claire came from a good Christian home. Her parents had worked very hard to bring her and her brother up in the most godly way. They read all the books, attended all the seminars and followed all the rules. But at the age of 11 Claire felt unloved. Her elder brother had started clubbing at the weekends, was smoking pot and having unprotected sex. He was having the time of his life. She did not want to go this way, but felt unable to talk to her parents about it because she knew what they would say. They were already deeply hurt and embarrassed by their son and his behavior, especially because he led the pack and even the pastor's son was now into the same lifestyle.

Claire felt hurt and betrayed by her parents' rules and superficial answers. She wanted someone more real to talk to, but because her parents were leaders in her church, she had few options. She was trapped.

(Compiled from the experience of several young women.)

How does one quantify Claire's position? Is it a case of abuse? She could be seen as a "spoilt brat" who has everything going for her. On the other hand, someone listening to her can hear an abused child, "beaten" into her present situation by relentless Bible teaching. She feels she can hardly breathe without breaking some rule or other. What can be done? From her perspective she has been damaged by "love," Jesus' love. To dismiss this as childish would be callous and probably lead to her abandoning church life and perhaps even her relationship with God.

It is very important to learn that it is not what actually happens to someone that determines abuse, but what an individual perceives or believes has happened to them. The most damaged area of our life is often an area where we are hurt but cannot easily objectively quantify or describe it. This perspective is the one most often ignored by people generally. This is made more complicated by our observation that if a person has been abused or hurt in the past, they will collect the pain. Then, when they later find themselves in a similar situation, it is all too easy for them to lay all the historic hurt on the person they believe is currently abusing them. Perhaps that person is not even harming them at all, but is merely someone who reminds them of their history. This is an occupational hazard to anyone seeking to help another.

But there is a level of abuse that is even deeper than subliminal emotional damage. In our therapeutic work we frequently find ourselves talking about how a person "feels." They may feel hurt or abused by another, but when you check out the facts, you find that the event could not have happened. The temptation here is to dismiss the person's view and—based on the facts—to tell them not to be silly. But this in itself can be abusive, denying the person the right to be loved and listened to. So much of the damage in life is not what has happened to us, but what we *feel* has happened to us. It is our perception of the experience that harbors the feelings of abuse, not the objective facts.

Another example of the complexity of this issue is seen at a societal level. In social psychology there exists the concept of "relative deprivation." It is the idea that people regard themselves as deprived in relation to the standards by which their experiences are being measured, rather than in relation to absolute economic or social criteria.[3] The person feels abused by "the system," perhaps without any specific act of abuse occurring.

The simplest or "soft" level of abuse is the infringing of personal rights or the single incident of threat of violation. Repeated occurrence, increased violence, add extra dimensions. Lack of independent corroboration is often irrelevant when defining whether harm has occurred. Often the more invisible the abuse, the more serious its long-term consequences. In seeking, as Christians, to love and honor the individual, it is very important that we take account of how the person perceives what happened. We should be careful not to bring to the relationship the "objectivity" that some traditional methods of counseling claim to bring. Christ always met people where they felt they were, not where He thought they should be (for example, Jn. 5:1ff.). We offer others the greatest healing when we also do this.

For the purposes of this book, a way of describing abuse is: *Where a person has been abused, in their own opinion, or where long-term damage is experienced by the person, whatever form that may take.*

God Sees the Heart

One flaw in this definition could be that there are some people, for instance, people in a marriage relationship, who are obviously experiencing abuse but are living in denial or simply do not see the long-term damage that is being done to them. Is it still abuse? From their perspective, it is not, but from the perspective of an outsider, it clearly is. Those who can see what is happening then have a responsibility to pray, probably without those being abused knowing, inviting the Lord in to help them through the difficult times. (In situations where risk is involved to children or the vulnerable, more action will be required. We cover this later.)

In adopting this description of abuse, we are moving closer to defining what is harmful and therefore abusive. But we are not suggesting that we simply take the person's word and act on it, beyond the bounds of the pastoral relationship, without seeking a more objective perspective. If someone has come to us for support in dealing with the pain, we are careful not to question their viewpoint as they do need us to see life from their perspective, even if they later realize they were wrong. But since there will always be a range of perspectives on violation against a person or a group, if anyone wants to take matters further, involving third parties, the facts become more important.

An additional complexity, when needing to take action beyond the immediate offering of pastoral care, is the question of who has the right to say when abuse has or has not occurred. Is it the victim or someone else, for instance, the courts? As already noted, it is also important to remember that some abuse is invisible, and is not even recognized by law (for example, spiritual abuse, as we illustrate later). The range of perspectives includes the victim's, the perpetrator's reasons for their actions, the legal interpretation of what happened and the peer perception or viewpoint, to name but a few. Moreover, the perspective of someone steeped in church tradition will be quite different from that of someone who is unchurched. To understand abuse fully, and to create a safe place that avoids such abuse, it is helpful to consider all these views. But other challenges also await us.

In law it is independent evidence that is the foundation of justice. This is right and proper. But Christ Himself changed the emphasis. He said that the sin was not just in the killing, but also in the carrying of sin in the heart. The heart feeds the mouth (Mt. 12:33ff.). "For out of the heart come evil thoughts" (Mt. 15:19). Moreover, as already noted, the heart is dark (Lk. 6:45). From Jesus' perspective, the sin is not just in the abuse, but is also in the intent to abuse or to deceive others with regard to the abuse. So when we ask who has the right to decide who has perpetrated abuse, and how, we must take into account Christ's idea that much abuse and deceit will emanate from deep personal deceit, even before any action has been taken. None of us is above reproach or exempt from guilt. Christ sets the standard in suggesting that it is the pure in heart who are most blessed, that is, those who do not carry, even in their hearts, the intent to abuse (Mt. 5:8). They are the safe people.

A safe place, therefore, is not just where a person is not being abused. It is also a place where a person will not *feel* abused in any way, at any level. This is the standard we are setting for this book. Our purpose is to help create a Christ-centered environment where being honest, transparent, and safe is the most natural thing in the world. We expect Tomorrow's Church to be an example of this.

But Aren't We All Guilty, Then?

It is worrying to realize that when we use an understanding of abuse based on "the secrets of our heart," we need to admit that we have all been abusive. We have all caused harm to others, since we all have dark thoughts. We all need to acknowledge that we are able to be deceived by our own dark self, both in our ability to abuse, and our refusal to accept that we are being abused. We all already suffer from damage in our lives so abusing or being abused will merely add to this. None of us has met the standards of a social Trinity and a life lived in Love. If we accept the teaching of Christ that it is our willingness to forgive (Mt. 6:14–15; 18:15–20, etc.) and the intent of our heart that will be judged, then we will be judged guilty of abuse, even if we did not actually act in an abusive way. This is a very hard position, but it is established by Christ.

One of the outcomes of reading this book might be that you realize that others have been harmed as a result of something you did or said, or that you are held to account for a hidden intent of your heart. The first person to whom you will need to say sorry will be God. Then if the other person knows about the damage, it might be appropriate to say sorry to them, too. But we would encourage you to be very cautious about doing this in case it leads to your being abused. If it is something the other person does not know about (that is, the intent of your heart), then there are very few occasions when it is helpful to make it known to the person concerned. In the penultimate chapter we look at this in more detail.

So how do we implement our definition of abuse, and who should we listen to in deciding what is and is not abusive?

Listening in Love

Knowing that we already have "a plank" in our own eye (Lk. 6:41–42) should soften our spirit when we listen to others. Our realization that we ourselves are not blameless should make it easier to empathize with the other person's pain and perspective and avoid being judgmental. According to Christ, we should be careful not to judge anyone (Mt. 7:1; Lk. 12:57–59, etc.). We should never sit in objective judgment unless we carry this duty in a court of law. Instead, Christ's teaching suggests that we listen to others and Love them. By this, we mean that we allow ourselves to listen from the Lord's and their perspectives. This is the approach that carries the most safety for both them and us.

We honor others by hearing them, and making their position our position while we are supporting them. In this way, we clearly let them know that we do understand and sympathize with their perspective. We also avoid the danger of judging them, and are able to honor them in their pain, anger or even desire for revenge. If they believe that we will listen without judging them or questioning their perspective, then they will be able to trust us. We will have created a safe place for them.

You will have noticed that we have sometimes capitalized the word "Love." We have done this deliberately in order to emphasize that none of us loves naturally and that some types of people are especially difficult to love. So in suggesting that we learn to love people, we are saying that this needs to be a supernatural love, a Love from God. Not a love that burns us out, but one that is of Christ in and through us (Jn. 15:12; 1 Jn. 4:7).

Exceptions to the honoring of people will be noted later in this book. But we do need to refer to some of them now. If someone confesses to crimes that are not already known or if there is a danger that an abusing person could still be at large, possibly abusing others, we must take matters further. In such situations, we do need to be more "objective," noting our duty both to obey the law and to ensure the safety of the congregation and wider community. Risk management factors also come into play: we might have a professional duty of care to report such information to the appropriate authorities. Again, we will be noting these instances later. But it will still be essential to honor people without judgment, thereby creating a safe place for them. If we communicate that we are standing in "objective" judgment over them, they will not feel safe. They will know that they are not being heard. Taking a position of honor with them is also consistent with our Lord's support of the widow, the orphan, the homeless and the poor. He took the side of the powerless, identifying and exposing deceit and consistently coming to the aid of those being abused.

Maintaining such a position is not easy at times, especially when the abused person is talking about a leader or someone you know, maybe even someone in your own family. At such times it is all too easy to brush what is being said under the carpet or to insist that it is not so bad. Many people make empty promises. They say that they will look into the matter, and do something about it, while having no intention of doing so. They appear to acknowledge that abuse has taken place, but then choose to forget it. We must all seek to gain a reputation for being trustworthy in such matters. When people begin to believe that we will honor them, then they will trust us and talk freely to us, knowing that we have created a safe place for them. This is the very highest compliment that anyone can give us. Let us give you an example from our own ministry.

We are working in Rwanda with both the victims and perpetrators of the genocide. Even after more than a decade many people are still afraid of talking about what happened to them, what they know. A comment we often hear is, "How will you protect us if we tell all?" It is only as they feel safe that they are able to share their perspective. One of the challenges of our work, therefore, is to create a safe place where people can be honest, engaging the appalling pain and trauma of what has happened to them. Women find it particularly hard to share what is really going on out of fear of reprisals, public humiliation or being judged. It is often instinctive for people who are damaged to blame themselves rather than to admit that an injustice has been committed and find the resolve to speak

about it openly. Linked with this, we have noted how surprised church members are when they learn what lies below
the surface in a local congregation.

Noticing Abuse

One of the most challenging groups of people that we work
with are those who are so deeply damaged that they no longer
recognize when they are being abused. There are also those
who are being abused but are genuinely unaware of it because
they have been told that this is acceptable behavior. When such
people are approached, they will often defiantly declare that
they are okay, and are not being abused. A typical example is
the choir member who is incessantly barked at by the worship
leader or humiliated publicly on making a mistake. They so
enjoy being part of the worship group that they deny that such
misbehavior is a problem.

Where people are denying or are unaware of abuse, a number of complex factors will be at work. They may fear saying
anything in case this brings about an unwelcome change in
their situation: maybe the abuser is someone who is supporting them financially or is in a position of leadership or is a
long-standing friend. Or perhaps by talking about it they will
expose the fact that they both love and hate the attention.
Others, though admitting the abuse, choose to defend or
excuse it: "We were just playing, it isn't that serious." Creating
a safe place for such people is always a challenge.

To some degree, how abuse is recognized and dealt with will
also vary according to the definitions being used in any situation. In an individual pastoral or therapeutic context, as we
have already mentioned, it is good to accept an individual's
perspective that they have been abused. Later in their healing
journey, individuals may realize that they were equally to
blame, and perhaps were even abusing others while claiming
that they were being abused. But if they are not ready to admit
this, then we should not be seeking to put it on their agenda. It
is the Holy Spirit who convicts, not a leader, counselor or
friend.

When There Is More than One Perspective

Listening in love and taking the perspective of the person who feels abused has an additional challenge. We are noting that we must never treat the abuse as if it is an objective "fact." It is all too easy to hear one side of an account, get emotionally fired up about the injustice and launch into the other person, without hearing their perspective on the events. It is also important to avoid letting what you have heard influence your attitude to others, especially those who have been specifically mentioned. The harm can be described in two (or more) different ways, each of which is likely to be real and true to the person involved.

If we meet the other party to discuss the matter with them, we must give them equal honor and invite their perspective. Such an approach is especially important when working with married couples or partners. To take one partner's side when with the other partner, will totally discredit you, preventing you from honoring either of them. It is important that we honor both equally, even when one admits guilt or misbehavior. It is not just the apportioning of guilt that is our responsibility.

Much stands or falls on how we conduct ourselves. We must not give the impression that we are condoning sin or misbehavior. Nor must we let people think that the problem is as simple as one person telling the "truth" and the other lying. This is rarely the case. In a congregational setting, it is advisable to hear both sides carefully and supportively before coming to any conclusion about appropriate action.

Following on from Nelson Mandela's observations (see page 3), it is important to remember that those who are abused or violated in one situation can then themselves become abusers in another setting, having learned how to abuse. Responses from those abused can include brokenness of spirit, despair, and deep paranoia, but abused people are just as likely to rise up with a bitter longing for revenge that focuses upon the abuser or anyone else who might get in the path of their rage. Most abused people have the potential in other settings to become abusers. Such cycles are all too common. Being a victim and being an abuser can even happen concurrently. A typical example is the woman being abused by her husband who then takes it out on their son, or the manager abused by his director who abuses the staff under him. This doesn't justify their actions, but should influence the spirit of our response. There are a range of steps that can help expose and break these cycles and we will be addressing them in due course.

We should also note that it is in some people's nature to take on themselves feelings of abuse when no abuse has taken place. This is sometimes called "over-sensitive syndrome." If someone has this over-sensitive perspective, then when they are ready we will need, as pastors, to explore this with them, helping them to reinterpret the actions of those around them. Alternately, there are some people who repeatedly put themselves into situations in which they invite abuse. Although resilience grows as they get healed, such people need special care as they learn to give their pain to Christ and to become proactive in minimizing abuse. Scripture cautions us to avoid being a stumbling block to others (Mt. 18:6). As they begin to experience significant healing, we need to show them how to take more responsibility for themselves, and to beware of the risk of an ongoing dependence on support.

It is also helpful to note that as we give our pain to Christ, we can often have feelings of abuse. Let us quote a reader of an earlier draft of this book: "At one time I felt abused by many women in my history but later on saw that much of this was primarily self-abuse that had used the other person in a way that abused myself. When you get this realization, you begin to accept that the real abuser was yourself."

Bringing Together These Ideas

By using such a broad definition of harm and abuse, we are suggesting that most of us will have been victims of abuse in the past or maybe still are. This also means that most of us are guilty of abusing others, even if unintentionally. We accept that this creates quite a challenge for this book. But it is our conviction that the world is crying out for a safe alternative to isolation, and we will be arguing, hopefully convincingly, that the Church is well able to respond to this cry for help. Admitting that abuse is far more commonplace, both in our society and our Church, than is generally acknowledged, is the first step in making the Church a safer place.

We have noted that abuse can occur when it is not noticed or intended by the person or others. It is important to recognize when a violation has taken place in order both to treat its damage and prevent its reoccurrence. But whatever happens, where people feel they have been abused and are willing to talk about it, they should be honored. They should not be judged, neither on what they claim to have suffered as abused people, nor on what they may have done as abusers.

Later in the book we will be developing the concept of "soft abuse" to describe situations where someone has been hurt negligently or unintentionally. It can be as simple as a leader walking past us in the church and not saying "hi" to us. Or it could be a friend forgetting a promise. Our life is full of such unintentional hurts. Part of the goal of this book is to raise awareness within the Church about what might constitute abuse even if others consider it acceptable behavior. As we will be illustrating, too much abuse goes unnoticed and unresolved in our congregations and in our society. Let us now go on to look at some of the numerous types of abuse.

Questions to Ponder

1. How would you describe abuse?
2. Why do you think it is so important to listen carefully to the person's perspective?
3. When is it right to dig for the "facts?"
4. How would you help Claire?
5. Is it true that we all have different thresholds of what is abusive?
6. In what way is a non-judgmental approach more Biblical?
7. What are some of the ongoing dangers facing someone who has been abused?
8. If you remember someone you may have abused, what should you do?

Notes

[1] Hooper and McCluskey, "Introduction: Abuse, the individual and the social," 18.
[2] For a list of articles and letters on abuse in the church go to <www.caic.org.au/zabusive.htm>.
[3] Thank you to Simon Clarke for noting this in his reading of the draft manuscript.

5

The Five Main Types of Abuse

In our own ministry we look at abuse in five main ways—verbal, emotional, physical, sexual, and spiritual. We will consider each of these in some detail and then ask some questions for the purpose of discussion, noting how all abuse is wrong.

One of our possible titles for this book was *Making the Church a Safer Place*. It would have been an audacious title since it suggests that many churches are not safe places. To say this in a generalized way is not helpful. So instead we are going to document it through the use of stories.

As a background and resource to this book, we have drawn upon the experience of the significant number of our own congregation who once were "former Christians." By this we mean that they are people who had had a history in the Church, but for various reasons had left congregational life. Many would still have called themselves followers of Christ, but when we first had contact with them they were no longer attending a local congregation. Some had left local church life because they felt they were in abusive situations. Some of the stories in this book are therefore quite shocking.

Other stories will seem more "ordinary," but still clearly reveal that considerable damage had been done to the people involved. A number of the stories are international, covering global mission work from both sides of the Atlantic. All the stories are authentic and are a sad catalogue of ways in which our churches are sometimes unsafe. We find similar situations wherever we travel—across the UK, the US, the Middle East, Asia, and Africa. Because of the nature of our ministry, which centers upon working with those who are in pain, we tend to attract many such cases.

Our goal in documenting types of abuse so specifically is to help create a greater awareness and sensitivity to it. If local churches are to become safe places, we as their leaders and members must be able to recognize when safety is being threatened or compromised. Denial, blindness, high-handedness, and complacency all contribute to an environment where abuse is tolerated and harm is caused. In Part 3 of this book we will begin making suggestions that congregations can easily adopt to help reduce the risk of abuse. We will also be suggesting policies and practices to help ensure that when abuse does occur, it can be quickly identified and resolved. But first we have to gain a better understanding of the various types of abuse that are to be found in the Church and that deprive it of the ministry of offering safety in a hurting world.

We identify harm and abuse in five major areas: verbal, emotional, physical, sexual, and spiritual. This term "harm and abuse" may refer to the manner in which the person is abused, for example, they have been physically hit. Or it may be the outcome of the abuse, for example, their sexuality is compromised. These areas of abuse are not exclusive. Many situations involve more than one type of damage, and the boundaries between them are blurred. For instance, verbal abuse can lead to deep emotional trauma that lingers for many years.

When considering how to make our churches safer places—how we may become Tomorrow's Church—it is helpful to be able to explore carefully each area of abuse. Most of the stories we will use have occurred within churches or church-related situations. Where these might be helpful, we will introduce some ideas that could be used as the basis for drafting relational guidelines.

The description of harm and abuse that we are using for this book is: "Where a person has been abused, in their own opinion, or where long-term damage is experienced by the person, whatever form that takes." This includes damage that the individual feels has occurred, even if there is no "factual" or "objective" evidence. This description also covers damage that the individual may apparently be unaware of, but that others notice. It also includes negligence on the part of a third party. A more specific definition of abuse would differ from person to person. Individual responses to the same event vary considerably, as does the long-term damage. What one person finds offensive, another may just laugh at. One person may be accustomed to being called an idiot and not consider it abusive, while another may reel for days at being addressed in this way. One person may be crushed to be told they are not loving, while another just shrugs, laughs, and walks away.

Verbal Abuse

A list of the different types of verbal abuse is almost endless, ranging from muttering an insult to more toxic confrontational screaming and shouting. Verbal abuse is extremely common, as television and the tabloid headlines illustrate daily. Whole television programs are built around the humor of insult. The thresholds for verbal abuse are moving so what used to be considered offensive is now more acceptable, and even funny. Swearing at oneself and others is abusive, yet is now part of everyday culture. Let us look at an example within a church context.

Verbal abuse by a minister

Ruth was 16, and a happy, committed Christian living with her family in a large city. But her father became chronically ill. The family decided to move nearer to her father's extended family, who would be able to give them better support. Ruth was just about to leave school and already had places in two sixth-form colleges so she decided that she would like to remain in the city and go to the local college. Needing to find accommodation, she advertised in the church bulletin. The minister and his wife offered their home, and Ruth was glad to go there.

After a very short while, however, Ruth began to be unhappy. The rules and regulations that were placed upon her in this home were very different from the family life she had known, and she found it particularly hard not to be able to invite friends around.

Eventually she told a friend how unhappy she was, and confided that she was often shouted at for no good reason. This "friend" broke confidence by speaking to someone else, and the minister heard that she had been complaining. Rather than talk to her quietly at home, he chose to shout at her in the foyer of the church after the Sunday service. Ruth, who was not given an opportunity to speak, felt humiliated. As soon as she could she moved into a flat share with a non-Christian. She left the church, and fifteen years later still hates the Church.

Redemption: None so far. Among other things, the minister's behavior has stolen her relationship with the Lord.

In this situation we see a number of mistakes. Ruth's naivety was probably the first real problem. She did not check out what she was committing herself to. (At 16 that was quite understandable!) Like many of us, she assumed that a Christian leader would be a nice man. Other folk in the congregation would certainly have known the kind of man he was. Perhaps it was out of a false loyalty that they said nothing when they heard what she was doing. The other obvious problem was the lack of integrity of her "friend." This was particularly sad as Ruth clearly trusted this person. This kind of betrayal often takes a long time to recover from. Ruth needed the support of a very understanding group of friends to see her through.

But the main problem here was the abuse of the Christian leader. This was totally unacceptable. The key principle with verbal abuse is the recognition of the power of words. Words can hurt or they can heal. This minister was clearly abusive with his words, yet sadly he did not accept this. For a man of the "Word" this is particularly appalling. He should have known the simple principle that we should avoid ever speaking to another person in anything but an honoring way. Also, we should never rebuke another person in places where we might be overheard or misunderstood by others.

Put another way, we should never speak publicly about any personal or contentious issues until we have the other person's consent and, ideally, not until difficult matters have been resolved. And we should never raise our voice. It is only people who perceive themselves to be weak or insignificant who feel the need to raise their voice; they shout to compensate for their feelings of inadequacy. Christ was capable of righteous anger, but few of us are. Moreover, if we need to raise sensitive or challenging issues, we should always ask ourselves whether it is better for someone else to be present.

Guidelines

+ If you need to raise a sensitive issue, consider carefully the most supportive way of doing this. For instance, first, talk it through with those you trust personally (but without gossiping), as their perspective will help bring balance to your views.
+ If you need to shout or raise your voice against another person, you are not yet ready to speak with them about the matter! Never speak out of unrighteous anger, that is, an anger that is intended to hurt the other person. We must never let anger be vindictive.
+ Never speak publicly about personal issues unless you have the direct consent of the person concerned or they have already talked openly about the same subject. The exception is when under supervision in a therapeutic context or as a mentor seeking advice about how to deal with a situation.

Emotional Abuse

Verbal abuse is often accompanied by emotional abuse. But emotional abuse can take place without any words at all. Indeed, the withholding of verbal affirmation can be a significant form of emotional abuse.[1] Some would argue that this can be one of the worst types of emotional abuse.

Emotional damage can also be gender distinct. Most women value relationships more highly than men so are more likely to be hurt when a friendship turns bad or ends. Many men, on the other hand, may not even be aware that a relationship has changed. Many other men, sadly, would not even care. In one sense, therefore, emotional abuse is more frequent among women than men. While men are far more likely to be emotionally abusive, whether they know it or not, it is women who often feel it most keenly.

Another key factor is that a man will normally have one or two relationships of deep value (wife, lover, children, professional colleague or training buddy), whereas a woman will have a wider circle of friends, which she will normally seek to maintain. For the man, an emotional exchange or breakdown with the few people he is committed to can have devastating consequences, as the number of male down and outs with tragic stories demonstrates. But for the woman, the loss of a friend or loved one will often be offset by her remaining network of relationships. These will normally fill the gap.

Emotional abuse is thus very different for men and women. A woman may live with abuse and absorb it more readily for the sake of the relationship, but will eventually take radical steps, such as divorce, walking away or having an affair, whereas the man, with far fewer valued friendships, will initially suffer more when one relationship is lost.

A vindictive God?

John and Maureen were working in central Africa and were expecting their second baby. Before the pregnancy began, they knew they were in great financial difficulties, and began to pray through the implications of this. Unless the Lord provided for them significantly, they needed to return home. Their colleagues on the mission station, who had the benefit of higher levels of support, were upset at the prospect of their leaving.

Months passed and the return date was fixed. They were to go back to the UK a month after the baby was due to be born. In the seventh month of her pregnancy Maureen went into premature labor, giving birth to a little girl. At first all went well as the baby was a good weight for her age, but then complications developed and the child died. Maureen was devastated. Following the delivery, she also developed a uterine infection, but continued looking after her eldest child. She was told by their senior missionary that the baby had been taken because they were leaving Africa, and God never meant the child to leave African soil. Maureen was not allowed to grieve and bury her baby, who was buried the day she died. Maureen was told that the best thing for her to do would be to return to her work in the hospital.

When the family finally arrived back in the UK, Maureen was exhausted, sick in both body and mind. As they had no home or work, they went to stay with her family, who were Christians. Maureen was longing for a little sympathy and understanding, but to her dismay she was treated judgmentally and branded a failure because "no Christian should ever be depressed." Once again she was told to put the past behind her, and get on with life. Her distress was further heightened when, on returning to her home church, she was again told that her baby had died as God's punishment because they had left the mission field.

Eventually Maureen's husband found work in London and the family had the opportunity to start a new life, but Maureen continued to carry the burden of failure and the guilt of feeling that maybe she had caused the death of her child by agreeing to return to England. There were times when she felt depressed, but she was afraid to seek help as she believed that by doing so she would be admitting her failure as a Christian.

Redemption: It was many years before Maureen found appropriate help and was enabled to deal with these issues, to grieve properly for her lost baby, let go of all the accusations and guilt, and move into a more joyful Christian experience.

What is evident in this tragic story is the appalling attitude that the leaders of this mission had toward God. They clearly believed that He was belligerent, vindictive, and uncaring, willing to take a child's life just because He did not get His own selfish way. It is shocking to realize that Christians can believe this of God. They had overlooked the fact that God is not human. He does not act like damaged human beings, for His nature is pure Love. So, first, we must note that those who hold such a view of God clearly do not have the right to lead other people. In our ministry we see it as sin against the person and the Lord to take unbiblical beliefs about God and irresponsibly lay them on others to their detriment or damage. No person has the right to do this to another.

Let me illustrate this with a reader's comments: "I had been taught that God was vindictive, but in small, more subtle, ways. When my father died, it was because I was naughty. When we left the mission field, we weren't doing God's will because we weren't spiritual enough so God could not use us. After a wrong relationship I had with a man, I was told I may have God's forgiveness, but I could never be trusted again. I was now a second-class Christian and I may do it again." This type of attitude about God is very sad.

The mental illness aspect of Maureen's story is also a serious concern. She was clearly suffering from a form of postnatal depression, but this was ignored. She was not supported and not taught how to grieve. She also needed to be shown how to separate the loss of the child from the complicated financial circumstances that surrounded this loss. No doubt she was also struggling over the loss of their ministry as a result of being forced to return home.

The words spoken over Maureen and John had a devastating impact on their lives. Even worse, this abuse was reinforced by other leaders. Soft, healing words need to be spoken over someone hurt in this way to help heal the tragic wounds.

We can draw many principles out of this example, but the principle that is most pertinent to emotional abuse is probably that we need to learn a better theology of both the human person and the nature of God. We must find a more balanced view of human emotion than many of us currently have. We must also pause long enough to ask what is really happening in any situation where people are hurting or being hurt.

Guidelines

• Take careful note of a person's emotional state, especially during times of suffering. Do nothing to make them more vulnerable, for instance, by telling them they are wrong or by being directive with them.

+ Never allow your own sin and negative views of God to be a judgment you lay on other people. It is so much easier to be negative than to seek out the facts and say sorry. Christ should always be our sorry.
+ Words can all too easily hurt those who are frail or vulnerable so we must speak honorable, loving words that help bring healing. We are called to build up one another, not to be negative and dismantle what the Lord and others are seeking to do.

Physical Abuse

It has traditionally been thought that most physical abuse is abuse of women by men. We both want to record how much we dislike the appalling history of male abuse against women. In any form it is totally unacceptable. Like all forms of abuse, physical assault impacts all areas of our life so it is essential that we take serious notice of any abuse against us, and do not pretend that "it's not a problem." Most abuse hurts more deeply than any of us realize, as is seen in our reluctance to return to the toxic emotions of the events.

Some people suggest that physical abuse is not as serious as other forms of abuse because it usually heals quickly. We do not agree with this position. All physical abuse, like all other abuse, leaves emotional scars, whether we recognize these or not. So it should always be treated very seriously. But another complicated issue should also be noted. Physical abuse of women by men can often cross the line into sexual abuse. So although we make a distinction here in this book, the reality is often not that simple. Sexual and physical abuse are often one and the same thing, especially when it is male against female or female against male.

Physical abuse is a huge subject in itself, covering abuse of children by adults, children by children, adults by children, and adults toward adults. It is important that pastors and Christian leaders remain alert to the possibility of physical abuse among those for whom they are responsible. The classic telltale signs are bruising, accidents (especially people saying they walked into a door!) or unexpected absences of people from meetings. Physical beating will also leave people looking fearful and traumatized. It is incumbent on all of us to remain vigilant to such hidden abuse.

Let us illustrate a typical difficult case.

Sexual or physical assault?

> A woman came to talk with Peter about a sexual assault that had occurred while she was attending a youth camp. A man had on several occasions physically manhandled her and hurt her by hitting her. As she plucked up the courage to describe the incident, she and Peter both realized that this had not been sexual assault at all, but physical assault. Over the years the woman had built up the events into a major sexual trauma. Not a day had gone by when she had not thought about it. Moreover, it had negatively impacted her relationship with the Lord. The damage had been so severe that she had not thought it could have been "just" physical abuse.
>
> Peter was able to show her how to engage the pain, trauma, and anger, to give it to the Lord, to let the assault go and get on with her life. The healing and redemption she found in the Lord meant that she was able to live free from the assault, as though it had never happened.
>
> **Redemption**: She is now married and settled in a local church.

In the case of this woman, it was important just to listen to her and to give her time to share her perspective. This honored her. Over the years, the sexual aspects of the events had loomed ever larger in her life so that she feared getting married. As she talked through what had happened, remembering the events, she began to see that the abuse did not have a sexual intent. This was a key revelation. On this basis she was able to let go of the fear of the abuse being repeated in her sexual relationship with her future husband. She was also able to begin to see hope of healing when we suggested to her that she did not have to continue to live with the trauma. Finally, after all those years, she was able to let go of the events emotionally.

Before leaving the area of physical abuse, we should address one further issue: the increasing levels of physical abuse by women against men in the home. On one website we were researching, the claim is made that violence of women against men is as high as 37 per cent of all cases of domestic violence. According to another site, although a higher percentage of women report domestic abuse, a higher percentage of women also commit violent offences. On a number of occasions men have told us of physical abuse against them by women. Several have commented on their reluctance or fear to go into the kitchen when she is there.

Physical abuse was once a male domain, but now, on a conservative estimate, 15 per cent of domestic abuse here in the UK is by women against men, and the figure is rising. There could be a number of reasons for this. Perhaps men are reporting such abuse more often than they did in the past or perhaps, with the rise of the feminist movement, women have a greater sense of injustice, and more frustration and anger, which boils over into physical violence. The trend may also be affected by the fact that women are less reliant on male financial support. Has financial independence taken away some of the need to be compliant? Is this leading women to be more willing to risk being violent against men?[2]

Guidelines

* Physical abuse can leave many hidden scars. Accusations should always be treated very seriously. For instance, we should not let our loyalties or prejudices stop us from hearing the person's perspective.
* We should be open and vigilant regarding physical assault by either men or women.

Sexual Abuse

As we have already noted, a great deal of physical abuse is also sexual abuse. For many of us who have experienced physical abuse, the line that defines the two is very unclear. For example, any physical assault against a woman by a man could be perceived as sexual assault. It depends where a person is hit or touched. The law in all these areas is very clearly defined through legislation, extensive precedent in case law and the established history of financial compensation. But to the emotionally damaged victim the line will rarely be so clear. Physical assault and sexual assault both abuse the whole person, including their gender identity. Sexual assault is the most intimate form of violation. Issues of vulnerability, accessibility, and victimization all play a part.

Although it is difficult for the victim to see it in this way, sexual abuse, like all forms of abuse, is a matter of degree. What is violent sexual assault to one person will be just a threat to another. What one person calls rape, another will excitedly call foreplay. It is important that, at the very least, congregations, denominations, and Christian institutions all stand by the definitions in law. The additional mandate from Scripture is that where possible there should be positive discrimination in favor of the sick, poor, and vulnerable, who should be protected and have their rights upheld. If someone is being abused, both law and the established procedure (for example, guidance notes and policies) of the local faith community should be seen to be seeking their protection and healing.

Let us illustrate with two examples of sexual assault.

Sexual abuse by youth leader

Victoria is the youngest child in her family, with three older brothers. Her parents were church leaders working within the medical sector. When Vicky was in her last year at junior school her parents decided to send her to a Christian house party. It was a holiday for junior boys and girls, and one that her brothers had attended in previous years. They had loved their time on the holiday.

One evening, the talk at prayer time was about receiving the Holy Spirit into your life. Children were invited to speak to the leader who had given the talk if they wanted to know how to receive the Spirit. Vicky's heart had been moved so she went to ask the leader. He took her into the woods to talk about how to receive, then proceeded to rape her, telling her that this was the way the Holy Spirit was received. The pain and trauma of this terrible abuse wrecked Vicky's life. She became a wild, unmanageable young woman who experimented with everything the world could offer her. She certainly had not found love and support in Christianity. She married and had a family, but then deserted them for affairs. She eventually sought to find her faith again, but could not sustain it.

Redemption None. Vicky continues to reject anything Christian and has had a life of damaged relationships.

The fear of abuse

Lucy is the middle child in a Christian family. She has an older brother, Francis, and a younger brother, David. Her early childhood was during the Second World War so her father was away much of the time on military service. Her young brother was born two years after the war ended, and her mother became totally absorbed with the new baby, leaving the other children to their own devices. Francis, the boy, was already showing signs of irrational behavior and began to seriously sexually abuse Lucy. This usually occurred outside the home, in outbuildings.

When the father was demobbed, the family moved to a new location. Lucy thought things would now be all right, since Daddy was home. However, the parents began to attend many church meetings, leaving the children alone at home. Francis took these opportunities to abuse his sister further, sometimes bringing in school friends who also raped her. One of her worst memories was a Sunday night when, in order to escape from her brother, she locked herself in the toilet. Francis pulled so violently on the door that the bolt bent and she could not get out when she heard her parents come home. She then had to face her parents' wrath on two counts: first, that she had somehow damaged the bolt; second, that she had not properly cared for her baby brother. She was only 10 and he was 3.

Eventually, Lucy decided that the only way to escape from Francis' attention was to accompany her parents to meetings. Rather than be left at home, she went to all of the services and meetings that she could.

As an adult, Lucy found herself overprotecting her own children, and even when they were young adults would not trust them in the house alone. She also had no real concept of the fatherhood of God, feeling that He must be remote and uncaring, liking meetings more than people!

Redemption: Following Christian counseling, and although still experiencing some difficulties, Lucy now enjoys a much more real experience of God.

What is evident in both these stories is the tragedy that such abuse could occur without others knowing about it. In both cases, the young women did not talk to anyone else. Neither of them seemed willing or able to talk to their parents. It is not uncommon for this to be the case, and also for parents to react badly or naively when sexual assault is reported to them.

Other issues also arise from these two stories, not least the long-term damage done to people when they are sexually abused.[3] As a young teenager I (Peter) was on several occasions sexually abused by an elderly man whom I trusted. It was over a decade before I was able to visit the events of the abuse and begin the process of letting go of all the pain. It is estimated that one in six boys in North America are sexually abused before reaching the age of 16.[4]

We mentioned earlier the need for faith communities to follow the requirements of the law. We will be looking into this in more detail later, but it is important to mention here that in both the UK and the USA, child protection legislation places a range of statutory duties on any professional who learns about a person being sexually abused, particularly if there is any possibility that the perpetrator could still be abusing. Every leader of a faith community, regardless of the size of the church or the leader's qualifications, has a duty in law to act properly in such matters. The police and others must be informed. All Christian leaders should also be up to date on such legislation and their duties in law.

Books have been written about people's journeying through such terrible experiences as sexual abuse so to draw just one or two principles is almost insulting! But some key practices do need to be highlighted.

Guidelines

+ Never ignore any rumors of sexual abuse in any form. Always ensure that the appropriate person checks out such suspicions, regardless of who the alleged perpetrator may be. But be careful, because a person's reputation can take years to establish but be destroyed in an instant by careless negative comment, even when it is not true.
+ When anyone comes to you to talk about being abused, treat what is said seriously and listen carefully. Talk it through with others you trust. Your actions must either be those required in law or have the victim's consent.
+ Be aware of revengeful or vindictive human nature. Sometimes things are not as they seem!
+ Build up effective relationships with local agencies who can be supportive in giving advice when you are unsure of how to handle an issue. For instance, in the UK, the police and the Public Protection Unit; in the USA, Christian legal professionals.

Spiritual Abuse

When speaking of spiritual abuse, what are we talking about? Within the Church, there is currently a great deal of confusion in this area. Do we say that all abuse includes spiritual abuse because all abuse affects our human spiritual nature? Or is it that spiritual abuse is a particular type of abuse, occurring when God's name is used explicitly or implicitly? Alternately, when abuse takes place, is it spiritual abuse if it happens in church? Is there a difference between spiritual and religious abuse?

Our own view is that all abuse impacts the human spirit. By the term, "human spirit," we are talking about the idea in Genesis (1:26; 2:7,21–22, etc.) of the breath of God being breathed into a physical body and then animating it to human personhood. The physical human body is sustained by His Spirit through human spirit. So the giving up of the human spirit brings the life of the body to an end (Mt. 27:50). Our human spirit is therefore impacted by everything that the human body experiences, and vice versa. We call this model of human make up "body–spirit unity," and use it in our ministry to describe how human personhood is constructed. The implication is that any abuse we experience will bring harm to our spirits.

Johnson and Van Vonderen define spiritual abuse as, "The mistreatment of a person who is in need of help, support or greater empowerment, with the result of weakening, undermining or decreasing that person's spiritual empowerment."[5] Although this definition is helpful in that it reminds us of our need to seek greater spiritual empowerment and anointing, it could be read as suggesting that spiritual abuse can somehow be separated from the broader experience of other types of abuse in everyday life.

But is there a specific type of abuse—spiritual and/or religious abuse—connected with the use of God's name, even if only by implication? If so, any abuse from a Christian leader, or within a Christian or religious setting, is also spiritual abuse because God is directly, or indirectly, involved. On this basis, heavy pastoral shepherding would always be spiritual abuse.

For the purpose of this book, we are leaving the question of a precise definition open, pending much more research. In our ministry, spiritual abuse is distinguished by its assault on our human spirit. Our spirit is that part of our nature that sustains our unique human personhood. It animates our personality and gives us our zest for life. The devitalizing of our spirit in any form is abuse against our spirit. Like all other forms of abuse, it reduces our humanness and our capacity to "bounce back."[6] We therefore see damage to our human spirit as little different from sickness in our body. Both need a period of restoring if they are to recover, and both need the help and support of others and God for this recovery to be fully achieved. By demystifying spiritual abuse in the Church in this way, one is able to call any form of abuse just what it is: assault against the person.

Most spiritual abuse occurs alongside the other four types of abuse already identified, but for one reason or another, the spiritual dimension is sometimes more prominent. Let us illustrate this type of abuse.

Spiritual abuse

> Some years ago I was working, as I had been doing for many years, in a lay pastoral ministry. I was helping a range of people who were seeking to deepen their relationship with the Lord. This involved helping them remove personal obstacles and baggage.
>
> This came to the notice of the leadership of the congregation I was attending at the time, and without stopping to ask whether I had either the anointing or call for this ministry, they demanded a complete list of all those I was "harming" so they could be protected from me. I was told by these leaders that I was not properly trained for such "specialist" counseling, and that these people needed to be told this. Much fruit was already evident in people's lives, and those I was seeking to help made this point when the leaders approached them. Nevertheless, I was banned in writing from offering to help anyone else, and the suggestion was made that it would be best if I stopped pretending that I could help such people.
>
> **Redemption:** Today, many years later, he has a pastoral counseling and teaching ministry. He has also published books and tapes based on Scripture, describing his approach. But for some time the experience left him wanting to have nothing to do with either the Lord or the Church.

The abuse lay in the act of judging the person and the spiritual gifting. As a result, the help people were receiving from this ministry was questioned and undermined. The implicit accusation was that it was not of God, even though the people clearly believed it was. As in many other cases, the witness of the people being helped was not trusted. Those in authority believed that they knew better, arguing that all involved were being deceived. So the abuse extended beyond the person's ministry to all those who had benefited from it and also affected the wider Church.

It often happens that the victim of abuse is not the only one to suffer. Much abuse yields wider-ranging loss than the creation of one victim. In this story, had the person remained under this "discipline," his skill and anointing would have been lost to the Church. Abuse often leads to barrenness and lost potential.

Guidelines

+ Listen carefully and transparently to all sides when it seems someone might be being harmed. But do not jump to conclusions without talking to others.
+ Do not use the name of God when giving your opinion. Do not seek to impose your view of reality on others. Respect diversity of opinions and practices in the Body of Christ. Seek to honor others, and encourage honor amongst others. The way we treat others is the way we will be treated by God (Mt. 6:14–15).
+ Remember that authority and standing in the Church are to build others up, not to abuse them in any way. Always be alert to the fact that it is much easier to be negative than positive, to believe bad things than defend or create good things.

One further comment needs to be made on the subject of spiritual abuse. Spirituality as a subject and area of interest now extends beyond the Church. It is fashionable in popular culture, business, and society as a whole.[7] Many of those who acknowledge the importance of the soul and of spiritual reality have no faith background. With this extraordinary growth of interest in spirituality there has come a range of new suggestions about what comprises "spiritual" abuse. For instance, it is now suggested that your doctor, teacher or parent—all people who are outside the Church—could "spiritually" abuse you. It is clearly no longer possible to "contain" spiritual abuse to faith community life. This may mean that "spiritual abuse" now occurring within the Church could reoccur outside the Church. It will be interesting to see how this evolves over the next few years.

In Summary

We've mapped out the terrain in terms of five main forms of abuse: verbal, emotional, physical, sexual, and spiritual. But it may be felt that this misrepresents actual experience since in everyday life they tend to overlap. It could even be argued that it doesn't matter how the abuse occurred, but that what is important is how the individual can be helped to undo it. We would agree that for abused individuals, the process of finding healing from the damage varies little, regardless of the nature of the abuse. But from the perspective of a congregation wanting to act in a proactive way to become more of a safe place, these details are important. Let us begin to explore how we can create a safe place.

Questions to Ponder

1. What distinctions can you make between verbal and emotional abuse?
2. Of all the types of abuse mentioned, which one is most common in your experience?
3. Outline some of the different ways in which men and women get abused.
4. In what ways would the main types of abuse outlined in this chapter vary from one local church to another?
5. Discuss what we meant when we suggested that all abuse has a spiritual dimension.
6. Where might spiritual abuse be found outside the Church?

Notes

1 J.K. Gottman and J. de Claire, *The Relationship Cure: A 5 step guide to strengthening your marriage, family and friendships* (New York: Three Rivers Press, 2002).

2 Some of the websites are: <www.oregoncounseling.org/Handouts/DomesticViolence Men.htm>; <www.dvmen.org>; <www.batteredmen.com>; <www.commun-ity.meath.ie/amen>.

3 See Williams and Holmes, *Letting God Heal.*

4 See <www.jimhopper.com/male-ab/>.

5 D. Johnson and J. Van Vonderen, *The Subtle Power of Spiritual Abuse: Recognizing and escaping spiritual manipulation and false spiritual authority within the Church* (Minneapolis: Bethany House, 1991), 20.

6 For a Biblical framework of human make-up, see Holmes, *Becoming More Human.*

7 P.R. Holmes, "Spirituality: some disciplinary perspectives" in K. Flanagan and P.C. Jupp (eds.), *The Sociology of Spirituality* (to be published).

Part 3

Creating a Safe Place

With our greater understanding of what abuse is, we are now ready to begin looking at how a safe place might be created. Having focused on abuse in wider society, and the five main types of abuse, we will now begin to consider how groups work and note the types of relationship required if a safe place is to be offered.

6

Group Dynamics and Creating
a Safe Place

*This chapter begins Part 3 with the challenge of trying to understand
group dynamics, that is, how we relate to one another, hurting and
healing one another. To help us in this understanding, we introduce
the idea of scripts and consider the way in which these tramlines dictate much of our behavior. We follow this with the concept of social
rules, looking at how these can be a help or a hindrance. We end with
some experiences of Christians, from which we draw some guidelines
for our conduct.*

We have so far considered in some detail the numerous ways
in which it is easy for churches to mirror the abuse that is present in wider society, thereby also becoming unsafe places. But
we now face a real challenge. How is it possible to make congregational life safer? How do we improve the situation? How
do we enable the Body of Christ to stand against the massed
practices of our society as a whole?

The remainder of the book is devoted to exploring various
practices and principles within congregational life that could
contribute to making Church a safer place. We are aware that
we are addressing a variety of denominations and church settings, and that therefore not everything will be appropriate for
everyone everywhere. But if some of these principles can be
adopted in some places, then the worldwide Church will have
become a safer place.

Christ in Unsafe Places

The first question we must address is whether it is even realistic to talk about a church or congregation being a safe place. Can any congregation be 100 per cent safe? Could Tomorrow's Church really exist?

On hearing that we were writing a book on abuse in the Church, one person commented to us that they did not believe anyone could provide a blueprint that stops people being abused in the Church. Abuse will always happen, regardless of any efforts to end it. Naturally, we gave this objection considerable thought, and we have come to the conclusion that we disagree. Although we accept that it might be unrealistic to think that abuse can be prevented by providing any one "blueprint," we are of the opinion that we can go some distance by outlining what abuse in the Church actually is, how to see it and where to draw the line. For instance, as people learn what abuse is, they can take steps to prevent it. We believe in the empowering of people and their right to know.

So can a congregation guarantee safety? Probably not! Fallen human beings who are seeking to grow in Christ-likeness are typically clumsy, selfish, and unthinking. Learning to welcome and minister to desperately sick and needy people outside of the Church is also a messy and untidy business! But we believe that we can all make our churches safer, and that there is a huge amount we can do to ensure that abuse and betrayal are minimized. Likewise, we can help ensure that when abuse does occur, it is dealt with openly, in a way that allows healing and reconciliation, rather than being left to store up bitterness and division.

We can be encouraged that Christ did not set Himself the limited target of creating "safe places." He did not seek to control environments or society as a whole. He did not regulate out disorder and sin. Instead, He sought the places and people where those who loved religious life were reluctant to go. He enjoyed the company of tax collectors, prostitutes, and foreigners. Note also some of the baggage and sinful behavior that the disciples used against themselves, Christ, and each other. He was accustomed to dealing with such betrayal in His community (Mt. 26:14–15,31–35,43–46,69–75; Jn. 13:21–30, etc.). He did not stop His friends making mistakes. He let things be, while teaching them how to live well in society. He did not seek to confront the powers, spiritual and social, in order to change them. Nor did He isolate Himself in an exclusive environment fit only for Him. Instead of creating a safe place, He was the safe place.

So do we need to create safe places? Is the idea of creating a safe place one that we should abandon? After all, any activity involving fallen and damaged human nature has got to be flawed or open to abuse, hasn't it? But, again, this is not how Christ approached the problem. From His perspective, undergirding all human relationships, including us with ourselves, was His expectation that we should live Love. Knowing that we are sinful and damaged is not an excuse. Tomorrow's Church may be unrealistic or even impossible in this life for some of us, but as and when we are willing to imagine it, we can then begin embracing some of its principles and practices. What we are noting is that Christ was the safe place, and by being the safe place created a safe place for everyone else.

The Dynamics of Relationships

In order to begin imagining how Tomorrow's Church might be a safe place, we must first consider some of the dynamics that occur when individuals come together. We must glance at relational life. We are moving here into the realms of sociology and social psychology to look at what happens when individuals start to interact with one another.

The whole of human life breaks down into social groupings. As well as being members of society as a whole, most of us are associated with various social groups, such as family, church, work, hobby and special interest groups, which all bring different possibilities of both safety and/or abuse. Few, if any, of us can avoid them because human nature, at its healed best, is social. Whether we like it or not, we are created for one another.

The simplest level of social life consists of one person interacting with another. Even the most morose of hermits among us must has contact with others at times, be it at the super-market, filling up with fuel or visiting the optician or dentist. During these relational encounters far more is happening than initially meets the eye. For example, when two people are talking they are communicating with each other in a range of ways, through speech, body language, what they are wearing (or not wearing), spirit to spirit. Even in the simplest of conversations, a wide range of things is happening.

Around 70 per cent of all our "conversations" are unspoken. So if you are a cerebral (in-your-head) type of person who lives by the words you say and hear, then you are in trouble. Most women, for instance, will ignore what a person says if it is contradicted by the accompanying actions, demeanor or body language. We do not have the space to go into greater detail about these very exciting, innovative, and growing areas of human knowledge. Understanding emotional intelligence (EQ) is at the heart of it.[1] What we are suggesting is that we need to understand social interaction and emotional signals, and what is now being called the "micro-inequities" and "micro-gestures" between people,[2] that is, all the naughty things we think and sometimes say or act out, but had not intended to say, and also all the tiny signals we communicate to one another at subliminal levels. Women are much better than men at reading and interpreting these.

But this is just the beginning of what happens when two people meet because people also have a significant range of values that they bring, unspoken, into any conversation or relationship. For instance, when a man and woman are talking together, they both carry a set of values and "scripts" about gender. He may instinctively "know" that this is a friendly or not so friendly woman, or the woman may be aware that he is a leader so can or cannot be trusted. Each, whether they are aware of it or not, will have collected during their lifetimes a unique range of hundreds of such values and scripts, which all help construct, for better or worse, the way they conduct themselves in any relationship. Typical generalized values are "women can't be trusted," "men are only out for sex," or "he will never notice me." So in any two-way conversation each person is working with a constructed, learned history and view of reality.

Introducing Scripts and Social Rules

Part of the history we all bring to relationships takes the form of many thousands of *scripts*. By "scripts" we mean our ability to store patterns of learned behavior so they become reflexive or instinctive. For instance, once we have learned how to make a cup of coffee, we remember it as a script. We no longer have to relearn the fifteen or more stages and decisions that are involved. We just decide to make a coffee. We have done it before so we use the script. In a similar way, as we learn to drive a car, we write a great number of scripts so that we no longer need to think carefully how to synchronize all our actions every time we get in the car. Driving a car, like most learned behavior, is made up of a cluster of scripts. For instance, where do we normally leave the car keys? Where do we normally park the car? How do we get into the car? One of the most complex of all the clusters of scripts is that used for learning a language. Every word is surrounded by a range of scripts or rules that guide its use. It is said that much of our life is lived out using such scripts.

Ordered, already learned, behavior always reduces stress. Indeed, scripts are essential to our well-being, for without them life would be intolerable. Imagine being faced all the time with situations that we have to learn for the first time, such as putting on trousers or carrying a handbag. Our lives would be highly stressful if we constantly had to face new situations that we didn't know how to respond to. Check this out in your own experience by noting what you are doing at various moments during the day. Are you following old scripts or writing new ones?

Society is socially structured, and is extremely complex, multi-layered and multi-faceted. I (Peter) once did an exercise exploring what one has to learn just to live in a Western culture. Even at the most minimal level one needs several hundred basic skills in order to live modestly as part of society. These begin with reading and writing, being able to count and articulate one's thinking. But much more complex skills are also needed, such as being able to find somewhere to live, complete the forms for gas and electricity services for our homes, use a laptop, select holidays and even partners. It is good that we spend a significant part of our life growing up, as we all need every minute to learn how to be part of such a complex society.

Much of this time we will be building healthy scripts to help us manage the demands of daily life. However, we all also use lots of scripts that may have been helpful at one time, but not any longer. For instance, as children, we may have been verbally abused by our parents. If so, we perhaps wrote a bunch of scripts that said to us that we should not be around them when they were angry. These scripts, which may have been essential in our early life, will still be lived out in adult life unless we have consciously sought to rewrite them. If we have not let go of them, when we meet people who remind us of our parents, we will act on the basis of these scripts.

Scripts remain with us once we have written them and lie dormant until a situation recalls them at an unconscious level. Most of us are unaware of the host of scripts and their values that are guiding us. We would do well to learn some of them, for instance, scripts leading to bad attitudes and sinful thoughts. When we give the Holy Spirit permission, He will often begin bringing these to our attention. As Christians, we have a responsibility to let Him talk to us about these toxic and unhelpful scripts, otherwise we will never know what they are or the values they carry.[3]

Earlier, we introduced four Biblical principles for living as safe people, culminating in having a Christ-like capacity to love others. This will require the dismantling of unrighteous scripts from our history so that in one-to-one relationships we can offer one another the safety and acceptance of Christ. For Tomorrow's Church to be a consistently safe place, a substantial number of its members must be committed to this type of ongoing positive discipleship change. This will involve the rewriting, as well as the deleting, of values and scripts.

Whereas a script helps us to manage the internal routines of our daily lives, *social rules* are written to help us in our relationships. When two people meet, they not only bring with them all their historic values and scripts, they also carry a range of social rules. These they will have written over the years and now bring to every relationship. Many men say things like, "I always say it the way it is," or, "I never get angry." Many women have social rules such as, "Never let on the way you feel," or, "Never trust anyone." Often our social rules will be positive contributors to our lives but when they begin to control our behavior, they can be destructive.

Social rules are the hidden patterns that have become the guiding principles of our lives in all our relationships. They are always predictable once we have adopted them. They impact us in just the same way as do more overt rules, such as that men should always use the men's toilet or that women should not try to be men. But unlike the law, and rules relating to, say, parking your car, social rules are usually unwritten, and are often implicit rather than explicit. Most of us don't realize that such social rules guide us, yet we dance to their tune all the time.

We all have a range of personal social rules—rules to fit any and every situation. We are conditioned by our experiences, and act on what we have learned. The term "freedom to choose" refers more to a faint echo of freedom than to a strong "free choice" or a feeling that "I can do what I like." None of us are entirely "free," because social rules always dictate to us how we should live and act. To act beyond these social rules would need a significant, intrinsic change in our values and scripts. "Original" or "unfettered" behavior is very rare. Stress is when we need to act or we experience reality, outside the comfort zones of our scripts and social rules. In our ministry, we are always looking for the voice of the Lord in people's lives and we most often recognize it by its originality; it is "outside the box" of the person's scripts and social rules. If it is predictable, then it is probably the person's own voice.

In popular parlance, predictors or social rules are often referred to as "hidden agendas." We need to commit ourselves to finding them by allowing them to surface in our lives. Some of us are shown them by the Lord, while many of us are just suddenly shocked to see ourselves using them, and are appalled and want to change them. Once they are changed they are deleted, replaced (hopefully) by new ones. If we deny they exist, we will continue to be influenced by them: the very act of denial can itself be determined by a hidden agenda. We have all had to face up to the man or woman who reminds us of someone from our past who mocked us or the friend with mannerisms that connect with the fear we carry from someone who abused us. Through such echoes come a whole range of values and scripts we will not be aware of.

One aspect of sin in our lives is our unwillingness to admit that toxic scripts and social rules exist in us. All of us are tyrannized by the things we deny in ourselves. When not owned and confessed openly to others, such scripts and social rules can be open windows for the Enemy to enter and abuse us.

Another key factor, rooted in scripts and social rules, is that abused people will always have the tendency to be abused again. For example, the scripts we write may tell us that the abuse will happen again, and we start anticipating it, thereby possibly making it more likely. Such a mindset is not dissimilar to being "accident prone." If we are the type of people who attract abuse, or self-harm, we will probably find it recurring in almost any church we attend. Likewise, at the other extreme, if we find it hard to learn from others, then we will also find it difficult to change from our old ways. Our scripts will re-enforce our arrogance because they tell us that no one else knows better than we do. Creating a safe place for those of us who have carried years of such damage is a significant challenge.

How Groups Do and Don't Work

One-to-one relationships are the basis of all social life. But Tomorrow's Church will not just consist of such networks. Scripture makes it clear that the Church is the Body of Christ, with each part of the Body belonging to every other part (1 Cor. 12:12–26). To be a safe place, Tomorrow's Church will need a sense of being a collective, a cohesive group of people.

Groups create their own social rules, and these might be quite different from those of the individuals who comprise the group. These social rules help construct and guide the way members conduct themselves in relationships within the group. Members of Tomorrow's Church must learn together life-giving social rules and relationships that mirror the harmony of social Trinity. These social rules will be quite different from the dynamic of wider twenty-first-century society with its selfism and abuse. They will offer a radical alternative. By allowing such Biblical social rules to emerge, the group will feel like a refuge, a haven for those in need. But when the social rules stop being subliminal and start to be "enforced," they can become the basis of judgment and once again carry the potential for abuse.

There are clues in Scripture that the Early Church experienced the culture of mutual support. Consider how they met together, provided for the needs of widows (Acts 6:1–6), and broke with the traditional values of the day. Read Acts 2:42–47 and 4:32–37 and note how many new social rules they were writing. The group social processes in the Early Church offered a tangible alternative, a "counter-cultural" way of life in the midst of the tumultuous Greco-Roman culture of the occupying power.

Within our own faith community in Deal UK, we discovered that social rules were evolving that promoted therapeutic wholeness as a discipleship journey. We probably have hundreds. Some that we have identified are, "It's going to hurt like hell but it's worth it;" "It gets worse before it gets better;" "Don't hide it, they already know;" "They won't judge you" and, "It's safe to be honest." All groups, as they exist together and mature, will create more and more social rules. What these are will depend on what is fed into the group and lived out by the group in social relations. In a dynamic or constantly changing group, social rules will also be changing all the time, being unconsciously reviewed, deleted, and rewritten. A group that is more traditional or stable will often have social rules that are more fixed. Some of the social rules may be to have no new or different social rules! In such situations, a careful joint effort is needed when it is time to change them! Some people may well resist such change.

For the dynamic of group social rules to be viable, the relational networks of the group must stay intact. It is suggested by social psychologists that groups can stay together in a cohesive way up to a certain number of members, after which they begin breaking into sub-groups. The figure normally suggested is around 150 people.[4] This means that in the UK, where churches often have no more than 40 members, most churches have a social configuration that allows them to stay one cohesive whole. In the USA, where many congregations are in their thousands, the picture is quite different. As the cell-church movement illustrates, people prefer small groups where "everyone knows my name," allowing *koinonia* (fellowship) life to proliferate. Within these larger congregations, social rule making is much more complex because every sub-group—teenage girls, leadership team, etc.—will write clusters of social rules.

Outside church life, some groups meet together only occasionally, perhaps monthly. Other groups have quite varied membership, with the "feel" of the group being quite different each time it meets. Such groups will find it harder to have a clear sense of group identity and membership, and social rules are more likely to be influenced by individuals rather than evolving as a direct result of group life. Other groups participate in the traditions and rituals of a larger organization, for example, a business or denomination. In these groups, social rules will in part be determined by the identity of the wider collective, although the members of each local group will influence how rules are adopted in daily life.

In any community, while relationships remain good, social rules are a helpful asset, but when a community begins to become insular or finds itself in a crisis of one type or another, the benefits can be lost as the social process and social rules begin to reinforce the damage, breeding, for example, ongoing mistrust, fear or mockery. When this happens, it will not be enough for the leadership simply to teach a different way of life or to impose "standards" of behavior. From among the group members themselves there will need to be a groundswell of protest that brings about a united desire to change the unhelpful social rules that have accumulated. The group can then begin to start again. We are describing here what is called "deep change," which can emanate from any level of an organization, but eventually permeates all levels. The change most often begins with deep change in the individual,[5] moving from the bottom up. Trying to do it the other way round, imposing change from the top, will almost always not bring about the deep change that is needed.

Having said that, we would add that people in positions of formal or informal leadership in the group do have the capacity to influence the group's social rules. For instance, someone who wishes to lead will bring into leadership all the good and bad experiences of their past, and these will color and guide their actions in the group. If they carry a basic, historic distrust of men, they may have an inability to trust men in the group. Or a woman with bad experiences of other women, experiences that have perhaps been festering from childhood, will, as a leader, be more likely to move toward working with men than other women. We will address some aspects of leadership in Part 4.

Our Church Culture Impacts Every Area of Life

If we are in any way committed to Christ or to a life in faith community, what happens to us at church impacts all areas of our lives. But if we are not careful, many years later we can still find ourselves being controlled and driven by past events. Let us share with you an example of this, which, though extreme, very clearly illustrates the point.

The black circle

> The spiritual damage I've carried was not the first thing that I looked at on my journey, but after four and a half years it showed up as a root. I had a sudden overwhelming feeling that I must walk away from most, if not all, of the things I held most dear. I was wearing an engagement ring and I loved the man who had given it to me. He was deeply committed to the Church, the journey, and to God. But if I accepted all that he was, I had the overwhelming feeling, "I shall be caged."
>
> I didn't understand, but I had always had a sense of needing to stay on the edge. Now I had to face it. So I sat down with God and I cried. I cried and cried. And I told Him how unfair this was, and I asked Him to show me why I felt like this.

I remembered being in the playground of my infant school. I was on one side, and it felt like around me was a black circle. Outside the circle, playing, were all my friends. I remembered at the time crying with pain because I wanted to be like them. I wanted to be normal. To laugh and run around, have fun, but I knew I could never have it. They were happy because they didn't have God. They didn't have to be in this black circle.

My family had been excommunicated from a Christian denomination, a denomination that holds the belief that they are the only truth and that outside of them truth cannot be known. When forced to leave, our family was seen as deceived and as going to hell—the "devil's children." As a child I had feared that without this community I would not know truth, and I wouldn't know God. They knew God, and we were outside of them now. I was terrified to move away from them because in the outside world I would never know what was true.

It caused my parents a lot of pain when it happened. For me, even before then, I carried a feeling that I was not normal. The denomination taught we had to be separate from everyone. When we left, I found myself needing to stay alone. I had always stood on the outside looking in on life. I felt that I was incapable of knowing the truth so was unable wisely to commit myself to any relationship, even with myself. "I don't intrinsically trust me in any area." I would never know what truth was.

I had thought these were just faded memories. Yet I still carried this desperate longing to be normal. I had to admit that I was still living as if I was in this black circle, cut off, different, frightened to join in with the rest of the world. Talking about how I felt, emotionally stepping over the edge of the black circle, sent me into so much trauma that I started to physically shake. I knew I needed help. I felt the terror, "I will be deceived again." I couldn't ever play freely with the other children because this would mean I would not know what was true and what was false. I could be deceived.

In order to dismantle these lies, I had to choose to say to myself, "That's not true," even though every part of me believed it was. The next thing was harder—to decide what's true and what's not true. To know who the true God is. I would say to myself, "I now know the Real God—the God who has taken away my pain." After some time, I realized I could step out of the black ring. I wanted, too, to join the children who were playing freely, with the Christ I now knew. I wanted to begin to trust myself.

From the time I chose to really see, I would say it probably took three to four months before I could step out of the black ring of accusation, because I really had to distance myself from what I believed was true. I would say sorry to God and say sorry to myself that I believed that lie. I wanted to feel free.

But I was also aware of the word "isolation." I felt very isolated from other people. I felt "outside," and this outside-ness was the result of what happened when my parents moved away from their church community and we, as a family, were accused of putting ourselves outside the group who claimed to be the only ones who knew truth. Getting married was me trying to join in, to be normal. It wasn't possible until I stepped outside my black circle. I can now say sorry to God, sorry to myself, and start again.

Redemption: She is now married with two children. They both continue in local church leadership, while her husband pursues a successful career in the financial sector.

This is a tragic example of the social rules and culture of a church community doing terrible damage to a young child, damage that she unwittingly carried into adult life. But social rules full of Love and life also have the capacity to influence who we are and who we become. They can give us all a foundation of Love to support us in the wider society.

It is a difficult balance to find. On the one hand, the internal values, beliefs, and practices of a successful faith community must always be stronger than the values pulling on the person in the culture around them. If not, a person will be lost to the Church or find few good reasons to be part of the faith community. For instance, where the values are the same in both the Church and the society around them, people lose any sense of the relevance of the Church to their everyday lives. Such values have to be distinctive so that people can make moral and relational choices for themselves.

But on the other hand, such internal values have to be just and righteous. They must not in any way build damage into the person. Rules should not be manipulative or controlling in an unrighteous way. People must feel they are free to make their own choices. Values become abusive when people feel they will be punished if they choose wrongly, or when they are unable to make a choice that they know will go against the wishes of their bosses, thereby incurring their wrath.

Freedom in Christ, therefore, is not the experience of all Christians. Many feel that they are on a tightrope and are afraid to move for fear of falling off. Such a statement may surprise you, but, sadly, it is true. Some of us do believe in a vindictive God who will punish us if we put a step wrong. For instance, we think, "If I don't sort out my feelings, I'll get sick." "If I don't sort out the bad things I've inherited from my parents, I'll hand them on to my children, and see them suffer." This is not what we are saying. We are hoping you will get the message that we all have an example in Christ of perfect Love, and this Love is available to all of us, ideally in this life through the local church or faith community.

Guidelines

+ Practice living and teaching by the example of Christ.
+ Learn to write Christ-like scripts and social rules that honor and build up people. Learn Love, not revenge.
+ Celebrate diversity, not a bland conformity. Maintaining relationships with others in the Body of Christ is more important than lecturing, judging, controlling them or laying blame on them. They could be right and you wrong.

In Summary

The observations we have made regarding social processes, the size of groups, scripts, and social rules all point toward a range of behavior based on our background, human experience and circumstances, both inside and outside the Church. Our actions and reactions are not as random or "free" as we might think, indeed, much of the time they can be predicted. With a dynamic of social rules emerging from close relationships, the church community can offer an alternative to the surrounding culture. But relationships will need to be solid and committed for these social rules to evolve. So in the next chapter we will look at what is needed for this to happen.

Questions to Ponder

1. Describe what we mean by social groups.
2. Why is it said that women are better than men at EQ? Do you accept this?
3. List some of the "micro-inequities" and "micro-gestures" we commonly use.
4. Talk together about some of your good and bad scripts.
5. List some of the basic skills needed to live comfortably in modern society.
6. Choose a group you are involved in and begin identifying some of the social rules in this group.
7. In what ways do negative scripts and bad social rules make congregational life unsafe?
8. In what ways can Church traditions become abusive?

Notes

[1] But a range of books is becoming available. See, for instance, D. Goleman, *The New Leaders: Transforming the art of leadership into the science of results* (London: Little, Brown, 2002); A. Pease and B. Pease, *The Definitive Book of Body Language* (London: Orion, 2004).

[2] J. Rawe, "Why your boss might start sweating the small stuff: New sensitivity training at the office focuses on all the little ways a tone-deaf manager can demoralize staff," *Time Magazine* (20 March 2006), 42.

[3] In our Introductory Workshop we devote a whole session to these scripts, teaching people how to remove them and write new ones.

[4] M. Gladwell, *The Tipping Point: How little things can make a big difference* (London: Little, Brown, 2000).

[5] R.E. Quinn, *Deep Change: Discovering the leader within* (San Francisco, Calif.: Jossey-Bass, 1996)

7

Relationships of Honor

In this chapter we will be seeing that it is the norm to live by rules in the Church. But we will also note that we need to put the other person ahead of rules. We will see that we must not develop a judging spirit because Scripture forbids such judging. Instead, we are called to Love, avoiding the danger of committing blasphemy against the Holy Spirit.

"Social rules" is a slightly misleading term. It implies something consciously and externally imposed that each of us reluctantly yields to. But in the context of the Body of Christ (or any other group), the term refers to the deeply-rooted patterns or values that drive our daily relationships. Scripture is clear that the greatest of these, the only one that should drive our lives, is Love. God is Love. When this supernatural, God-given Love is flowing in relationships, and is at the core of congregational life, then so is Christ.

But we are also noting that to have Love in our lives and in our communities, to be safe people and create safe places, each of us has work to do. Where we do not achieve a life of Love together, we inevitably end up resorting to lesser alternatives. In this chapter we are going to compare the life of Love that would characterize Tomorrow's Church with two of the most common obstacles to that life: living by rules and the negative practice of judging.

Living by the Rules

In saying that people live by social rules, we are not suggesting that a safe place is created by setting in place the right rules and guidelines and then merely implementing them. To live-learning-rules in this way defeats all that we are seeking to say. We hope that as you read the rest of this book, you will begin to understand that a safe place is nothing less than a safe place. In a safe place people feel safe: that is the atmosphere they breathe. But to achieve this, we have to create an overall culture of safety. In taking this perspective, we are adopting what is often called a "holistic approach" to congregational life.

By the term "holistic approach," we mean that instead of addressing each part of the organization separately and making each area safe, we focus on the group as a whole. It is the group as a whole that carries the anointing of Love and is rooted in divine social community. In baking, you might have twelve perfect ingredients but it is the process by which they are combined that creates the delicious cake. Likewise, it is the spirit that each of us brings to our life together as a group, combined with the Spirit of the social Trinity, that enables the group to live and breathe, thereby creating a safe place. In my (Susan's) research it is this synergy that transforms a group from an efficient, functional environment into a living, dynamic place of refuge and sanctuary.

The following story shows that love and safety cannot be created merely by imposing helpful or Biblical rules.

A Bible school of rules . . .

I went into shock when I began Bible school because I didn't realize the extreme regime I was entering. For example, women and girls had to wear skirts all day. No relationships were permitted with any boys, no social life. I was already 21 to 22 so I should have known better, but I felt really small inside. Every day during the first week we had "assemblies" where we would start with worship and after that it was about getting rid of our past. There was this big huge bin at the front and people would get rid of their pasts by throwing away all their old music or clothes and tee-shirts that reminded them of their pasts. I got rid of a ring that reminded me of someone. But I was still going out with this man, whom I hoped one day to marry. He wasn't a Christian and all that pressure got churned up so I eventually broke up with him. It was actually one of the most abusive things that I have ever done to a non-Christian, but the pressure was so great, and the judgment and condemnation meant I had to get rid of him.

Also, everything was compulsory. You were expected to read your Bible certain hours every day. Also, we all met in this huge hall, and we had to pray in tongues for 15 minutes, out loud so everyone knew we were praying in tongues. If you didn't know how, that was a bit tragic, so you got prayed for. If you were sitting quietly whilst everyone else was jumping around praising the Lord, someone would come up to you and say, "What's the matter with you?" They partly thought you were rebelling, but also were more on the Enemy's side if you weren't doing these set things.

Redemption: The woman who wrote this did get over it and is now married and part of the leadership of a local church.

When others are leading the way, and managing the relationships or situation incompetently, it is important to understand what is happening. This woman was part of an institution that had very fixed ideas of what was good and holy, and the leaders had no intention of changing or even reviewing their practices. This we find very sad. They did not stop to see what they were creating. They did not see that the social processes were not helpful to this woman and were probably not helpful to others.

We see two problems. The first is that there was no awareness of the social processes that were being created by the rules. The second is that the leaders seemed unwilling to stop and ask how these rules might be made more "user friendly." We can imagine some of the social rules that were at work in an environment such as this: "Smile, regardless of how you are feeling;" "Don't admit to your hurt;" "Keep separate;" "Show everyone how full of praise you are." They are the types of guidelines that would feel threatening, and induce fear in many people, especially those feeling fragile or needing help. Such social rules would not promote a safe place.

What we are leading up to, and beginning to suggest, is the need for a major shift in the way the Church looks at people.

Instead of putting the rules first, we need to learn how to put the person first.[1]

Putting the Other Person First

By introducing us to the Holy Spirit, Christ has given us access to social Trinity Love (Jn. 14:26–28). With this new relationship comes the assumption that we can live Love despite our damaged human nature. For instance, even before it happened, Jesus answered Peter's betrayal with the command that the disciples should Love, and this Love should be lived among them (Mt. 22:34–39; Jn. 13:31–35). Christ expected the disciples to Love one another. This Love was to be a fundamental part of their lifestyle, witness, and reputation. He assumed they were able to do this. His Love for us, that we can know now, becomes the basis of our capacity to Love ourselves and others (Jn. 14:21–23). And He gave us specific guidelines, for instance, He told us how we should respond when hurt by another person (Mt. 5:21–26,43–48; 18:15–17), as well making an exacting requirement with regard to our duty to forgive others (Mt. 18:21–35; Lk. 6:37–42).

Instead of seeking to correct other people or to get our point across—which we sometimes do even at the expense of the relationship—we should think in terms of grace. The creating of a safe place means that it is essential that people should trust us, especially our reactions to their values, actions, and misbehavior. It is transparently obvious from the huge number of people who approached Christ that even though they *came* in need, they came. He could be trusted, He was approachable, even when at times His disciples were not (Mt. 19:13–14). One of the reasons why people came was no doubt because Christ offered them the hope of becoming whole (breaking the sickness, poverty, and deprivation trap) and of being all they could become, even excelling Him in His ministry (Jn. 14:12).

In terms of daily congregational life, this life of Love can be summarized as putting the other person first. To adopt it as the norm requires a whole lifestyle change in the way that we live and act. It is incompatible with selfism and the background noise of abuse that most of us carry, experience, and inadvertently condone. In asking ourselves what is best for the other person (as they, and not we, see it!), we are shifting all our resources from what is best for us to what is best for them. This is a huge exertion, since human nature will always first be faithful to its own agendas. To be more like Christ means that we need to stop this way of thinking that puts us first.

When we say that the other person should be put first, we are not talking about slavery under them or a kind of self-hate or self-loathing. Instead, we are describing a mutual honor. Our observation is that some people, in honoring others, end up dishonoring themselves: that is not what we mean. We are also assuming that this is done in the context of what is acceptable to the community as a whole, rather than at the expense of the community. Finding the balance in this life of putting the other first takes practice.

As we become safe people, we each have a greater capacity to put the other person first, and to set this principle at the center of Body life. In Tomorrow's Church there would be a core group of disciples committed to this way of life. Although each would focus their energy on a life of Love with others, each would also be the beneficiary, the recipient, of others who are living this way of life. So there would be a solid mutuality of Love, which newcomers and those in need would be able to draw from.

Who Knows What Is Best?

At this point we need to re-emphasize a word of caution. In saying that we should ask what is best for the other person, we are not suggesting that we judge for ourselves what is best for them. No. We must talk with them. Ask them. Listen to them. Nothing is more therapeutic and friendship-building than being listened to, especially when feeling unsure, shaken or hurt. This is probably the most important thing we will do for anyone seeking help. By listening without judging, we are touching into the essence of creating safe places. But unfortunately there are times when all of us are not such good listeners. Let us give you a rather extreme and tragic example.

When healing fails . . .

As part of the leadership of a local church, I was asked to go and visit a woman in hospital who, although only 35, and a very fit person, was dying of cancer. The leadership team had called days of fasting for her, and the whole church was believing the Lord for her healing. It even reached the local papers.

On sitting with her, I asked her what she wanted. To my surprise she looked at me with a radiant face and said she wanted to die as the Lord had made it clear to her that this was her time. I asked her whether she had told the other leaders this and she said she had. This puzzled me. Then why were they so fired up trying to get her healed? She then went on to say that she knew the church's prayers were keeping her alive when all she wanted to do was die.

With her permission I prayed with her and commended her spirit to the Lord. I also went and told the other leaders what we had talked about. She died the following day and the church was devastated. But the leadership still decided not to tell the members what had really happened. Although I protested, they held to their decision. I could do nothing. I left the church shortly afterwards.

Redemption: There was little redemption at the time, but the family, still in the church, eventually began to talk about the woman's wishes and the leadership team were finally forced to make a public statement. Listening to the woman in the first place or, failing that, tendering a simple sorry early on, would have saved considerable pain and bewilderment.

This was not a woman who was depressed or mentally ill. Neither was she accustomed to being ill and the center of attention. Apart from the cancer, she was very healthy. But she had peacefully come to the conclusion that the Lord was calling her home. She was able to explain quite clearly and honestly why she wanted to accept this, and why she was not asking the Lord for anything else. But it seems that there had been a presumption on the part of the leadership, and even the congregation, that the best thing for her was to live, not die.

From this woman's perspective, the conclusion of the leadership and congregation was devastating. It was standing between her and the Lord. But for us, the most tragic aspect of this account is that the leadership of the congregation believed that they knew what was best for her. They were wrong, as we all so often are. Their judgment of the situation had an arrogant distastefulness about it. It clearly never occurred to them to take serious note of what she believed was best for her, and what she believed the Lord was saying. When they learned that they were praying in a way that was against her, they were still not willing to put her first or love her in the way she invited love.

In Tomorrow's Church, when this woman became ill, there would have been a core group listening carefully to her wishes and supportive of her heart's desire to be with the Lord. This would have been sensitively discussed among the leadership, and then with the congregation, so that when He took her home there could have been a celebration of her life instead of the confusion and despair of a "failed healing."

The Curse of a Judging Spirit

The previous story is a good example of one of the deep, persistent failures of human nature—our compulsive addiction to judging. This can (unhelpfully) be called discernment, and may be as subtle as merely having an opinion. At its worst it is the purposeful judgment of others in the arrogant belief that one already has the full counsel of God and therefore has the capacity to judge another person's life, theology, values or actions.

Judging is the process of testing whether the other person comes up to our own perceived "high" standards or God's standards as we see them. We "sit in judgment" over the other person. Such behavior is often cloaked with the most noble of intentions: that it is "for the Lord's sake," "defending the

Lord," "protecting truth," "showing concern" or testing whether a thing is "Biblical." But in most situations it is high-handedly seeking to rule over another and over their beliefs and actions. It may be done in the sincere belief that this is what being a Christian is, but to the person being judged it rarely feels like Love.

Behind such a judgmental attitude is the mistaken belief that one has enough knowledge of Scripture, Christian tradition, social psychology, theology, anthropology, and even Church history to be able to test whether what another person is saying is "Biblical" or "the will of God." It is assumed that the person doing the "judging" has more of God's mind on the matter than the person being judged. Such an attitude raises its head in a variety of ways. It is seen when we believe the lie that we are intellectually superior or that we have the responsibility to judge others. It comes with the sly question, "How will we know what the truth is if we don't test what everyone else says?" Or, "Isn't such 'discerning' essential to 'defending' the gospel?"

The judgmental attitude might be motivated by a genuine desire to hear and defend the Lord. At times this is necessary, for instance, in matters of doctrine or behavior. As we mentioned earlier, the core teaching of Scripture, enshrined in the creeds of the Early Church, needs to form the basis of both doctrine and behavior. We must discern what is true in these matters. But we should also be careful to avoid assuming that we know all the answers and have the right to decide whether others' views are okay. Look at how the Pharisees judged Christ's theology! One of the simplest ways of testing the difference between unrighteous judging and righteous discernment is to ask whether Love is present.

But before we all condemn the Church for such sad behavior, we need to notice that judging is not confined to the Church. Every one of us judges all the time. Judging is endemic in our society—it is part of daily life, an expression, often, of a critical, questioning spirit. Some sections of the media are notorious for reporting "a good story" before doing the research. Many a person of integrity has been crucified before anyone has checked out what really happened or was said.

The scandalous undermining of people and organizations by a critical, judging media and public has left all of us with warped views of people and situations.

As human beings we tend to judge almost everything, from the most innocuous (that color doesn't suit him), to the galactic (*they* have destroyed the natural world). We test everything by our own sense of right and wrong, based on our own (alleged) knowledge of life, society, Scripture, human experience, and learning, even quantum physics! As a result, much evil has been unleashed against the Church, while many Christians have left the Church because they were judged without being given the chance to respond and be heard. Listen to this man's story.

"You're wrong!"

As a graduate in theology, I was deeply involved in church leadership. Among other things I was a house-group leader and part of the preaching team. One Sunday I spoke on the importance of people's human spirituality, saying that without a personal knowledge of our own spirituality we would have great difficulty conceiving of both human spirit and the person and work of the Holy Spirit.

The following week I was called to a special leaders' meeting, the purpose of which, I was told, was to plan the preaching rota. But when I arrived, the other three leaders (all men) informed me that they wished me to step down from leadership because they could no longer tolerate my "New Age" beliefs. They were convinced that anyone who spoke about "human spirit" in the way I had was not teaching Scripture. Despite my protests, I was forced to leave the church. They also publicly stated the reasons they had asked me to step down, while refusing to let me respond. My wife and I were devastated. We left the church in shame, losing our whole network of "friends."

Redemption: The couple went to another church, where they were welcomed, and today he has a recognized ministry. His wife has also recovered and is herself active in the leadership.

But at the time their relationship with the Lord took a nosedive and their confidence in the Church was undermined.

Judging can be sinister. Judgmental people have decided that those who disagree with them are wrong. Having such judgmental people as friends and leaders means that one cannot accept one's own viewpoint or trust it for fear of the accusation of being deceived. So the group, or the dominant individuals, increasingly control what you think and who you are. No other opinion or perspective can possibly be right, only theirs. Judging treats with contempt what others teach or believe. Such judging is bad enough among church members, but in leaders it can be pernicious, especially when they add to this toxic outlook the use of the name of God to back up all they say. In Tomorrow's Church the life of Love, putting the other person first, would preclude all such judgments. Social rules would ban this attitude, and a teachable spirit would sweeten the leader's approachableness.

Guidelines

+ Let's remember that none of us has any more than a small fraction of the knowledge of Christ or Scripture. So none of us has the competence to judge.
+ Defending Constantinian Christianity is fine, but never cross the line into forcing personal views on others.
+ Judging other people dishonors them and makes us less human. Judging is the domain of God.
+ Better to Love than to judge, but remember that loving is much harder than judging.

What Do Jesus and the New Testament Say about Judging?

The New Testament has a great deal to say about the evil of judging others. Christ condemned judgmental behavior (Mt. 7:1–5; Lk. 6:37; 12:14,57; 19:22; Jn. 5:27; 8:16; 12:47, etc.). Paul likewise condemned the practice of judging (Rom. 2:1–4; 14:10; 1 Cor. 4:3; 5:12–13; Col. 2:16, etc.), though he did concede that this would be the role of the saints at the return of Christ (1 Cor. 6:2–3). Christ, Paul emphasizes, is the only one ordained to judge (2 Tim. 4:1,8; cf. Rev. 20:4). Even James (4:11–12), Peter (1 Pet. 5:5) and Jude (15–16) warn of the dangers of judging others.

What becomes clear from such passages is that none of us is qualified to judge others. We do not have the responsibility to judge what is right and wrong. Christ requires us to make a commitment to prioritize Love, while letting Him be the judge (Jn. 5:22). Our duty to Love includes our enemies (Mt. 5:43–48). The reason Scripture is so clear on this point is that judging others divides people, turning them into the judge and the judged. When people are judged, they will often become unwisely dogmatic in their assertion of the opposite view. (Whole denominations have been birthed this way!) Judging moves us away from the possibility of unity, breaches reconciliation and undermines the social Trinity model of divine harmony. It does all of these by instilling division, distrust, and doubt—"I'm right, you're wrong." "I know more than you so I can judge you . . ." In essence, judging creates an unsafe place for us and everyone else.

We could all contribute to making congregational life a safer place if we resisted the temptation to correct everyone else, and stopped seeking to impose our "right" theology and views on their "wrong" theology and views.

Some, however, may accuse us of being relativistic, and of allowing people to drift from the absolute truths of Scripture. This is far from the truth. Our own congregation was recently described by a pastor friend in Houston, after he had lived for a time in our faith community, as "conservative, mystical, charismatic, and orthodox" (Mike Gammill). We passionately believe in the absolutes, but would not want to see the defense of these precious truths associated with the offensive practice of judging. God is Love.

Some wonder how you make decisions about others if you do not judge. The answer is deceptively easy—you ask the people concerned. As leaders, many of us believe that our cozy relationship with God gives us a duty to make decisions for everyone and then tell them what they should do. But we are merely in danger of imposing our prejudices and opinions upon them. Is it not better to ask them than to guide them by our own wisdom?

Love Instead of Judging or Prejudice

So the grace of Christ is what we should seek to live: a life where we do not judge one another. Many of us have lots of petty prejudices based on years of experience in the Church, sometimes stirred up with passionate theology. Yet such prejudices prevent us from being able to put the other person first. To make Church safer for ourselves and others, our judging prejudices must be brought to an end. We must stop telling other people what we believe they should believe, and where they are wrong.

Not only do we judge others, we also judge whole denominations, other churches, and those outside the Church. We treat them all with suspicion, believing that our opinion alone is the only one that is valid. So often church members and leaders have a ghetto mentality, which leads them to see everyone "in the world" as the enemy. As an extreme example, look at the habit churches have of judging one another's theology. Rather tragically, many Christian leaders find it is inconceivable that they could "fellowship" with someone who does not believe as they do. Let us illustrate.

Christ at the center

> A local church leader joined our community and began to get involved. He and his wife already knew a number of members, mostly Christians who had become disillusioned with traditional church life. He brought with him a strong suspicion of other Christians, especially leaders. We had talked with him about this, but left it with the Lord to speak with the pastor when He wished.

The pastor's Evangelical background was deeply challenged one day when he bumped into the local Catholic priest in the High Street. They had known each other professionally and stopped to talk. The priest began by saying that he had heard that the church leader had left his church and joined the new congregation in town. This he admitted to. The priest then asked the man a surprising question: "Does this new congregation have Christ at the center?" The church leader responded by saying that this was the case.

"Then nothing else is important," replied the priest.

Redemption: The pastor had assumed that the priest would be more religious and less centered on the Lord. For the priest to express the very values that he himself held was a real shock to this pastor. That the priest could have a relationship with Christ was a new idea to him. It impacted him in a positive way, both in his relationship with the Lord and the wider Church.

The leader discovered that he and the priest had the same values, even though the priest was part of the "bells and smells" brigade. Had he been wrong all these years in thinking that everyone who didn't share his beliefs was wrong? Did these other people really believe and know the Christ he knew? How could the priest be a Catholic and still believe in Jesus? For many, it is shocking to discover that those they have previously seen as the "enemy," or "deceived," actually have the same basic values and relationship with Christ that they have. Christ often confronted such prejudices in the religious leaders of Israel, especially the Pharisees (Mt. 21:23–27; 22:23–46, etc.).

Guideline

+ Our prejudices are usually based on our baggage rather than God's objectivity. Instead of judging, be careful to practice Love, because the way we judge is the way in which we will be judged. None of us is ever right all the time.

Blasphemy against the Holy Spirit as a Form of Judging

One of the problems with judging is that we are taken in by our own belief that we know better than others. We allow ourselves to be deceived into thinking that we have the intellectual and spiritual skills and anointing to fully know the "Truth," while assuming that others do not. What arrogance!

God has given us the privilege of receiving His self-revelation in our world, but Scripture tells us clearly that we can all abuse this privilege. We would know nothing about God were it not His desire and intent to be known. Natural theology—that is, seeing God's hand in the created world—and the incarnation of Christ-as-God-as-Man, are two of the ways in which God, taking the initiative, has introduced Himself. The immanence of spiritual reality co-mingling with our physical world, with all the resulting angelic activity, illustrates the means God uses to make Himself known. If we abuse these privileges, we do so at our peril, since none of us is able to be sure where God is actively involved in human affairs. We don't know what He might be doing, and where He is to be seen and found.

Because of the "veil" that is between us and God, because we are not "all knowing" with regard to God, Christ has some sobering words for us all. We should be careful, He says, not to blaspheme against the Holy Spirit. Christ is very specific about what constitutes this blasphemy.[2] He cites, as examples, the Pharisees, as they had a habit of judging what they were seeing Christ do—"It is by the prince of demons that he drives out demons" (Mt. 9:34; 12:24, etc.). By attributing the miraculous healings and deliverances of Christ to the work of the Enemy, they were denying that they were the work of the Holy Spirit through Christ.

Christ's response to this attitude is very clear. In Matthew 12:22–37, He suggests that the Pharisees' attribution of the work of the Holy Spirit to Satan is blasphemous (verses 30–32). Christ also notes that when people speak in this way, the Holy Spirit does not retaliate by defending Himself (verse 32), though Christ and His Father seem to come to the Holy Spirit's aid in not forgiving those who blaspheme in this way (verse 32).

We are not told why. One reason could be that these people have put themselves in a position where they are incapable of hearing anything that the Holy Spirit might say so are incapable of repentance and therefore cannot be forgiven.

Put into modern language, blasphemy against the Holy Spirit is when a person denies that something is the work of the Holy Spirit and instead attributes it to Satan. This is a process of judging from a human perspective what is of God and what is not from God. Some contemporary Christians judge others' claims or experience of God in this way. In suggesting that something is not valid, not Biblical, they are stating that this is not how God works. They believe that as Christians they have the ability and, some claim, even the duty(!) to judge in this way. Christ's words are clearly meant to add caution to anyone tempted to be dogmatic about what is and what is not the work of the Holy Spirit.

Christ, clearly reinforcing what He has already said, then goes on in the same passage to warn us all about our careless words (Mt. 12:36). We are all in grave danger of making blasphemous judgments out of carelessness. A typical contemporary example is the way we sometimes innocently attribute things that go wrong in our own lives to the work of the Enemy. It would not occur to some of us to see Christ behind such events. In such ways we may all be in danger of abusing God in a blasphemous way.[3]

To some this may sound a little far-fetched. The traditional view of blasphemy against the Holy Spirit is more restrictive. But the view we are suggesting is well supported, and was clearly the Early Church's perspective. The *Didache* is a Christian document written about 60 years after Christ. It is one of the few manuscripts we have that was written in the period between the ascension of Christ and the formation of the established Church at the end of the second century. In the section on Christian behavior, one passage reads, "Do not be a grumbler, my son, for this leads to blasphemy. Likewise do not be too opinionated, and do not harbor thoughts of wickedness for these, too, can breed blasphemy." It goes on to say, "Accept as good whatever experiences come your way, in the knowledge that nothing can happen without God."[4] The *Didache* suggests that the Early Church assumed that moaning and murmuring could also lead to blasphemous words, turning what is of God against Him.

Guidelines

+ It is not our place to judge whether or not what happens to others is from the Lord. We must all seek wisdom in our relationships with others, but honor must come before judgment.
+ We do not have a duty to correct other people's beliefs when we think they are wrong. Instead, we should encourage others to read Scripture for themselves, and mature in their own views, even where these are different from ours.

In Summary

In this chapter we have identified several practices that steal from making the Church a safer place. These include the abusive power of rules, and not putting the other person first. We then noted that the New Testament forbids us to judge others, calling us instead to live a life of Love. Finally, we noted the possible and subtle dangers of inadvertently blaspheming against the Holy Spirit. In the next chapter we will explore a radical positive alternative to the practice of judging—discerning the Lord's voice.

Questions to Ponder

1. How can we obey the command to Love?
2. What makes us a safe place for others?
3. If we start putting the other person first, how does that change our relationship with them?
4. In what ways do we judge people and things?
5. When, if ever, is judging right?
6. Why do you agree, or disagree, with what the New Testament says about judging?

7. How do you stop the habit of judging?
8. On the basis of the explanation given above of blasphemy against the Holy Spirit, in what ways, if any, do you need to change your attitudes, words or actions?

Notes

[1] I (Peter) have covered this subject in another of my books, Holmes, *Trinity in Human Community*.
[2] Christ's teaching is that "the wilful, malicious slander of the work of the Holy Spirit through Jesus, by attributing the Holy Spirit's work to Satan, would not be forgiven" (W. Grudem, *Bible Doctrine: Essential teachings of the Christian faith* (Nottingham: Inter-Varsity Press, 1999).
[3] For a very helpful comment on a misuse of Scripture that can be abusive, see M. Hickin, *Uncomfortable Reality: Abuse, the Bible and the Church* (Swanley: CCPAS, 2004).
[4] M. Staniforth (trans.), A. Louth (ed.), *Early Christian Writings: Apostolic Fathers* (London: Penguin, 1968), 228–9.

8

Your Unique Contribution

In this chapter we will be looking at the challenge of passivity and control. One aspect we will be noting is what we call the "spectator congregation." We will see what it is to be "empowered," and what can happen in a positive way when all the members of a faith community begin to hear God for themselves. We then move on to look at what we call "social dissonance," that is, the way we live in both the Church and outside the Church. We end with a warning about the dangers of "petty Hitlers!"

In the previous chapter, we looked at the place of Love instead of judgment in helping to create the safety that should be typical of a local church. But, of course, the risk with such a strategy is that there will always be those who demand to be loved unconditionally. This is another way of compromising safety in the Body of Christ. It is a very different type of problem. Rather than in the arrogance of judging others, the harm is in the unreasonable expectation that one person places on others.

Loving others does not mean that we become their slave. God has the capacity for unconditional love, but none of us has this capacity. Nowhere in Christ's descriptions of love does He ever give the impression that we should allow ourselves to be abused. Instead, the love that He lives is proactive, requiring the involvement of all in the mutual exercising of their gifts. In this chapter we are going to explore how churches can help to ensure that social rules based on Love do not result in those who are doing the giving being taken for granted and burning out. Tomorrow's Church will be a place where every member of the Body plays its part in loving every other, and where everyone's contribution will be equally valued. Those on the fringe, the sick and the weak will be treated with special care.

Passivity, Dependency and Allowing Others to Be Responsible for Us

In seeking to find the key to making a place safe, we have already noted that it is us. We have to learn to be safe for others. Yes, it is true that the leadership have a key role, and later we will devote several chapters to issues of leadership. But a safe place is about each of us being a safe person. So the responsibility belongs to all of us to do everything we can to create a safe place by being safe. For a congregation to be safe, a substantial number of its members must be safe. They must then take responsibility for keeping it safe for one another, especially for newcomers and those in need. If individuals do not accept their personal responsibility to be safe people, then everyone suffers. This raises a big issue that we have alluded to and will now address.

In some ways, we have created a spectator Church. The basis of much abuse in the Church seems to be an attitude that many members slip into whereby they surrender any independent thinking or sense of justice or personal responsibility they may have had, choosing, instead to become passive and let others be responsible for them. This may be explicit: members make known their needs and require others constantly to meet them. In these situations, loving, giving, and serving are perceived to be the responsibility of a few toward the many.

But a more subtle passivity also occurs. Here, members remain outspoken, and appear to be very much in control of their lives, but inwardly they have stopped thinking for themselves, presuming that the leadership will always know better and have their best interests at heart. They are choosing to be "shepherded" by others who they assume will look after them. This may be a state of mind encouraged by the leadership, who communicate that they carry this responsibility willingly before God for each member of the congregation. Or it may be that the leadership resist such a notion, but members adopt it anyway: we pay you to sort us out and be responsible for our spiritual well-being.

As members move into this passive state, they let go of a lot more than personal responsibility. They open themselves up to all manner of subtle abuse, which can mislead them, use them and then just as quickly reject them. They may be looked after, perhaps without much to do for themselves, and be able to glide along smoothly in passive submission. But it creates an unrighteous dependence on others.

Congregations in which the majority of members have abdicated responsibility to the leaders and to those willing volunteers happy to shoulder the burden, are rarely safe. The leader(s) do all the thinking, much of the work, and come up with most of the ideas. Everyone else merely follows, the whole congregation passively, admiring the preacher/leader. Boredom, passivity and sameness are among the curses of the Western Church. While leaders act with integrity all is well, but when they lose focus, life can become cultish and dangerous.

Remaining the same

> I met one of the new members of the church last week and had an interesting chat with him. He and his wife are professional people, high wage earners and were very well respected in their last church. During the conversation I asked him why he had sold up and moved across the country to become part of our community. He then said quite spontaneously, "Oh, that's easy. I had been in my previous church for 18 years, and was still the same person that I was when I joined."

This story is tragic. If this man had been around Jesus for 18 years, it is unthinkable that he would not have changed. There would have been demands, challenges, rebukes, growth, learning, success, and failure—all hallmarks of a discipleship journey. But they clearly were not the norm in the congregation he had been part of. Passivity can feel comfortable but we would suggest that it is an unrighteous kind of comfort. In

Tomorrow's Church such unrighteous comfort and false security would not exist. Instead, one would live in a culture of dynamic challenge and ongoing personal growth.

Guidelines

- Remember that leaders should point us to Christ, not themselves. Be careful if a leader begins to expect an unrighteous loyalty.
- It is each member's responsibility to look to Christ, not the leader or anyone else.
- Passivity is a sickness that any of us can catch, and it makes all of us vulnerable to abuse.
- No leader is "god."

Being Empowered

As an alternative to passivity, in a safe place all members feel empowered, knowing that their voices are heard and that they are expected to act, contribute, and make a difference. In Tomorrow's Church their opinion is valued, indeed, sought. Everyone who wants to be involved is involved, participating as an equal alongside other newcomers and the more experienced, all learning from one another. Likewise, when one part of the Body suffers, all suffer (1 Cor. 12:26). All this is the kind of dynamic we would expect to find in Tomorrow's Church. Support and training are, of course, needed, and readily available. But, as we shall see later, involvement must be balanced with family commitments and a healthy relationality with others.

The gospel of Christ should be an empowering experience for everyone who surrenders to it. But, sadly, as we have already noted, by entering church life we can become spectators, sometimes even of our own lives. People's sense of powerlessness is more common than many church leaders are prepared to admit. Although some types of Christianity do make us responsible for our own lives and decisions, others are particularly good at stripping us of our freedom and choices. Being able to distinguish between types of church leadership is particularly important for those who have come from abused backgrounds. When they are ready and able to take responsibility, they will need support in learning how to become empowered.

Some people feel vulnerable in these places of powerlessness. They feel they have no authority over their lives, are not listened to, have no vote in influencing events and no voice. From a member's perspective, this is especially one of the dangers under the "prophetic" type of leadership, sometimes called "charismatic." This is a strong, clear, triumphalist, and often authoritarian leadership where decisions are made at the top. It can create the feeling of being led, but also of being "sat on," confined or constrained. Some of us submit, beginning to believe that keeping the rules and "asking no questions" is the best way forward, and that few alternatives exist. Other people just leave. Some merely freeze, not knowing what to do.

Moreover, because the leader speaks with clarity and authority, we believe that God is on his or her side, not ours. This can have the effect of further isolating and separating us. Such an environment can be a very unsafe place. But compounding this is our own tendency to see God in a similar vein so that we begin to believe that He also is this authoritarian type of person, and we wait for Him to tell us how to act and what decisions to make. We will be addressing this issue of the "Lord's will" in Chapter 13. Types of Christianity that disempower do not reflect the empowering of relational social Trinity.

Guidelines

♦ Christ liberates us from our sinful damaged pasts, allowing us to be more of who He created us to be.
♦ Empowering people to possess the person God created them to be is fundamental to the gospel of Christ. He is our "Yes!"—intellectually, emotionally, and spiritually empowering us.

Hearing God Personally

Another helpful way to ensure a culture of safety in faith community is to encourage every member to hear God's voice for themselves. Many Christians, when we first mention this, respond by saying either that they do not understand or that their congregation already teaches this. Over the years we have both been surprised to see how many people accept that they have a personal relationship with Christ without it ever occurring to them that they could personally hear His voice. Even among those denominations and congregations where there is a culture of hearing the Lord's voice, numerous subtle social rules hinder members from being free to hear the Lord and to share with others what He says to them.

Required to conform

> When I first became a Christian, I heard the Lord's voice inside me, but when I tried to explain this in my church they looked at me as if I didn't know what I was talking about. So I then assumed I was wrong. After all, hadn't they all been doing the stuff for years and knew God better than I did?
>
> So I conformed, and spent 14 years feeling like I was just talking to the ceiling, and wondering why what I read in the Bible didn't seem to hold true for me. I always wondered if I was really saved because no one had believed my conversion story. I also felt like I had to pretend everything was okay because to say it wasn't meant you didn't have enough faith to believe that God had sorted it.
>
> **Redemption:** This judging of her had a terrible negative impact on both her relationship with the Lord and her trust in the Church. She later found her way to a church that did not judge her, and has done a remarkable journey based on being honest about her relationship with the Lord. She has now gained a university degree and is enjoying being part of a community that understands her.

In this story, the woman had several problems, but in essence she was part of a church that was not able to encourage her in hearing the Lord's voice clearly for herself. This meant that she was unable to move ahead as she should have in the Lord. As a young Christian she should have been able to learn quickly how to use her natural gift more fully. Instead, she closed down. So sad.

From Scripture we see around thirty ways in which God speaks to people. Teaching others about these ways of hearing the voice of the Lord so that they hear God for themselves should, for a range of reasons, be liberating for both teachers and those taught. One reason is that it lifts a huge pastoral responsibility off the shoulders of those who carry pastoral care—no one person can be responsible for hearing God's voice for each member of even a modest group. Then to teach people that they need to hear the voice of the Lord for themselves is to introduce them to a real adventure! By hearing the voice of the Lord and then talking to others about this, people are able to move on and begin to believe in *their* relationship with the Lord. They become interdependent rather than dependent.

In the following, particularly sad, story the church members and leaders were too quick to give an opinion. They should have helped their friend build up the confidence she needed to hear from the Lord for herself.

Should I marry?

> I was 24 when I began going out with a man who had a number of interests in common with mine. Our faith in Christ and interest in mission was at the center of our relationship. As we began to get more serious, he proposed to me so I asked the Lord whether it was right. I thought I heard the Lord say no, but when I talked to my boyfriend and other friends and leaders in the church they thought it was a good idea. We married and within a year we had separated. It was the worst year of my life. I am now happy to be single!

Such behavior by friends and leaders allows people not to think for themselves. The woman's instincts were better than her boyfriend's or those of leaders and friends. But she found fault with herself and chose to believe others. When things go wrong like this and we go ahead (even with reservations), God can be lost and all relationships questioned. Can we trust even those close to us? This woman had no doubt asked herself what would happen if she questioned the leaders' views. How much should she say? Women will tend to close down at such times, while men will often walk away and ignore all opinions. When it all goes wrong, the person is left with a range of emotions and fears, including a felt need for revenge. At other times they will have to cope with the accusation that they lack faith or the suggestion that their relationship with Christ is not right. Why else would they question what has been told them?

A Whole Congregation Hearing God for Themselves

Some Christian leaders look at us with horror when we mention to them that this is a good way to live. The idea of having a whole congregation hearing the voice of the Lord does not at first sound like a way of making a place more safe. You feel as though it must surely create chaos, and indeed it sometimes does! People start to have ideas, take responsibility, become self-organizing, get enthusiastic, change their minds, forget to keep one another informed. We could go on! Is this really safe?

Our response would be that if we were to take this idea in isolation, then, as with any of the themes we are discussing in this book, the form of group life it leads to could be disastrous. But Tomorrow's Church is a place of Love where people are growing in their discipleship journeys and are learning to put others first. All are aware that they belong to one another, and new, supportive social rules are continually being grown to help ensure that the congregation retains its effectiveness as a safe place. It is in the midst of such synergy that each person takes on the responsibility of hearing God for themselves. This is life giving for all concerned.

Counter-intuitively, therefore, teaching and supporting all members to hear God's voice does make a place safer because it helps remove one of the most subtle forms of abuse in church life: passivity and dependence. It forces growth and learning.

It also removes the potential for the unrighteous power of a few leaders. In a congregation where everyone is encouraged to hear the Lord for themselves, a leader can be questioned. He or she really is not the only one to hear the Lord's voice.

Non-Christian people are especially astute in hearing the Lord. Inviting God to talk to whoever is willing to listen is a beautiful way both to honor people and to let God into your community. Fear of being deceived is healthy. But most of us would rather trust others in these areas than trust ourselves and the Lord. In Tomorrow's Church all members would grow in the experience of knowing social Trinity resting in their midst and all would have the ongoing experience of hearing His voice.

But churches today struggle with ways of letting this happen. From their very first *Rapha* workshop, we encourage and teach people both to hear and act on the Lord's voice on their discipleship journeys.[1] As they discover how to hear the Lord speaking to them about themselves, they grow in their familiarity with His ways, increasingly being trusted with His perspective. Nothing strengthens faith like knowing that God talks to you.

Standing up in front of a church full of people can be an intoxicating, addictive, and powerful experience. For strong leaders, there is a fine line between speaking in the name of the Lord, as Scripture is shared, and declaiming, "thus says the Lord" as if God Himself is speaking. For a place to be safe for others, it is important to restrain such first-person declarations. It is generally preferable to let each person hear for themselves the Lord's direct affirmation of the word that is shared, rather than simply telling them that they have heard the Lord because the preacher has spoken His words. Sadly, some leaders will, for selfish ends, always cultivate the idea that they are the only ones who hear clearly from the Lord, and are the only ones trained to do so. It should be the leader's anointing, not their appointment to the office, that keeps them in leadership.

When people begin to hear from the Lord, they should also be encouraged to share what they have heard. In the early days, this sharing should ideally be with a small group of supportive friends. Most of us carry a lot of fear in this area, believing that the Enemy is more able to deceive us than the Lord is able to protect, teach, and guide us. Despite this fear, over many years of teaching people to hear God's voice, we have met very few who have been unknowingly deceived by the Enemy.

Sharing in a small, supportive group is a helpful way to begin when you are starting to hear from the Lord for others and for the church, too. It is especially hard to speak if what you have heard is a rebuke or something that could be unpopular. Most congregations and Christian organizations do not have structures and policies to cope with such feedback. In fact, in some organizations and congregations it is positively discouraged. We cover this topic in greater detail, from a pastoral perspective, in Chapter 15.

One example of feedback within our own community was when the Lord began to talk to us about how upset He was with our indifference to all He had given us. It would have been so easy just to say nothing, even though several folk in the community were hearing the same thing from Him. Instead, we decided to stop Sunday services and have a period of retrospection behind closed doors. During this time we reflected both on what the Lord was saying and how we should respond. Only after a whole month did we as a community feel that we were ready to begin to move on. It was some months before there was a groundswell of sorrow and repentance amongst us, and we were ready to respond with greater integrity to His word.

We have also experimented to find the best structures and channels for disseminating this knowledge as it is gained. At the time of writing, we have just set up a team of about twenty members who are one of the leadership teams of the community. We call them the "hearing God" team. They are preparing recommendations on how best to share what they and others are hearing from the Lord so that it becomes available to all members.

Guidelines

• Encourage one another to hear from God for themselves. This also builds greater discernment in hearing from the Lord through others.

‣ Live as the Body of Christ, not as a group of isolated, private individuals.

The "Social Dissonance" of the Lord Speaking

There is another reason why hearing from God is dangerous. It means that we have to act on what we hear or run the risk of living in dissonance with Him and others.

Social dissonance is when one part of our world is out of kilter with all the other parts. It might be that the way we live in our congregation is one "hat" that we wear, but that outside church we have another wholly different, and perhaps in some ways contradictory, worldview and lifestyle. Another form of social dissonance is when what we read from Scripture about how we should live is contradicted by how we see most church members living. A third form is when we know what the Lord wants of us, for example, to give up pornography, a "friend," a compulsive habit or irresponsible spending, but we refuse to do it. It all remains secret, hidden. Any form of social dissonance undermines our being safe for others, and, indeed, our inner conflicts and stubborn denial will make us a danger.

Christianity is initially very convincing to newcomers, even when it is abusive, but if it is flawed or unrighteous in any way, they will in time begin to see through it. Let us illustrate.

Church culture and being honest

I began to see things in the congregation that were not always very positive. There was a hierarchy that had nothing to do with ability, commitment or genuine character, but simply familiarity. There was a different standard for those who were part of the "in crowd." Also, church organization didn't allow women to lead. "Converting the lost" seemed to me to be little more than a number-crunching exercise. Very few seemed to stay for long. I found leaders to be quite manipulative. My friends and family found church a very uncomfortable place to be.

These observations became more acute when I moved to London and started to attend a large local church going through the process of a church split. Of course, no one called it a church "split"—it was a church "plant!" The politics, manipulation, deceit, and power-games were simply obscene— even more so as this split was presented as a "wonderful thing that God was doing."

Evangelism seemed to me to be little more than a means of manipulating people into discussing things they were either unready or unwilling to talk about. This was "giving the gospel." Living like Christ and "being a good witness" was all about outward behavior: not swearing, smoking, sleeping around or getting drunk. There was no emphasis on inward transformation of character. "Telling my story" (or "test-imony") was all about my conversion experience and not about my ongoing relationship with God (which hadn't really devel-oped since conversion). Doubts were explained away—if you were spending your time praying, reading your Bible and going to church, then you shouldn't have doubts, or if you did, you should just "get on with it," that is, bring more people into the church.

Redemption: The young man is now part of the leadership of a local church, where, understandably, he is seeking to ground the faith of the community in pragmatic reality!

Such a culture can promote high levels of deceit. Members of the church will be self-deceived in that they will believe that this is all that Christianity is, and they will consequently deceive anyone else who comes into the church. With the emphasis on evangelism, not discipleship, the church is likely to end up with a number of people who make a confession of faith in Christ but then have no higher calling than a sense of duty to bring in more newcomers and get them saved. This is one way to grow in numbers as a faith community, but raises serious doubts about whether such a congregation can then Love and serve people, helping them to grow.

Newcomers need a good reason to stay, and there is one that cannot be bettered: to positively change by becoming more like Christ. Unless they can find a good reason, they will nor-mally remain for only two to three years, then move on to another church or just drop out altogether. The Body of Christ has not been safe or meaningful for people like this.

When these kinds of social dissonance occur, as they do more often than many of us are sometimes willing to admit, it can prove to be a double bind. As a result, we can end up denying our own experience, and submitting and conforming to the party line, which makes it harder for us to continue to hear God's voice on other matters. To avoid this, we can uphold our own experience and do something about it in a righteous way. If this is not possible, we end up leaving the Church. Let us illustrate this problem with a story about praying for deliverance.

Abuse?

> I was part of a deliverance team that was asked to pray for a man who was possessed. This was fine, as I had done it a number of times before. But when we began to pray, I felt uneasy. He seemed to go into trauma, rather than "manifest" signs of evil. As the session continued, we ended up chasing him around the room and eventually he hurt himself on the door by running into it. That brought the session to an abrupt end. I went away asking myself what I would have done differently if I had led the team. The next time I prayed for someone I adopted some of these new principles that I was thinking about.

> **Redemption:** The man continued his journey and developed a more sensitive way of helping people who carried trauma, teaching them first how to separate themselves emotionally and spiritually from the darkness in them.

On this occasion, the pastoral team member used the dissonance to help shape his developing ideas of what was best for this type of need. Instead of allowing it to be a source of conflict and fragmentation in his life, he drew on the experience to help guide him into a new way of thinking. If God has His way in our midst, there will be many times when He wants to teach us something new. People with dogmatic, preconceived ideas about a situation will not be able to create the safest place for those in need.

In almost every area of church life there can be times when one or more of us is at odds with what is happening. Often the difficulty is that when we try to talk to others about this, we do not receive support, perhaps because they do not want to question or discuss what is going on. So the only people we can talk to are those who are not part of the church or are on the fringes of church life. This can be troublesome, for when we gravitate toward other disillusioned people within the congregation, we create a third front that becomes divisive. Neither option is helpful.

From research done in the UK Church, it would seem that increasing numbers of Christians are finding that faith life and daily life are becoming more and more dissonant, and they are being forced to make choices.[2] Many feel that such conflict is not helpful, but abusive. If this cannot be resolved, we will increasingly find that people will leave because the type of Christianity they are being taught conflicts with their social, family, and professional life outside the Church.

Guidelines

- If we are to invite the adventure of hearing God's voice, we have to be willing to be honest, and act on what we hear from Him, especially about how He might see us.
- In learning to hear the Lord for ourselves, we should be careful not to believe that we are always right in what we hear or what we say.
- Speaking in the name of Christ is a deep privilege that should never be abused, especially in a way that exalts us.
- All of us must learn that we will be accountable to the Lord for every word we say. It is helpful to treat others in the honorable way in which we would like to be treated.

Sharing Responsibility; Not Being Possessive or Controlling

There are times in congregational life when empowerment can become over-emphasized so that people cling to this power as theirs, thereby losing some of the benefits of relational faith community. Such behavior is often evidence of an underlying vulnerability in the person's life. It inhibits the development of a safe place as the dogmatism and possessiveness that accompany the taking up of responsibility begin to trouble or harm others.

This type of person, sometimes called the upstart leader or the petty Hitler, can be found in many churches. Often there is a modest responsibility—handing out hymn books or counting the collection. But the power begins to overtake the love. Such people have a domain to rule over. They cannot be questioned so woe to those who try to assist them, to do the task differently, or to cast doubt on their handling of the responsibility.[3] Such behavior can be very abusive to the people themselves and to others. No one feels safe around them.

One of our social rules in CCD is embodied in the phrase "light touch." It is the principle that anything that we do, either for the Lord or others, is done without any attempt at control. It is done as though the Lord were receiving the service, not other members. "Light touch" also emphasizes the need to look beyond the task or duty to the greater significance of what one does. It is for the Lord, not for us.

Guideline

• Beware of carrying responsibility in a possessive way that excludes others. Practicing a "light touch" is a good discipline.

In Summary

We began this chapter by mentioning the idea of God offering all of us unconditional Love. Acceptance of God's Love is a prerequisite for the creation of a culture of safety. We then went on to note what we describe as a "spectator" church, where the congregation is an audience observing the performances that others are giving. We also looked at social dissonance in a range of different aspects. We ended by warning about petty Hitlers. We must now move on to look at specific relationships and see how these can be safe or damaging.

Questions to Ponder

1. Do you agree that postmodern values are sometimes different from those held by the Church? If so, in what ways?
2. In what ways do we abdicate responsibility for our lives?
3. How can we empower one another?
4. According to the Bible, what are some of the ways in which we can hear the Lord talking?
5. What are some contemporary ways of hearing God, which are not mentioned in the Bible?
6. When God speaks to us, is He more likely to say nice or nasty things? Why do you think this?
7. Name some of the possible problems in a "hearing-God-personally" church.
8. Where there are "petty Hitlers" in a congregation and even denomination, what can be done?

Notes

[1] We have a Bible Note online on this theme. See <www.lifegivingtrust.org>.
[2] P. Brierley, *The Tide is Running Out: What the English church attendance survey reveals* (London: Christian Research, 2000), 86.
[3] J. Chevous, *From Silence to Sanctuary: A guide to understanding, preventing and responding to abuse* (London: SPCK, 2004).

Part 4

Leadership in a Safe Place

Christian leadership has a special responsibility to create a safe place for all those seeking Christ in a deeper way. The nurture of newcomers to Christ is the essence of shepherding/pastoring in Christ. In these next two chapters we will look at several aspects of this very challenging role.

9

Professional Leadership in a Safe Church

In this chapter we will be looking at the tendency we sometimes have to put Christian leaders on a pedestal, and the resulting danger of feeding the "messiah complex." We will also look at other aspects of the abuse of power, the "paid to love" problem, and abuse from one leader to another.

The transforming of congregational life into a safe place that we are exploring in this book requires that we all take up some level of responsibility alongside those in "leadership." This would help ensure that the abuse so prevalent in the world around us, and so intrinsic to our own fallen natures, does not become the norm in our local church. Tomorrow's Church has a view of shared responsibility quite different from the conventional model of a full-time leader perhaps assisted by a full-time or part-time team. Traditionally, it is the leader's job to ensure that things run smoothly, and that the values of the community are maintained. But no leader in any organization has the power to make that organization a safe place. For a place to be made safe, everyone must be involved.

What we are suggesting in this book is that all of us must stand alongside and support the leadership, thereby lessening the "gap" between the "professional" church leader and ourselves as members. As well as making every member accountable, Tomorrow's Church welcomes diversity and a multiplying of gifting and anointing to help carry the congregation farther into Christ. In addition, such a way of life helps minimize the difficulties caused by specific individuals having an inappropriate amount of power.

We are not going to attempt to define what leadership is. We have done this elsewhere.[1] The model for leadership that underlies these chapters is the servant model of Christ Himself. In both His relationship with Father God and with all those around Him, He showed all the qualities of true leadership, including honor of people, a transparent honesty, an in-depth capacity to love and a non-judgmental approach to every relationship. This we can summarize in His "brokenness." Even with the Pharisees, Christ did not rubbish or condemn individual Pharisees who came to speak to him. Although He knew He would be the Judge at the final accounting, He chose not to exercise this power in His earthly ministry. Instead, He acknowledged judgment as the role of His Father (Jn. 12:47–48).

In contemporary faith community, some form of leadership structure is essential, even if it is a structure that disperses power throughout the organization. We wholeheartedly support the need for the highest level of training and spiritual anointing for our leaders. Church should be a culture of excellence, and we should be willing to pay for this.

Most churches today have salaried staff, and we do not have a problem with this, though our model in CCD is slightly different. But what we are emphasizing here is the need to diversify the role of leadership so that each member is involved. In this chapter we will address issues that are specifically associated with the challenge of having a church leadership that is professional in its way of working and helps facilitate safety. We will start by considering the special case of an ordained ministry.

The Power of the "Ordained" Leader

Priests, ministers, and Christian leaders have power invested in them, the power to help and, as we are suggesting, the often more unhelpful power to take responsibility for the individual. The handing down of authority, through rituals such as the laying on of hands, is intended to be an empowering for servant leadership. It gives the minister and the congregation the clear message that these people are special, both as servants of the faith community and as the mouthpieces of God. Rituals such as the Eucharist; the power to teach and preach; the giving of spiritual direction; the wearing of vestments, all emphasize a separated role. Leaders feel themselves to be in a favored place with both God and those in their pastoral care. Ordination gives priests, ministers, pastors, and other professional Christian leaders the delegated power to use the authority of God's name. For better or for worse.

This power should not be underestimated. When church leaders speak, they are to varying degrees perceived to be speaking in God's name or talking "Truth." Some leaders use this authority more than others, but when Christian leaders stand up to speak, there is an assumption that they have a level of "power" over the people who have chosen to submit to them by being there or by listening to them, that they would not have, if, say, they were managers in a toy factory. This is important to note in any desire to create safe places. When Christian leaders stand up and speak, sometimes wearing clerical vestments to signify their God-given authority, what is said has a force that any normal conversation does not have. Most members take their words far more seriously than if the speaker had been their boss at work.

This extra authority as God's representative can leave both leader and congregational member vulnerable. There are always some people who will become abusers when put in positions of power and Christian leaders are not exempt from the danger of abusing the authority they have been given by church members. There is sometimes a very unclear line between speaking the thoughts of God (with authority), and acting in an abusive and manipulative way. Members, for their part, often forget that leaders are just fallen human beings, as we all are, and can have a level of expectation of the leader that is unrealistic.

Will Tomorrow's Church have ordained leaders? That is the choice of Tomorrow's Church members, and is not ours to decide, but probably, yes. What we do say is that Tomorrow's

Church leadership will be characterized by qualities that maximize social-Trinity-safety, both personally, relationally, and in Christ.

Don't Be Put on a Pedestal

As church leaders ourselves, we know what it feels like to be adored, and to be abused and hated. Both can happen all too easily. Adoration comes quickly if the leader is a good teacher or preacher or loves people. Members then begin to equate the effectiveness of ministry with personal holiness: "If God uses them, then they must be holy!" So leaders find themselves being raised on to pedestals. But in time others will begin to resent this hero worship and will seek to subvert the honoring of the leader. When leaders carry the anointing of the Lord, they can be accused of acting in a "godlike" way. Before long they are being attacked. This places the leader in an impossible position with any decision being experienced as wisdom by some and unhelpful, or worse, by others.

In Tomorrow's Church, members and leaders will resist the construction of any form of pedestal because it will distort the principle of equal personal responsibility—the so-called perichoretic principle (see Chapter 19). The gifting and anointing of all members will be recognized in accordance with the Biblical principle of belonging to one another in the Body of Christ. Some gifting will be more mature, other gifting growing; some more public, other gifting not seen. But everyone will recognize that Christ is the giver and sustainer of His Body. Not any one person, trained or not.

The passionate loyalty of many members to their pastor or leadership team is a source of wonder to us. We have heard it so many times: "My church is better than your church, our pastor is . . ." It is as though church members need to believe this in order to continue being committed. Perhaps it somehow justifies their abdication of personal responsibility. It is sometimes true that the more competent the leader, the less concerned we are about the need to take responsibility for our own lives.

It is inevitable, however, that at some time the leader(s) will do something that hurts or upsets those who believe in them. This can have devastating results. Once something like this has happened, members can find their whole world in chaos. Having lost confidence in the leader (and, psychologically speaking, in God Himself) people will begin to doubt everyone and everything, including their own judgment. Some may recover quickly, but many, if they are already dependent, will find themselves so deeply hurt or abused that they may quietly leave or see God in this failed experience. Let us illustrate.

A trust betrayed

> I was a newly-converted, very enthusiastic teenager, working hard helping to lead the youth group when I wasn't at school. The man who led the group was also part of the worship team with me and in my house group, too. He was happily married so it never occurred to me that he was interested in me sexually. I was very naive. One of the other deacons told me he was, and immediately I felt my world collapse. He (and his wife) both denied it so I was the one who had to leave the church. Out of loyalty to the church I never told anyone.

> **Redemption:** After a period of sickness, this young woman is now an active member of another local church. She has a more realistic view of leadership. But in the short term, she saw a serious deterioration in her relationship with the Lord, and loss of trust in the Church.

The remedy for such adoration, then victimization, is for everyone in leadership to be more human. All of us should be able to laugh at ourselves, admit faults and be willing to say sorry. It's okay for people to honor leaders, but that should not be allowed to extend to adoration or worship. As a leader, give the Lord permission to keep you humble, and accept the reality that some will always see you as someone greater than you really are. We will be talking later about what to do when things do go wrong in this way.

Guidelines

* Adoration should be given exclusively to Christ. Leaders have a duty to point the community to Christ, not to themselves.
* As a leader, choose to humble yourself before the Lord. If He then exalts you, stay in the place of brokenness.

The Dangers of Becoming Messianic

Some leaders claim far too much authority and control over their members, some really believing that they are "the mouthpiece of God." This is bad enough, but when they go on to believe that they are the *exclusive* mouthpiece of God for the congregation, then things become even more problematic. Rather than encouraging the congregation in their own relationship with God, teaching them how to hear His voice and grow together in maturity in Christ, the leader can begin to take the place of Christ.

We are describing what we call the "messiah complex"—the incomprehensible belief that one is messiah to the flock. Some Christian leaders have clearly suffered such delusions.[2] It is then only a short step to creating a regime of tyranny, fear, and control, where members can no longer act for fear of upsetting "God!" It is all too easy to use the pulpit as a channel to vent one's anger over a compliant congregation. Let us illustrate.

When a church implodes

> David preached, and kept repeating: "Your obedience is paramount." If those words were from God, they were actually for David, but he wasn't listening. Instead, he was trying for the umpteenth time to bully us into accepting that we must obey him. Week after week it was blame, blame, blame because we weren't doing, couldn't do, the kind of outreach he said God wanted. Some left, the older men particularly, then their wives and their wives' friends, and then some of the younger men. Those of us who remained could barely drag ourselves to

Sunday worship. We were papering over the cracks, living a lie, no longer able to bring anyone with us. If this was Christianity, who would want it, anyway? We all kept our own counsel, believing that we were acting out of love and loyalty. On the rare occasions when hurts were confided, the result was more anguished torn loyalty.

The pain and false loyalty began in the leadership team and spread slowly. The four members who would later stand down (the beginning of the end) did an amazing job of concealing what they were suffering at the hands of their supposed "first among equals" colleague. David's autocratic ways got worse over a period of years, taking a while to be registered as unacceptable. Even I, coming to the church at quite a late stage, didn't immediately question what I found.

I discovered that there was a rigid process by which contributions were to be submitted upwards to the leadership, but that such comments then seemed to disappear into oblivion. It was a long time before I discovered that David was the one who had ideas. He heard from God. There would be no invitation to work with him. But he was not even fulfilling the stuff he had promised, which really shocked and angered me. It was a case of covering up while demanding loyalty. When he did give tasks to people, any failure, if it happened, would not be their fault but it would look that way, and it would be very public.

As the year wore on, we heard less and less from most of the team and David and his three closest colleagues seemed to be becoming increasingly unapproachable. We kept hearing the same message, based on the same scripture: God was not pleased with us, and they would continue until we were ready to move on. People were hurting.

David had close family ties with at least three of the other seven members of the leadership team, the three who didn't resign, while he and one of the other four lived on either side of a land boundary that had been in dispute for centuries. Also, the leadership had not had, and were not going to get, any training in the day-to-day, nitty-gritty of leading, nor any guidance in how to meld eight vocations into a team. In the dynamics of survival, existing lifelong ties took hold, ties that had been picked up in the cradle and perfected in the playground, with David and his "inner cabinet" gradually smothering all other initiatives. Other voices fell silent and left. What do you do when a promising young Christian grows into a deluded dictator?

Redemption: In time many came back together, now much more loving, open, and caring. The lady who wrote this piece moved on, found a community she was able to settle in, and began the journey of letting go of all of the betrayal. She is now part of the leadership and is finding a range of interesting things she can do in contributing to faith community life. She is valued.

A safe place is where everyone knows both their strengths and weaknesses and where they can talk openly and supportively about differences, fears, and concerns.

Connected to this "messianic attitude" is the often-heard complaint from church members that the leadership never listens. This can be for the simple reason that they are too busy, or it can be for far more complex reasons connected to the baggage in both parties' lives. The danger comes when leaders no longer feel the need to listen because they believe that all that they do and say is from God. They get their guidance directly from God, therefore it cannot be questioned.

When a man or a woman has this mindset, there are many telltale signs. Typical are an unwillingness to be questioned, an incapacity to hear what others say, and the denial of serious problems when they occur. Another classic sign is that such leaders expect all their wishes to be immediately obeyed and look for a kind of awed homage when they speak ("thus says the Lord"). Behind their behavior is an arrogant self-righteousness that all too easily abuses others and makes congregational life unsafe.

Guidelines

+ Christ is Messiah—His followers should never try to be!
+ All of us have the duty to humble ourselves, while allowing others to honor us.

Power and Its Unrighteous Consequences

As Christians, we will often choose to trust our leaders in what they say, and for most of us this is right and proper, a key ingredient in our personal growth and maturity. But where trust does not exist, or has broken down, relationships are ruptured and the individual suffers, along with the whole community. There is no safe place.

Much long-term damage has been done to people who have fallen foul of abusive Christian leaders. Deprived of their calling by an egocentric leader of a congregation or mission, their deep love, devotion, and trust can turn to profound hate and a desire for revenge. Such attitudes and toxic emotion must not be allowed to fester. When a leader loses the way and begins to do such damage, it is essential that the congregation, and other leaders, find ways to recover the situation. They must not be seen to be closing ranks or protecting someone who has been causing harm to others. Trust must be re-established or the Kingdom of heaven and the wider Church will both suffer. When one person leaves, others usually follow. In a church with the average UK congregation of around 40 people, this can be fatal. Also, by leaving, members have no opportunity of resolving the hurt.

Some leaders will always become intoxicated by the power of being in control. They will pay almost any price to get there, and once in leadership, will allow no one else in. Being in charge feels safest for them. They may attack others as a form of defense, frequently forget to do things, manipulate situations and relationships, and turn one person against another. Power is more important than the servant heart or spiritual anointing. And set alongside a cocooned life, remote from church members, it is dangerous. The leader becomes unassailable.

How would Tomorrow's Church be different? Recruitment would be by anointing, not formal appointment; proven gifting and anointed experience would reduce the risk. There would also be less likelihood of an outsider being brought in instead of someone who shares the values of the church. Even if someone were brought in, existing team members, as people who know brokenness in their lives, would be well practiced in being open with one other, ministering to one another and being accountable to one another.

By brokenness, we are describing that profoundly deep moment in our life, sometimes several moments or a part of our journey, when, in the presence of Christ and others, we allow ourselves to acknowledge our dark side, our self-harm and/or the utter despair of our fragmented life, saying sorry to ourselves, others, and God. Many joke that they have been there, done that, but when one authentically does this, it leaves its permanent mark, sometimes a new meekness, sometimes a "knowing" that allows us to see the arrogance, pride and self-possession that is in us and others. It is frequently a place, of tears, which we find many times during our subsequent ministry, a place in us that Christ can touch, bringing us back to our knees.

To achieve a healthful wholeness we all need to go through the deep waters of being broken, when we see the sin in our life and the destitution of our life without the righteous purposes of Christ. It is here that we learn in the deepest way that we are nothing without Christ, that we cannot live without His support, and are incapable of living as safe people without the supernatural change and sustaining of His saving grace and Spirit. Such a place of "brokenness" gives us all the capacity to surrender to one another, to Love as unto Christ, and to honor one another as He honors us.

In the example quoted above, David showed no such brokenness. In Tomorrow's Church, as he started to become abusive, the congregation or leadership team would be able to address the problem quickly. They would appeal to his meekness, and mutuality might rule. Likewise, members of the congregation would have safe ways of expressing concerns, confident that they would be heard and dealt with appropriately. The abuse would not be allowed to continue. In Part 7, we will note the kinds of procedures that might be helpful when things go wrong.

Guidelines

+ As a leader, be under Christ, but also learn how to submit to other leaders and members.

- Always carry a "sorry" in all that you do. Practice embracing brokenness.

Leaders Abusing Leaders

With professional Church leaders facing the challenge of abuse, it would be natural to assume that they would be effective in supporting one another. Sadly, it is evident to Christian leaders who have served for some time in the Church that they have as much to fear from their fellow leaders as they have from anyone else. The fragmentation of the modern Western Church is in part the fruit of thousands of stories of Christian leaders in conflict. Working together as local pastors seems to be particularly challenging.

As we are noting, Christian leaders can believe that they have the right, ability, and responsibility to correct others. At times they need to, as in the case of justified Church discipline. But we are also suggesting that unrighteous judgmental attitudes are endemic in the Church because in some parts of the Church judging is assumed to be a duty of leaders.

But judging is just the tip of the iceberg. Some Christian leaders seem to believe that it is incumbent upon them to defend "Truth" (as they understand it). So anyone challenging their body of "Truth" should be confronted, exposed, and corrected. We accept the tension that differing views of Scripture and tradition can create and the offence felt by adherents of one belief system when confronted by what may seem to them to be objectionable beliefs. But this is not what we are speaking about. Rather, we are noting the lack of integrity that some leaders show in their behavior toward others. Christian leaders can sometimes criticize before checking the facts, and act in very unprofessional ways. Leaders need to make a fundamental shift from the arrogant belief that they alone know best to a position where they believe in the priority of relationship. If this is not done, there is no possibility of seeing mutuality among Christian leaders.

In some parts of the Church, such a rapprochement has begun, but there is still a huge distance to go. Few fellowships of local ministers, for instance, include everyone. They are often made up only of those who share similar beliefs. Most would not celebrate a diversity of ideas. Likewise, some congregations, and even denominations, act as though they have an exclusive on "Truth." We see this as an absence of the grace of Christ, as arrogance and fear of the wider Church. If others really are the "enemy," then we should Love them. Instead, a kind of separatism seems to prevail, particularly in the case of Catholic and Protestant denominations. A local Catholic priest and close friend acknowledged to me his feelings of sorrow and anger at being ostracized in the past.

What is needed in some cases is for Christian leaders to lay down their prejudices and even be willing to say sorry for their arrogance to others. In seeking "Truth," we should not build prejudice, because when rumors or whispers fit our prejudices, all of us become reluctant to search for a different perspective. Members of Tomorrow's Church will be noted for their unwillingness to judge, and for preferring, instead, to value relationships over conformity, and to celebrate diversity while personally holding to their own beliefs.

In Summary

The role of leadership in contemporary society is more complex than ever before and is increasingly challenging. We are moving into a time when diversity is valued more than conformity. As well as being known as the age of women, the twenty-first century will be characterized by the high value it places on teams, on the importance of EQ, on the benefit and gift of human emotion, and the capacity to live life well. If faith community cannot be seen to be embracing some of these ideas, it may follow the history of the dinosaur.

Questions to Ponder

1. Who is your model of leadership?
2. In what ways can the authority given to Christian leaders be abusive?

3. In what ways can we unrighteously trust our Christian leaders?
4. When we describe someone as having the "messiah complex" what do you think we mean?
5. In what ways can a pastor or Christian leader make life unsafe for himself and others?
6. What are some of the indications that a pastor or Christian leader is a "control freak?"

Notes

[1] See our website at <www.lifegivingtrust.org> for a range of Bible Notes on these subjects.
[2] G. Davies, *Genius, Grief and Grace: A doctor looks at suffering and success* (Fearn, Ross-shire: Christian Focus Publications, 2001).

10

Shared Leadership Responsibilities

In this chapter we will be looking at a range of different problems that confront contemporary congregations. We will see some of the benefits of teams, and consider what further training may be needed by leaders. We will think about how we should manage when things go wrong and note the danger of financial abuse.

We have looked at some of the pitfalls that threaten the ministry of professional Christian leadership. But in Tomorrow's Church all will grow into some measure of leadership. All will be entrusted with the responsibility of taking their place in the Body of Christ. All will be responsible for creating a safe place. Running a modern church needs much more talent than any one person has. Specific leadership responsibility will be affirmed by the congregation, and leaders will introduce professional practices and expertise. There will be no discrimination in terms of status, power or influence. All members will work alongside one another, exercising complementary gifting.

Creating Diverse Leadership Teams

In Europe, where congregations are relatively small, a solitary pastor is still the norm, whereas in North America many congregations and their denominations have staff. We believe that the future of the Church rests with the ability of leaders to become increasingly team-oriented. So while we fully support the traditional idea of a pastor, we see a growing need for the pastor to be part of a team. This team will often be a mix of paid and voluntary members, all working closely together.

Many Christian leaders seek to create team life for their churches, believing that only in this way will they successfully meet all the needs of contemporary people. Diversity, they feel, is both inevitable and essential. They have a number of different teams to cover different aspects of the church's life. But team members must co-inhere in the Holy Spirit. This requires having the honesty to admit that no one is a god or messianic. At the heart of such teams there must be a mutuality whereby leaders and members alike honor one another as equals. "Pulling rank" would be alien in Tomorrow's Church, making it more difficult to "close ranks," bury, or simply deny any wrongdoing. A more transparent team life and the counsel of many help to avoid such abuse.

What type of team is best equipped to create a safe place for all members? Would the needs of newcomers be best served by having a newcomer on one of the teams? More controversially, what if someone who was sympathetic but not yet a Christian joined a team (subject to membership policies)? They would offer a completely different perspective on church life and could draw attention to possible abuse and vulnerability that others might miss. Would their opinions be welcome? Along similar lines, some of the most spiritually gifted are also some of the most awkward of people! Would the leaders have the integrity to choose people who were likely to threaten or excel them? Who wants an upstart claimant to the throne?

If someone joins a leadership team because they have gifts or natural talents, they may quickly move from a place where it was grace that put them there, to believing that they have the right to be on the team. They move from the honor of serving, to believing that they have earned their position. Alternately, if they are there by grace of the leader, they may feel indebted to the leader and so fudge over wrongdoing. In this way, "fake" teams can be created.

In our own community, it has been an interesting experience to build leadership teams. One of the numerous benefits is the moderating effect the team has on any extreme behavior by any one person. As a team and a leadership, we are together able to absorb it. Having no "full-time" or salaried leadership has had a leveling effect, with no one person exercising too much power. We even rotate jobs and responsibilities to avoid building mini-empires. Such leadership teams draw on a range of gifting and life-of-learning experience for the congregation. There are always some on the team who have more experience, but if they are continually seeking to share responsibility and train others, a lay-team leadership can prove very effective.

Leadership Training

We mentioned the idea that contemporary people are looking for much more than many congregations are currently offering. One of the problems is that a lot of training for Christian leadership does not seem to take this fully into account. We (Peter and Susan) are not experts in this field, nor are we theological educationalists, but it seems to us to be self-evident that many leaders do not have basic training in areas like management, emotional intelligence (EQ), team building, and leadership. We are saddened by the number of times we hear, "Snap out of it!" spoken to someone suffering from chronic depression, or the more devastating, "If you knew the Lord better, you wouldn't have these problems." A theological education alone does not prepare Christian leaders for the needs of all those they will meet. For instance, in modern society, many people see themselves on a journey toward deeper spirituality, but in Protestantism neither a life journey toward Christ-likeness nor even maturity are emphasized. Postmodern people see human make-up in three dimensions—IQ, EQ, and SQ (spiritual intelligence). Many outside the Church would say that we in the Church are okay sometimes with the IQ, but the EQ does not exist, and neither does the SQ.

As mental illness increases, leaders of faith communities will encounter higher numbers of damaged people and will need to know how to respond without causing more damage. They will also require vocational guidance skills, including a knowledge of psychometric testing, and the ability to talk through academic choices as well as personal relational issues. They will need a better understanding of how male and female are different, including the most appropriate ways to teach Love. In addition, a basic knowledge of social relations and group processes, and of psychology and its related therapies, will all be very helpful. As authors of this book, neither of us has all these skills, but they are available to us in our own "group IQ" in our faith community.

Bringing in Other Professional Expertise

We are suggesting that if you have a lawyer, scientist or administrator in membership, get to know them. Talk to the financial experts. Use them. If you have social workers and probation officers, talk to them. Learn from them. Ask them to teach you their health-care perspective. What would they do with some of your problem cases? If you are a Christian leader, stop pretending that you and Christ together can meet every need. Let others help shape the policies and practices of your faith community.

Each local church is unique, and so also are its needs. Training, however good, is never enough. All areas will need regular reviewing. For instance, what are your confidentiality policies? What should you do if you hear a rumor of sexual abuse in the community? Are you using all the available resources? Where conflict of interests might arise (you are wearing too many hats?), your advisor helpers will tell you so (if you give them permission). To be a safe place, we all need to have a teachable spirit and an insatiable desire to learn. In this way, no team will ever be fake. Moreover, such diversity will create a safe place for everyone.

Tomorrow's Church will seek the highest standard of professional expertise from a wide variety of sources, rather than judging the "world" and its ways, by seeking to be exclusive. The following is a rather severe example of church leadership keeping control instead of embracing the expertise of others.

A controlling, institutional leadership

As a young mother and a teacher in a new church in Australia, I was inspired by the idea of developing an alternative approach to education, an approach shaped by the Christian tradition. So along with other parents I helped set up a school that became very popular and successful with parents both inside and outside of the church.

The church itself had a membership at the time of over 1,000, and a very substantial income that supported many leaders. It had above average numbers of young professional families and also a strong tradition of intellectual enquiry. A number of us began to study theology, and were particularly inspired by Neo-Reformed theology. That critical enquiry led us into conflict with traditional Evangelicalism—and this was particularly evident in issues surrounding the leadership of the school. My personal and professional view was that the school was there for education. However, there was a strongly held, and often unexamined, belief amongst church leaders that the school was there to protect our youngsters from "the world" and to "get them saved." Parents were hugely supportive of the school financially.

The school governing body included representatives of the church. However, the church leaders assumed that they had "spiritual authority" to decide on the strategic direction of the school, and I, with others, found myself increasingly at odds with them.

I was also working at a national level with other schools—both Christian and other types of alternative and independent schools, to seek changes in the law that would enable schools like ours to receive government funding. The wider Christian community was divided over this issue, for the same sorts of reasons that our home church was divided. Some of the "elders" of those other church communities (whose churches and schools were completely integrated) began contacting my own church leaders, suggesting that I had problems with authority, basic personality flaws which made me dominant, deceptive, and dangerous—the three D's that Christian women must avoid at all costs. I was not submissive enough, especially to men to whom God had given spiritual authority over me. I was dangerous. Eventually a male colleague wrote me a letter saying that he thought I had "evil powers" that I used to dominate and control people.

My husband and I decided to take this letter to the church leaders. Either it was true—and I needed help—or it was not true and there needed to be some apology. The church leaders took it seriously, but were indecisive. However, they did suggest that I have special counseling with one of their number deemed to have special powers in relation to personal counseling. In a private session, I admitted that I didn't know what was true any more, and as a result there was an exorcism session in which I had "demons" cast out of me. Later, in a full church leaders' meeting, in breach of confidentiality, notes from that counseling session were brought out and read aloud.

I was unwise to have allowed myself to be put through such humiliation. However, at the time the power of the community was very great—it was all we knew. I knew full well that I wasn't perfect, that I had unresolved issues of my own to deal with, and therefore could not completely disagree with the fact that in some situations I could have handled things better or behaved more lovingly.

Redemption: The story has a happier ending. This chapter of my life caused me and a whole generation of my friends significant suffering, which is still surfacing. I later studied more theology in a way that has led to my own growth and development, particularly through the theology of lament. Also, seven years later two of the people concerned sought me out and without reference to the other each apologized unconditionally to me for what had happened. I realized then that we were all victims of a bigger system, and that each individual, including me, was capable of both perpetuating that system and being wounded by it. For me the cross is not about wiping out sin, but enabling us to hold together in suffering tension our common human brokenness with our common humanity.

Here, the author, a professionally qualified person, found herself being told what to do in running the school, and being told, moreover, by a group of church leaders with "spiritual" oversight, who were not educationalists. They should surely have known how much they did not know. Although some would disagree with this woman's perspective, this story has a sadly familiar ring. Male arrogance rears its ugly head again.

The person writing was also a key part of a movement that the Church today is still much in need of. The arrogance of the congregational leaders meant that they stole from the wider Church a vision that was significant in the field of education. Today, years later, that experience has begun to be redeemed in this woman's life. But it is similar to many other types of abuse in which we see potential stolen from the wider Church. Such gaps are difficult to fill when they occur. Those with "spiritual" oversight believed their privileged access to God gave them a better perspective than the professionals who were writing the success story. This self-deceit and arrogance created a setting for abuse, loss of vision and numerous hurt people. Such carelessness is one of the most common forms of abuse by both church members and leaders.

Guidelines

- The more you learn, the more you realize how little you know. This is a helpful attitude to have.
- Always have a teachable and humble spirit. Never pretend you know when you don't, as this can be abusive of both yourself and others.
- Regularly ask: In what areas am I weak as a leader? With the Lord's help, how can I grow stronger as a leader?
- Always be aware of who you need to consult in order to give better help to those in your congregation who are currently outside your area of expertise.
- Build a trained and diverse team in your faith community. Call on others, share the load.
- Welcome being taught by others, even when they disagree with you.

Confidentiality

The type of pastoral care strategy we are suggesting for Tomorrow's Church offers a resolution of one of the sources of abuse—that of confidentiality. Traditionally, the pastoral relationship, like the one-to-one counseling model, has been a private one. In the USA, initiatives like HIPPA, the national standards to protect the privacy of personal health information,[1] re-enforce this. But in an age when confidentiality in any form is becoming the holy grail of medicine, we would like to question the wisdom of allowing this to creep further into congregational life.

The issue of confidentiality can create a number of problems. At one extreme are the pastors and leaders who keep an iron grip on all relationships and disclosures. They insist on knowing all confidential information and often seem to think that it should come to them alone. This increases their power over those who seek help. At the other extreme are churches where openness is encouraged to the extent that people do not feel safe around their leadership because they might use confidential information about them in sermons and conversations in the church lobby. Finding a balance can be difficult. Let us illustrate.

Are you a virgin?

> While I was living in the States, our youth group went to a youth day congress where they had loads of different speakers and numerous praise and worship bands. There were probably 1,500 to 2,000 people there. It was in a huge stadium and my brother was there as well, together with a whole lot of youth I'd got to know while I was out there, together with youth leaders. Eventually a speaker came on and started to talk about the commitment of waiting and having no sex before marriage. Then he asked everyone who was a virgin, and everyone who was committed to waiting, to stand up, in this huge stadium. I had a choice whether to just lie because, anyway, no one would know, and maybe it was with a little bit of rebellion, but I thought, "Actually, I just need to stay sitting." So I did stay

sitting, but it was so undermining, shocking, condemning, judg-mental. There was no reference to circumstances or to how a person might have since changed. I'd say probably over half the stadium stood up—that's what it felt like, certainly everyone around me was standing—that didn't help. They all had to applaud themselves and so the whole stadium was roaring and I was just sitting there crying, thinking, "What a big sinner I am. Now everyone knows, and my brother knows that I haven't waited and maybe I won't go to heaven." Then everyone just sat down and we continued as normal. That was it. My brother was still loving towards me, and didn't react.

Redemption: She did get over it, and later married. She is now an administrator for a church.

What becomes evident here is that not everyone was accus-tomed to talking openly about their sex life, and many were probably not being as honest as the person writing this story. Telling people to stand up might have been intended to encourage transparency but ended up feeling abusive.

In the USA, legislation regarding confidentiality is different from that in Europe. Our perspective at CCD, noted in other writings, is that God is a Trinity community, three persons as one,[2] and to reflect Him we need to learn greater transparency of relationships in a community forum. We do not, as do psy-chotherapeutic professionals, promote private exclusivity. Pastorally speaking, the more people there are to support someone on their journey, the deeper will be both relationships and authentic community.

Working pastorally with individuals on a one-to-one exclu-sive basis can lead to the proliferation of privatism and if people do not get what they want, can open the pastor to the accusation of abuse. Involve a third person, and this is unlike-ly to happen. Encourage people to talk openly about what they are going through, and they will break the power of secrecy over their disorders, however bad they might be. We are sug-gesting the recovery of the ancient Christian tradition of "con-fession one to another" (Jas. 5:16), thereby taking our progress with our journey into a public forum where the whole community benefits. Christ did most of his healing publicly, especially with men, so why do we do so much of it in private?

Before we move on, we should mention the legal duties that guide conduct in families, and especially our duty in law with children. Here in the UK, the Children Act 1989 established the principal in law that the paramount consideration is the protection of the child, while the Protection of Children Act 1999 established a range of guidelines for organizations working with children. The most recent UK Children Act (2004) moves further, following the Green Paper *Every Child Matters* (September 2003). Such legislation, similar to that in the US, lays down a whole range of duties on all those who work with children.

A Narrative Culture

So how would Tomorrow's Church find the balance between helping people feel safe in a pastoral setting, and promoting greater openness in congregational life? Tomorrow's Church would have an open "narrative culture" where people are encouraged to tell their stories in all their sordid detail. Everyone has a story, and once they begin their journey, each story is a testimony of healing. In these stories, people explore why they do not have greater intimacy in Christ and ask what is standing in the way of greater fulfillment in life. The two are the same in Christ. Sharing in this way helps break the power of shame and guilt that many live under. When you experience the acceptance and forgiveness of others, it makes the amazing forgiveness of God much more of a reality.

In times of revival people are led by the Holy Spirit to sort out conflicts in relationships, resolve old tensions, and confess sin. Through such public testimony the Lord is glorified. What we are suggesting is that where the power of secrets rules, there you find the playground of the Enemy. A narrative culture where we can all openly tell our stories is liberating. It is so much easier to be in deep relationships of trust when you no longer have secrets, and no longer fear people knowing your past.

In Tomorrow's Church there may well be a break from traditional one-to-one therapeutic practice, and there will be sensitive openness among members. Congregational life, following
Trinity relational community, will be marked by our living in
open, harmonious transparency where nothing is hidden that
needs to be said. Traditional views of confidentiality will have
been rewritten. Such a culture is particularly helpful to people
with no Christian background because when they move into
congregational life they are able to hear everyone's amazing
stories, and this is compelling. If everything goes on in private,
with very little told, they begin believing that church is lived in
secret. The safest place on earth is where there are no secrets.

Guidelines

* Be open to the idea of creating a narrative culture.
* All matters should, at the appropriate time, be talked about
  openly in such a way that no one is in breach of the law. Be
  open, even when it is painful.
* Where there is sin, confess it together; where there is injustice, resolve it. Have the matter settled in such a way that
  members are satisfied that it cannot happen again.

The Desire Not to Betray God or One Another

Christians are on the whole very protective and committed to
their leaders. If you are committed to Christ, then you will normally be committed to His appointed leaders. A leadership
team that works closely together can also develop a deep loyalty. It would be natural to assume that a shared leadership
team in Tomorrow's Church would function with such close
ties. But this allegiance can go too far. Safety can be compromised when a commitment to loyalty runs deeper than a commitment to openness and love for the needy.

In Tomorrow's Church, the honor of all members of the congregation and particularly of the needy, the oppressed, and the
vulnerable, would have a greater priority than loyalty to

fellow leaders. There would be an acknowledgement that all leaders make mistakes. These would be talked about openly, and a remedy quickly sought. We are talking here about a no-blame culture that allows anyone to make mistakes.

Victims of abuse are often betrayed by leaders who insist on cover-ups when they should be establishing evidence of holiness. By virtue of their office they have special responsibility for giving ethical shape to their authority.[3] Such leadership can only operate in a no-blame culture, where forgiveness is a lifestyle norm.

An unrighteous cover-up

> I was part of the leadership of a local congregation and in the elders' meeting one evening one of the elders mentioned in passing that he had had a scare the previous day with his grandson. He would not say more. But in the meeting I asked him if it was a matter that should be talked about. He told us that he had talked to one of the other elders and the matter was closed.
>
> Totally unconnected (I thought), a few weeks later we heard that the elder had been arrested by the police on suspicion of downloading hard porn and pedophilia on to his computer. The case went on for some months, went public, and the man was forced to resign from leadership. It was only a year or so later that we heard the whole story, though even then not from him but from his wife.
>
> They had had their teenage grandson staying with them one weekend and he had spent much of the time on the grandfather's computer. During these hours he had downloaded and hidden a lot of porn. The police, some time later, were following up a different matter, and took the grandson's computer away for examination. When taken in for questioning, the grandson told them he had been taught to do this by his grandfather—if they did not believe him, he said, they should look on his grandfather's computer. They did, and arrested the church elder.
>
> **Redemption**: None so far. The elder lost everything and now blames God. His colleague, too, no longer attends church. (Compiled from two unrelated incidents.)

Had the leader spoken out when the matter came to light, then the church would have been able to stand with him in the injustice. Talking openly at the time would have been much easier than going through the subsequent humiliation. The other elder was forced to resign for serious misjudgment and collusion in the cover-up.

Deceit by leaders takes many other forms. At the soft end, it may be reading about others' experiences, then pretending they are ours. Some leaders do not stop at this. We have both found ourselves in situations where we have been asked to give a testimony, but have been told what to say. It is hard to correct a Christian leader who requires you to embellish the story a little. Likewise, it is very easy to exaggerate what the Lord is doing in one's life.

The worst is when people are tempted to lie or speak a half truth. This could be telling others that the Lord is providing for them when they are living on their overdraft or credit cards. Or making showy gifts that put them into greater debt. They are moving from reality, to wishful thinking, then into deceit. Probably the greatest area of dishonesty is the lack of authenticity with Christ. The need to achieve this can tempt people into pretending. Some have shared things with us "from the Lord," but we have read the same books. Or, somewhat more sinister, they quote the Lord, knowing they have made it up.

Our desire to show that we have a deep allegiance to Christ can warp our focus on both truth and integrity. If we are not careful we can find ourselves either being deceived or deceiving in the name of the Lord. We cannot create a safe place where we do not know what is true and what is not. Neither can we create a safe place if we are not safe in ourselves.

Guidelines

- Be honest at all times, but be careful that your honesty or "speaking the truth" does not come across as abusive to others.
- None of us needs to defend the Lord's actions, or inaction.
- Hold steady in what is true, but be open to correction from the Lord and others.

Financial Abuse

One final area is that of finance. Here in Europe we have in the Church a culture that assumes that if you are working for the Lord, you should work for nothing, or, if you need a salary, keep it as low as possible. Working for a pittance is a substantial area of abuse in some parts of the contemporary Church. In fact, where this is not the case, and a person does earn a just salary, others in the Church will sometimes feel that this is "unspiritual" or self-serving. Motives can be questioned. Much Christianity in Europe is therefore managed and led by people who are willing to work for very little income or even nothing. In some cases this precludes churches from employing the best people. Such penny-pinching attitudes mean that at times we are all in danger of having the people we deserve working for us, and not the people we and the Lord actually need. Thankfully, this is not such a problem in the USA.

What view would Tomorrow's Church take about financial matters? This would in part depend on the denomination and the wealth or poverty of its members. A range of people and gifting serving part-time on a job-share basis can make the Body of Christ more effective. But when people are employed, they should be offered a wage that is appropriate to the service they are providing.

Tomorrow's Church would have its own financial guidelines, rather than just being content to adopt those of other organizations. But it is important to be transparent in what you are doing, not in any way seeking to act behind closed doors or in a strident manner. At times, it is necessary to put spiritual/relational issues first. For example, creating a careful budget won't be sufficient if a curse of poverty remains.

Guidelines

* People must be honored financially if they are serving the Lord.
* As Christians, we have the duty to create wealth, but it should never be at the expense of relationships or integrity.

• There should be transparency in a church's management of its finances.

In Summary

In this chapter we have looked at a range of issues related to the growing need for diversity in leadership structures and the people chosen as leaders. We have also, in passing, noted the need for far more diverse areas of training for traditional leaders of faith communities, for instance, the need for more professional people and training. We have noted the importance of not betraying God by unwisely covering up potential scandal. And we would include a caution about having husband and wife teams in leadership.

Questions to Ponder

1. What, if anything, makes you get defensive about God?
2. What are some of the problems of being a solitary pastor or Christian leader?
3. To "spread the load" in your faith community, what are some of the things that could be done?
4. If someone came to you admitting addiction to pedophilia, what would you do?
5. What are the professions or skills of most of the key members of your congregation?
6. Write guidance notes on how confidentiality could be practiced in your congregation.

Notes

[1] See <www.hhs.gov/ocr/hippa>.
[2] Holmes, *Trinity in Human Community*.
[3] R. Ammicht Quinn, et el., "Postcript" in R. Ammicht Quinn, H. Haker and M. Junker-Kenny (eds.), *Structural Betrayal of Trust* (London: SCM, 2004), 130–5.

Part 5

A New Model of Pastoral Care

So far we have ascertained that a congregation that is a safe place is comprised of safe people, who are growing and positively changing in their relationship with Christ. It is the responsibility of pastoral care to help support this process.

11

Looking Again at Pastoral Care

In this chapter we will suggest a new definition of pastoral care based on Scripture and postmodern values. We will consider the risks of leaders whose own needs are ignored and will comment on how our uniqueness in Christ can reshape the way we do pastoral care, by involving all as "experts-by-experience".

The purpose of pastoral care is to help see Christ be formed in us and one another, to bring people into a deeper, more intimate relationship with the social Trinity, themselves, and others. If done well, it carries significant potential for creating community as a safe place. In some ways, all of us are responsible for contributing to the pastoral care of others in the Body. But this also means that others are responsible for offering pastoral care to us. We will look in the next chapter at pastoral care as leadership. But, first, we will explore the mutual giving and receiving that comprises pastoral care in Tomorrow's Church.

What Is Pastoral Care?

In Tomorrow's Church we have assumed that the majority of people are committed to the ongoing journey of growing in Christ and living *imago Dei*. Indeed, it is because Christ is in us, and abiding with us, that Tomorrow's Church is a sanctuary. Pastoral care is Body life promoting the formation of Christ in us among us.

In some ways, it is radical to say that we all have a part to play in the ongoing formation of Christ in one another both by giving and by receiving. If we believed this, we would treat each person as our neighbor (Lk. 10:25–37), and be as little children (Mt. 18:3). When the disciples were squabbling over who was the greatest, that was the opposite of pastoral care as we see it (Mk. 9:33–34). On the other hand, the way the disciples loved, supported, and protected one another during the formation of the Early Church was authentic pastoral care in action.

The outworking of pastoral care is unique in every congregation, mirroring the needs of the individual members. Earlier in this book, we noted that to put the other person first means to love them in the way that *they* need to be loved, to let them choose. Pastoral care is therefore not an imposition upon faith community but requires maturity of relationship and personal guidance for every individual. We must ask what is best for each individual from their perspective, how they think they can best be supported in their journey toward Christ-likeness.

For some, this will sometimes mean "putting clothes on their back and food in their belly" because they need first of all to experience God's faithful provision through other members of His family. This is building bridges of trust with them. With others, those without a faith, pastoral care might mean being a support in a journey of enquiry, vulnerability, friendship, leading eventually to meeting Christ. For those more experienced and more mature in their faith, pastoral care might mean mentoring and coaching, discipleship, shared prayer and Bible study. For those who are suffering, pastoral care could mean sitting and weeping together, holding their hand while they touch into their anger and pain. Christ meets all of us at the point of our need. Pastoral care is our participation in this ministry to one another.

Achieving this kind of pastoral care requires from all of us a certain level of risk tempered with trust, a chosen vulnerability. These are essential qualities for all of us who seek to progress toward more Christ-likeness. But wherever there is vulnerability, trust, and transparency, there is the possibility of abuse. So it is easy to understand why many churches opt for a more formal model of pastoral care in which specific individuals have responsibility for pastoral care and the rest are happy to leave it to them. Which of us wants to make our needs known? In a safe place, pastoral care still requires a servant heart, a humble view of oneself, and a belief in the personal work of the Holy Spirit coupled with a growing confidence in the power of the atonement.

We are suggesting that pastoral care is a corporate duty, the responsibility of all members of the faith community, not just the job of the pastorally trained elite. Its scope should be wide. There should, for example, be training in the likes of EQ and SQ. And it is to be undertaken purposefully to create a safe place both for the needy individual and the wider congregation.

Before exploring practically what this type of pastoral care might look like, imagine how difficult, and unsafe, congregational life can be for even the most committed Christians. Most of us know leaders who have served in local churches in deeply sacrificial ways. Week after week they have arrived early, or opened their homes, been available on the telephone, or taken responsibility for a youth group or Bible study at short notice. But the toll on their personal life, and their relationships with partners or children is often very severe. The overall culture that they find themselves in can feel abusive, simply because of the cumulative impact of the demands. Imagine what might happen if the needs of the individual leader were to be given priority over the goals of the church.

This may seem to some of you an extreme idea but we hope it will help you identify what a safe place could look like. At the end of the chapter we will be suggesting a pastoral care approach that is based on a strategy of involvement by the members, not just by the "leadership."

Much congregational life today is about sustaining ambitious programs and keeping the buildings and ministries going. To achieve this, most congregations, and even some Christian organizations, rely on zealous voluntary help. But the maintaining of structures can become more important than the well-being of the individuals seeking to sustain them. At the heart of the problem is the sad fact that the individual begins to exist for the survival of the structures of the church. In some congregations and denominations less and less attention is being given to what these programs do to the people making them happen. In this way congregations and Christian institutions become abusive to the people in them.

We believe that congregational life should exist for Christ and for those who are committed to Him. It should not exist to suck the life out of willing and able workers.

For day-to-day relationships to be safe in congregations, every person must choose both to give and receive. Imagine if the church makes a priority of together ensuring each person's needs are met. In Tomorrow's Church perhaps every leader is in their own support group.

We know a substantial number of "former" Christian leaders who are still committed to the Lord but want nothing to do with congregational life. It has been suggested that in some parts of the UK there are now as many "former Christians" outside the Church as there are regular church-goers. At some point, leaders need to become the center of others' love, as Christ suggested. Without this there is a significant risk that they are driven into burnout or compassion fatigue.

Personal Uniqueness

A make-believe scenario . . .

> Two converts come into the church damaged, with their lives a mess, incomplete education, an inability to do relationships, and a lot of debt and toxic relationships. They are in need. As a pastoral team we might be tempted to set about sorting out their lives. In most congregations there would be pressure to get them into jobs (like "we" do), to encourage them to study (like "we" have done), to sort out their relationships (like we believe "we" already have), and teach them all we know about God (because "we" know more). In no time at all they are like us.
>
> "We" celebrate this achievement. Understandably, perhaps, we assume that "godliness" for them would be similar to the "godliness" in our own lives. Our response to them might be completely different were we to acknowledge that the godly

people that they are to become might be uniquely different from the expression of godliness in our own lives.

In this book we have avoided discussion about which "personality type" is more prone to abuse and which more likely to be abusive. We are suggesting, rather, that we are all unique in Christ. Although we are not against personality profiling, we are disturbed by its pigeonholing of people. Our concern is that we may end up inhibiting their broader development since we all have a tendency to fulfill the labels we are given. Uniqueness in Christ means that as we mature we become "wider" than any specific type. To reflect Christ-likeness more fully, our personalities should broaden to include a greater capacity for wholeness than any narrow "type" would allow. In other published work, we explain in more detail this alternative way of seeing growth in Christ. We call this the *gender continuum.*[1] Tomorrow's Church will meet you where you are, and then help you become the mature, well-rounded, unique person Christ intended you to be.

But in saying that one should pursue one's personal journey, we are not promoting the kind of selfism that we noted in Chapter 3. Instead, we are suggesting a model of pastoral care and maturing in Christ that involves substantial input to and from others. We are not promoting an exclusive, personal, private model but a relational one that is inclusive. For the majority of members to feel that they can contribute to the pastoral care of other members of the church, there needs to be a clear, shared, and achievable goal for pastoral care. We would suggest that at a practical level, the goal is for each member to support other members in their ongoing and unique journeys into greater Christ-likeness.

In Christ we are all unique, and carry a divine uniqueness both in who we are and who we might become. Our biological nature, our DNA, our finger prints, eye signature, saliva, and shape and size are all unique to us. Similarly, we are also unique spiritually, in our spiritual growth, gifting, calling, and potential. In every way, at every level, we are unique. While accepting that we all have a duty to do a journey toward greater maturity in Christ, we also see this as a shared journey together. This approach of doing the journey together makes it safer for all of us and profoundly changes the definition of what pastoral care is.

Pastoral Care as Personal Relational Change

We noted in Part 4 that some leaders have a tendency to create a culture of cloning, requiring other members to be like them in order to be more like Christ. Such a view is in marked contrast to the postmodern emphasis on personal uniqueness. What Christ envisaged is that all of us need to do a personal journey that will bring about radical positive change in our attitudes, outlook, personality, and values. We must become more child-like (Mt. 18:3). We need to develop a simple child-like trust in the Father, and in our relationships with one another, which gives us all we need. Pastoral care in Tomorrow's Church would be a shared involvement of mutual support on this pastoral journey.

Such change in us, traditionally described as a discipleship journey or a process of sanctification, is mandatory for all of us. In some Church traditions, change in a person is expected before and as they are converted to Christ. This is usually outward behavioral or attitudinal change. Traditionally, this is taught, not caught. Within the Protestant tradition, once we are committed, little further change is required in us other than a lot of cognitive learning.

This is in marked contrast to the Early Church where the deep change that was required was social and personal, beginning after a person had joined a faith community, not before.[2] It was caught through involvement in the relationships of the community rather than through formal teaching. New Christians entered a new counter-cultural world that focused on Christ and His relevance. Local faith community was a culture of ongoing personal positive change that promoted the forming of Christ in one another. Change was at the heart of allegiance to Christ.

To achieve this type of corporate body life is not easy because we all love conformity. Rather than face change, most of us are more comfortable having clockwork-like routines and order in our lives, whether through a uniform, examinations, qualifications or by practicing long-held traditions. Although, paradoxically, there are some changes that most of us relish—a holiday, new car, home or wardrobe—human nature dislikes the type of change that requires painful effort on our part or a change in the way we are. We rebel when such change is forced on us. Whether it is losing our favorite pen or having to change our attitudes and prejudices, we normally resist all the way.

In our churches, many of us celebrate a type of holy conformity—"We've always done it this way!" "It's always worked in the past." "We need to increase our efforts, not change anything." Many seem to have chosen to believe that there is something sacred in what they already do, and the way that they have done it for so many years. To change would be to lose that sacredness. We are not saying that these highly valued traditions should be trashed, but that they should begin to take second place to the needs of members and newcomers.

What we are suggesting is that what Christ requires goes against most basic human instincts. Part of our reluctance to make this deep-rooted change is our need to admit that we may have been wrong. Few of us do this easily. None of us is naturally Christ-like or naturally safe for others. And if we must change, we would rather do it privately and stay in control. Instead, however, we must all learn to celebrate ongoing positive change in ours and other people's lives, and their growing uniqueness alongside us.[3]

When talking to people with no Christian background (and we now have many in Europe!) we often hear the comment that the Church seems to make few concessions to contemporary culture, and does not try to change in order to be better understood. Although in many instances the truth may be the opposite, what usually happens is that newcomers to faith community, rather than receiving support in celebrating how different they could become in Christ, will find they are expected to conform. The longer they remain in their new faith community, the more like everyone else they are expected to become.

We are not suggesting that belief in our growing uniqueness leads us into an attitude in which everything is relative. We do not mean that we should make our own rules based on our whims or feelings at the time. A belief in our own uniqueness does not give us permission to practice a situation ethic, choosing what we want to do in every situation. Rather, it means that we hold to what is called Constantinian Christianity—the core values taught in Scripture and the creeds of the Early Church—while adapting these to our own and others' needs where Christ meets them.[4]

In Tomorrow's Church, the foundation of all we would seek to do is the celebration and encouragement of a person's maturing and uniqueness in Christ. This is important, as many of us suffer from the idea that we are no one special, that our lives are not significant and never will be. To live in a culture where this uniqueness in Christ is not only believed but lived is very important for the redemption of both the person's life and the future Church. Such a positive culture can and will be a safe place. Being in permanent change can make a faith community a very safe place.[5]

Many Christians are so insecure about themselves and their faith that having someone around them who is different (or better) is bad enough, but having someone who enjoys being different can be hard work, even condemning. So in order not to abuse, it is essential that we begin to change our attitude to others, enjoying their uniqueness as well as our own. Ongoing personal positive change, when welcomed and enjoyed, creates a safe place. It is Christ-like.

Guidelines

- Welcome diversity of interests and beliefs among your friends and fellowship. You have Christ in common.
- Be personally willing to change in positive ways in order to become both more unique and more like Christ. Your positive change makes you safe to be around.

"Experts-by-Experience"

Over the last decade or so we have developed a therapeutic model of care for those on the journey toward Christ-likeness that allows the mentoring of people in need while strongly emphasizing their responsibility to care for themselves, even when they are in extreme emotional and mental ill-health. At times they will need medical support, but by far the best environment for many of these people is the support of others who have already overcome their own problems. Those who offer this support are mentors or "experts-by-experience."[6] The more of this shared expertise there is in a faith community, the safer it is.

In response to the ever greater emphasis these days on acquiring academic or professional qualifications before one can help others, as a congregation we have looked again at therapeutic practice and returned to a more traditional therapeutic community (TC) model (see page xix). In this model, although a qualified professional may oversee day-to-day conduct, each member also makes an important contribution. The principle is simple. What one person has learned, and the positive change this has brought about in that person's life, has the potential to be shared with someone else who has arrived more recently. It can then become part of that newcomer's success story.

Over a period of time, the individual achieves through learning from others, and in turn is able to pass this on. In our own faith community, we specifically encourage people to become mentors, and we also offer training in mentoring. This practice is not as dangerous as it may sound since mentors are only mentors as and when others seek them out. It is not a status bestowed by the leadership, but a role achieved when others ask for help. So the whole process is "self-leveling." If you are in a bad space or are not wanting to mentor, then you take time out. This is your decision.

After nearly a decade of working in this way, we can usu-ally find someone to help any newcomer with their unique combination of problems. Then they in turn, by seeking Jesus and His healing, can themselves become "experts-by-experience." This reproduces a pastoral care and discipleship model that focuses on human need. This practice of having "experts-by-experience" also does something else: it encourages a narrative culture. Individuals who are gaining some measure of success on their journeys, or even struggling, are expected to talk about it. Although there is no pressure, and people only share their stories when they want to, it is assumed that they have a story to tell. Sharing this story, and being willing to help others, means that they contribute to the "therapeutic IQ" of the whole community.

In Summary

At the beginning of this chapter, we noted a new way of looking at pastoral care. Instead of leaving it to the highly trained professional or pastor, it becomes the responsibility of all of us. We looked at two sides to a tragic story that could be found in any congregation or Christian organization and we noted some of the things that should have been done differently. We then began to identify our uniqueness in Christ, and saw how this impacts and changes our view of ourselves, others, and pastoral care. Finally, we noted the value of becoming "experts-by-experience." We are now going to look at how we can make these ideas into a safe place.

Questions to Ponder

1. What is your definition of pastoral care?
2. Do you see in your own congregation any of the abuse experienced by the couple?
3. What are some of the pastoral problems associated with the idea of personal uniqueness?
4. What would an unchurched newcomer be uncomfortable with in your faith community?
5. How would you teach the benefits of changing to become more like Christ?
6. Outline some of the changes that would take place in your faith community if you assumed that you all needed to change positively to be more like Christ.

Notes

1 P.R. Holmes, *Trinity in Human Community*, 175–6.
2 A. Field, *From Darkness to Light: How one became a Christian in the Early Church* (Ben Lomond, Calif.: Conciliar Press, 1978/1997).
3 P.R. Holmes and S.B. Williams *Becoming More Like Christ: A contemporary Biblical journey* (Milton Keynes: Paternoster, 2007).
4 For some illustrations of how this works for different people with differing problems, see our book *Changed Lives*.
5 S.B. Williams and P.R. Holmes, *Therapeutic Community as a Salugenic Place: Four stages of insider status in a synergistic model of community* (Association of Therapeutic Communities Windsor Conference, 2006, available at <www.lifegivingtrust.org>.
6 See <www.mentalhealth.org.uk/page.cfm?pageurl=expertsbyexperience.cmf>.

12

A Safe Place for Those Needing Help

Personal uniqueness becomes invaluable as a foundation for pastoral care when we begin to consider the diversity of need in the Body of Christ. How is it possible to offer a safe place for all those who come? Toward the end of the book we will be considering types of structure and policies that enable the local church to keep safety paramount at an organizational level, but in this chapter we will explore some of the circumstances and different types of need that present a challenge in contemporary pastoral care.

Our Call to Help Those in Need

Much of the Church's cultural life is expressed in day-to-day relationships within the faith community. These relationships either do or do not create a safe place. We are suggesting that it is not enough for congregational life to be a safe place for the majority or for any specific group in the congregation, such as the longstanding members, the leadership or families, but it must also be a safe place for everyone. Christ noted that we all find it easy to love our friends (Mt. 5:46), suggesting that human nature will always take the easiest path, regardless of the consequences. We love those who love us but avoid (either intentionally or unintentionally) those people who would be trouble, challenging or demanding.

But for any community to be a safe place, it must also be safe for God's "awkward squad," those who we would not naturally love or want to spend time with. We are speaking here of the type of people who Christ chose as disciples. They were not the cream of society, but those on whom He felt best able to build an eternal Kingdom. He ignored the well-trained, outwardly godly and religious leaders such as the Pharisees. During the time He was with them, His chosen disciples proved to be rewarding, but difficult. They would be unlikely seminary material today.

Over our years as pastoral leaders in the UK Church, in front of our very eyes there has been mounting evidence that has forced us to some radical conclusions—conclusions that now form the cornerstone of our ministry. We have found that those who are most damaged emotionally are often those who turn out to be most gifted. Buried underneath the damage of the years there is often significant anointing. Once these people have been taught to let go and give to Christ the damage in their lives, they become remarkable treasures for the Body of Christ. It is almost as if, during their early years and long before they ever knew Christ, the Enemy saw the gifting and anointing they carried and set out to damage them before they could have an opportunity to hurt the Enemy by bringing glory to Christ.

Put another way, those who most of us would not naturally seek out, the sick, failed, and damaged, are those on whom the Lord often builds His Kingdom. They are the ones He tells us to go to first (Mt. 9:6; 11:4–6; 25:34–40, etc.). He gave us a mandate to help those who both need, and would value our help. We are all called to care for those who cannot easily care for themselves. From Christ's perspective, this is what true love is (Mt. 5:43–45). For at times it is Love alone that creates a safe place. To do so, to create a safe place for those who in themselves would not be able to find such a place, is a unique mandate to the Church from Christ. No other institution, organization or group of people on earth have this requirement placed on them. So how sad that at times these are the kinds of people who we are most likely to ignore or even inadvertently abuse. So often our instinct is to create successful places, full of triumphal Christians, rather than faith communities that are primarily safe places for the sick and damaged. We are suggesting that congregational life should know the "solidarity of the shaken."[1]

Pastoral Care for the Vulnerable

One of the sub-groups identified by the UK Violence Research Programme is the vulnerable adult. Following on from this research, the Department of Health has published a report entitled, *No Secrets: Guidance in developing and implementing multi-agency policies and procedures to protect vulnerable adults from abuse.*[2] Another vulnerable sub-group is children and young people—and schools are likewise seeking to draft guidelines to help lessen abuse. For instance, *A Legal Toolkit for Schools: Tackling abuse, threats and violence towards members of the school community*[3] outlines a number of measures that can easily be implemented.[4]

Many churches are blessed with large numbers of people from the professions. These people know their rights and are articulate on the subject of what is and is not acceptable. But some congregations find themselves with vulnerable people, even, perhaps, like us, with a majority of vulnerable people. If you carry extensive damage in your life, you will be more vulnerable to abuse. Because of the fear of abuse, you may be unable to hear things clearly in the way that is natural to most of us. A passing comment might be heard as a blasting rebuke, a word intended as positive come across as damning. Those who it is hardest to support are those who do not realize how damaged and vulnerable they are.

Here in the UK one in four adults will at some time in their adult life have an extended period of mental or emotional illness. Over half of all absenteeism is the consequence of emotional stress,[5] and it is anticipated that the number of people with mental and emotional illness will only increase in the decades ahead. A substantial number of all health-service beds in the UK are occupied by those with emotion-related illness, much of it long term. Again, this number is expected to increase. Such illness will leave many people in deep need, yet there are few resources to support them in traditional health care. Many are already finding their way into churches or para-church groups where they are seeking help. Perhaps you, reading this book, are one of them. Sadly, not all find traditional church life helpful. Let us give you an example.

Disregarding his mental state

I became a Christian when I was 22. I was very mixed up. I'd had a breakdown when I was 19, being sectioned under the Mental Health Act, an experience from which I had never really recovered. I had an unchurched background, but had made contact with a local Charismatic church through a messed-up friend who had told me the church might be able to help. I had ended up going on an Alpha Course, and it was shortly afterwards that I "gave my life to Jesus." I never really considered the decision properly.

I had desperately needed to change so when people had talked about Jesus being able to perform miracles I really had nothing to lose. My conversion was dramatic. I genuinely felt the presence of a spirit that seemed to cleanse me emotionally. My behavior and lifestyle also changed quite fundamentally. I stopped taking drugs, getting drunk, smoking, and I started to exercise regularly again. Being around a group of people with a positive outlook on life seemed to have a positive influence.

But I found that there were many young men coming into the church who, like me, were currently experiencing mental health problems. They were going up to the front to be prayed for, but with little positive effect—several days later they would be back in hospital. There seemed little support for them. One experienced church worker admitted to me, "We just don't know how to help them."

Eventually I went to my pastor to talk out my doubts. I really felt like I needed some form of proper discipleship because I was scared that I might get ill again. He answered me by saying something like, "Well, these doubts are normal, you've just got to get on with things." "You're still coming to church, isn't that enough?" And, "Sometimes you've just got to make a decision about what you believe, and go for it regardless."

On reflection, I think I was moving into another breakdown. I was showing all the signs of another depression. Going to my leaders for help proved to be a complete waste of time—they communicated a complete incapacity to help me, even in the most basic of ways. The last time I met with my pastor, he launched into this attack on me: "I don't care what you do or where you go, just as long as you make a decision either way," and, "You're no good to me whilst you're like this—either stay and get on with things or just go." I began to admit that I was not important as a person, only for what I could do for the church. Those who were vulnerable (who had a "good testimony") like me, were used by the church, but not helped.

Redemption: He left this congregation, seeking help in another faith community. Long term, his relationship with the Lord has suffered serious damage. He has since gone on to complete his degree and is now doing his doctorate. He is also a key member in the leadership of a local congregation.

What is clearly evident in this sad account is the gross incompetence of the leaders of the congregation. There was a complete failure to understand this young man and his damaged past. At the beginning of the twenty-first century, it is wholly unacceptable that there should still be a stigma attached to mental illness, even by the Church. The Christian leader in this story was reacting in a stereotypical way in not wanting to understand what the young man was experiencing. He expected him either to be normal or to leave (go somewhere else!). If the young man had arrived with a leg in plaster, it is likely that he would have received a different response. The invisibility of his illness made him very vulnerable. His illness also meant that he needed a big investment of time, an investment that this pastor was clearly not willing to make.

This man was fragile. He was in a serious state and was showing several signs of another psychotic episode, yet no one stopped to listen to him and ask how they could serve him. The leadership's response was, "What can you do for us?" In this congregation at least he was unlikely to find the level of understanding and support that he needed. The congregation was not a safe place for him. It was a place of abuse. If we are to build the Kingdom of God as Christ did, with broken and damaged people, we have got to learn how to love and help such people. There may come a time when sick people like this man are the only ones seeking help from the Church.

In Tomorrow's Church, how would this man be received? He would be listened to and it would soon be realized that his experiences in hospital, and earlier factors, had left him feeling deeply emotionally abused. Priority would be given to his needs and he would be supported in a way appropriate to him. He would be invited to participate in activities and to take on responsibility that he felt comfortable with. But if he felt at any time that these activities were not in his best interests, then there would be no pressure to continue. It is also likely that additional support and advice would be sought from specialists, with an attitude that said, "Please teach us more about how to love such people."

Guidelines

• Seeing potential in even the most clumsy and awkward of people helps them to believe in themselves, too.
• Those who are fragile or emotionally ill need extra pastoral support, often in conjunction with specialist professional services.

The Problem of the Demonic—a Pastoral Practice

The problem of the demonic is very specific, and this section is not relevant to all branches of the Church. If you are one of those who have no tradition of dealing with this kind of problem then do feel free to skip this section.

Confronting the Enemy and casting out demons is a command of Christ (Mk. 3:13–15), but what is not so clear is when and how it should be done. It is fraught with difficulty. Even Paul brought great trouble upon himself when he cast out a spirit from a slave girl fortune-teller (Acts 16:16–24). The Church has had a very checkered history in connection with this issue and has often taken up extreme positions ranging from absolute denial of this reality to a view that all of us are demonized in one way or another.

Our Lord seems to have had two approaches to this part of His work, one method more for men, another more for women. With the exception of one or two passing references (for example, Mk. 7:24–30; Lk. 13:10–13, etc.) most of the deliverances He did publicly seem to have been on men. He seems to have taken more care to be private with regard to deliverance on women.[6]

We should remember that Christ was fully equipped with the spiritual maturity and discernment to know what was going on in people's hearts (Mt. 12:25; Mk. 12:15, etc.). The emotionally ill are particularly vulnerable if this issue is not handled well, and in our work we seek to make a clear distinction between emotional damage and trauma, and those issues that have a more direct demonic root. We will (almost) always deal first with the emotional damage. We help the person understand the contributing factors and experience that they have been through, and the way these are exploited by the Enemy. We also focus on the profound restorative impact of meeting Jesus in His love. This enables them to repent of unwise choices they have made, engaging and letting go of their sin, anger, hate, etc. In seeing some of this as sin, either theirs or others', they will begin to grow stronger in Christ's power to help them. As the sin is confessed and taken by the Lord, the Enemy loses his footing in their lives. If any demonic issues then remain, they can be tackled more distinctly.

To discern spiritual darkness is not easy and requires spiritual gifting. Interestingly, one of the few references in Scripture that moves toward a definition of maturity is Hebrews 5:13–14 where the writer suggests that to be mature one needs the ability to discern between good and evil. To have such ability one would need to be at ease and to be able to see clearly in both worlds, the material and the spiritual. For this, common sense is needed as well as spiritual gifting and, as many have discovered, the former is not as common or easy as one might think. Let us illustrate.

The demonic or an emotional disorder?

> I had been for prayer several times and had felt a real benefit
> from it, but still had panic attacks and irrational fear episodes.

So the leadership of my local church decided to pray for me, to deliver me. I was not too familiar with what this meant, but agreed.

The prayer time started routinely enough, but then one of the men began to raise his voice and I recoiled, crouching down in fear of his voice. But my action just seemed to encourage him the more, and he stood up over me, shouted at me, and began to wave his fist at me. It didn't feel as if he was talking to me but to something in me. I was terrified, and showed it, at which point another of the men leapt into the fray and began to shout at me as well. I panicked, leapt up and began to run for the door. A woman stood in my path, blocking me. I screamed, but to no avail. They descended on me again and stood over me as I crouched in a heap in the corner of the room terrified of them. I began to shake violently, clutching my face in my hands, now becoming hysterical. I passed out . . . waking some time later with them still speaking over me, rejoicing that I was now free.

The woman had to help carry me out of the room to the car as I was now in a deeply traumatized state. I was off work for several weeks and never went back to the church again.

Redemption: She did eventually learn what were the causes of the trauma and panic attacks, but continued taking medication until she found a therapist who could help her dismantle the factors in her private world that had required her to live in fear.

Much of our work is with folk who have difficult and damaged pasts so we have adapted the traditional practice of deliverance to accommodate such people. We describe it as "deliverance through gentleness." The principle is simple. We assume that most authority of the Enemy in our lives is given to him by our own stupidity or sin or the damage that we are still carrying from what others have done to us. So to remove his influence, we must say sorry for this sin, as we welcome the authority of the finished work of Christ. It is a shift of allegiance toward Christ in a particular area of our lives. Most of the time it works well, as you can see in the eyes of people when they have done the appropriate "homework," repenting of the sin, and saying sorry.

By approaching the problem of the demonic in this way, we are taking the focus away from his power to abuse us, to the power of Christ to cleanse us. Deliverance in different areas of our lives then becomes routine, though many who use this approach are never aware that deliverance is what is happening to them. All they know is that they feel more clean, and are now able to live in a way that they could not in the past. We have Bible Notes and Bible Studies that help people understand what they are experiencing. They feel safer where an emphasis is placed on Christ, and not on the power of the Enemy to rule over their lives.

Self-Abuse

Abuse takes many forms, as we have seen. Most of the abuse we have discussed so far has an external dimension. It has been brought on us by someone else or by circumstances. But in a review of a pastoral care approach that will meet the needs of everyone, it is important to consider the problems created by those of us who are our own worst enemy. Some of us abuse ourselves.

The most serious form of self-abuse is, of course, taking one's own life. In most developed cultures the act of killing oneself is viewed as a criminal act—self murder. There are statutory guidelines in place to protect and support those who have become so sick that they threaten to self-harm in this way. It is important that the Church should be aware of the latest legislation, and know how to respond.

As a congregation, we have a policy that anyone who seriously threatens to take their own life automatically excludes themselves from community. We usually refer them to the local GP or health-care professionals. Once help has been received, if the person is then able to choose to no longer self-harm, we welcome them back. But we need to hear them say that they want to learn to live. We will also lay down appropriate guidelines so that they and other members of the community are not abused, and we will work with the local agencies to support them in their recovery if that is appropriate.

There are far more church members whose self-abuse is less severe but is nonetheless very damaging. Two of the main areas are compulsions and addictions. With several hundred addictions to choose from, it is hard to avoid catching a few. It is our view, based on many years of clinical experience, that all of us abuse ourselves in some way or another, in part because of the disease called sin, and also because of our human gravity to darkness. Virtually every person coming to us for help and support, will in time, with the Lord helping them, discover areas of self-abuse. It could be as mild as caffeine and chocolate or as sad as living beyond one's means in the chaos of credit cards and overdrafts. Whatever it is, this fundamental lifestyle disorder,[7] will be a relevant issue for each of us as we pursue a journey of having Christ fully formed in us.

Addiction to pornography is a typical male form of self-harm, while for women it could be self-hate or a loathing of one's body. In its worst form, pornography leads to vices like pedophilia, lusting and lewd acts against children.[8] Congregational life is recognized by outside agencies as an "ideal" place to deviously pursue such addictive disorders because of the high degree of trust that is presumed in most churches.

What we are suggesting is that a great deal of self-harm and abuse of others is driven by our own deep needs, appetites, and baggage. We should note this dark side to all of us, and take into account these hidden or subliminal drives. In pastoral care, one of the most helpful ways of supporting people suffering from any form of self-abuse is to ensure that such matters are openly discussed in congregational life, and that there is no judging of people when they talk about them. Rather than feeling judged and shamed, people need to feel supported in their decision to admit the problem and seek help in addressing the underlying issues.

Another area of self-abuse is finance. This can take many different forms, from a simple decision to borrow money but without the cash flow to service the debt, to being victimized by other family members whose behavior creates poverty or continued dependence. The ease with which we can get credit, together with a culture of borrowing money, guarantee that most of us will at some time or another stretch ourselves beyond our personal means. This is often made worse by unfortunate changes in our circumstances, perhaps job loss, the break-up of a relationship or the failure of a business. Other causes can take a range of complex forms that may begin with our own irresponsibility but end up being compounded by others' abuse of us. A good example is when credit agencies report our debts and we get a bad credit record.

Some forms of financial abuse are much more subtle. It could be a bad attitude to money, with the result that it is not valued or perhaps, at the opposite extreme, a Scrooge-like mentality that means we will never part with it and abuse others by refusing to help when we can. Much of this could be engendered by unrighteous fear, or our unwillingness to trust. In our pastoral work, as we delve into the person's circumstances, values, and attitudes, we often note patterns of poverty. Such patterns may suggest that someone is under curses or scripts that ensure that they will never get ahead or break the cycles they are in. Whatever the drives or background circumstances, all forms of financial abuse are on the increase, especially in the area of identity theft. We believe it will increasingly become a leader on the pastoral agenda for many congregations.

Although it is important to recognize and admit to self-harm, what matters more is what the person does with this knowledge. The easiest path for most individuals is to ignore it, and just go on. The responsible thing to do is to seek help in breaking these cycles. If we know that there are others in the congregation who have successfully dealt with these issues, this step will feel much more manageable. Imagine having heard someone share their story, admit the problem and talk about how they broke the habit and got rid of the underlying drives: wouldn't this make you feel much more comfortable about talking about your own issues?

In addressing the problem, the all-important question to ask is: "What benefits do I get out of this self-harm?" The immediate response of most people will normally be, "None!" However, as they begin to get more honest, they can usually find between fifteen to thirty reasons why they are living as they are. Some of the most obvious are refusing to take responsibility for one's life, not being able to believe one could be free from the pain, and using the self-harm to take revenge on someone else. Self-harm is abusive of others, and can lead to the congregation becoming a place of secrets, deceit and double lives. We should be ready to offer support in a non-judgmental way so that as soon as people are ready to deal with these issues, they know they have someone to turn to. This is basic pastoral care, and creates a safe place for such people.

Guidelines

+ Let's remember that self-abuse is still abuse, and as such it makes us unsafe. Becoming safe people will mean inviting the Lord to help us undo these areas so we can help others, too.

Difficult Relationships

As part of their offer of pastoral care, churches also have to respond to relationship breakdown. One in two marriages will fail. That is the statistic in the Western world and sadly it is little different for people in the Church. This means that huge amounts of emotional damage, anger, pain, and betrayal are accumulating in our society. But our own observation is that this pain is often greater in the Church where the requirement to stay together, to love, is so much higher than in society in general. The shame is also greater, and the judgment against those who admit they are struggling is very severe and can result in deep self-loathing. Surely this cannot be the most helpful pastoral care strategy? Let us look at two short accounts.

A broken marriage

They started going out, and before long everyone in the congregation had noticed. But he began to have doubts so went to the pastor to talk it through. He thought at the time that the conversation was helpful but on reflection he realized that he was actually being told that now they were "going out," he could not shame her by backing out of the relationship in front of all her friends. So he went ahead and married her, with disastrous results.

Redemption: None so far, except that he is a much wiser man.

"We love each other, but . . ."

They were both following the Lord when they married and they had a very good life together. That is, until she began to question his faithfulness. He was coming home late, made little reference to the reasons why, and had changed from the type of person he had been. When she talked to friends in the church, they agreed with her. So she went to the pastor, a woman, who also expressed some concerns. So the pastor summoned him in "for a chat." In the conversation, she implied that he was having an affair, but did not actually come out and say that. Nor did she ask him to account for his mysterious behavior.

He went into deep shock, not understanding why his promotion and longer hours were such a problem for her and others in the community. It got so bad that he left the church, but this just made things even worse, as the women, in supporting his wife, closed ranks on him. They had a time of separation and then later she divorced him.

Redemption: Some years later, in therapy, she realized that this had happened to her mother. She had been "betrayed" by a man who went off with another woman. She also realized how much she missed him, and wanted to restore the relationship. But by this time he had remarried.

Not every relationship gets as bad as this, but there are many couples who do go through similar pain yet cannot face the prospect of divorce. They love each other, and want to stay together, even though they feel as if they are killing each other. Many couples in Christian leadership find themselves in this position. We are always surprised at the indomitable human spirit that somehow continues to go on regardless of such conflict and betrayal. Both parties will have contributed to the problems in the relationships. It is never just one person's fault.

Where men have abusive wives, they will tend to ignore the abuse if they can, but then try to push the problem away by telling the wife to go to the therapist. The husband will rarely see himself as part of the problem. When these strategies do not work, men will seek alternative ways of coping with the damage or will even take revenge by being unfaithful or unavailable to their partner or by seeking solace in addictive behavior. Sometimes the vengeance may be more subtle, such as hogging the TV control, finding an expensive hobby or doing further study that she is not able to part of, even though she may be financing it!

An abusive husband will get a very different reaction from his wife. Most women are remarkably loyal, and will absorb great amounts of abuse, either out of love or because of the calling they both have. But when the situation gets too bad, she will initially seek to talk with her husband about it, sometimes persisting when all he wants to do is run. If this does not work, she will want to get the two of them to a therapist. Her husband will resist, often because of the humiliation of admitting that he cannot manage or resolve the situation. She will also talk to her friends, and perhaps the pastoral team, which makes him feel even more isolated and ashamed.

What is needed in Christian marriages, as in any marriage, is honesty, a confession of how bad things are, and the recognition that they will not get any better. Both partners will need to talk things through and resolve to act positively. But this will be a much bigger step for the husband than for the wife. He is most likely to be willing to seek help if he has a network of men who he feels he can trust. Very few men have such a network.

Many of us assume that problems with marriages are private, and are not really relevant to church life. But where the home is not a safe place, the faith community will not be safe either. Damage will inevitably spill over into other relationships, often after desperate efforts to keep it hidden. To attempt such secrecy is to live in false loyalty to each other and to God. Many churches focus on families as the building blocks of congregational life. In such churches, the damage can be immense. In communities like ours, where over half of our members are single, the damage will be much less. But it will still be present. Let us show how parents' baggage can impact a child.

Parents' emotional abuse

> I found I was good at art and the encouragement of my art teacher, plus the encouragement of an uncle, helped me decide to become a graphic artist. My father had other ideas. No daughter of his was going into the art world. In one short statement it was announced that I would not be taking O level art but chemistry. In that sentence my choice was eradicated, my voice ignored, my dreams dismissed—and my world fell apart.
>
> No emotional response was allowed; any reactions other than obedience to my father's will would have been met with a blow. In the silence of my bedroom, I nursed my pain, silently cried and carried on, according to my father's will, realizing that my hopes and dreams were predetermined by "family." My voice was of no consequence. Unable to cope with the family dynamics, I ran away. I had no money. It was hopeless. I secretly hoped that if they came after me, then that would at least prove I meant something to them. On this occasion, it would be their role and status at stake, not mine. I was caught, felt broken for a while and unsuccessfully ran away again, deciding on my return to be a nun.
>
> I chose an approved career with training, sought a mixed college of education for that purpose and had my pride and belief system dented by being refused a reference by the head teacher to any college other than a Christian one. Again the hypocrisy reverberated for a reference would have been granted if it had been for a university. My father delightedly supported the school. I went north to a Christian college of education, believing in freedom at last.
>
> **Redemption:** In this story we see a wealth of complex relational abuse. The decision of the father was to impact the woman for many years until she began to emotionally set herself free from him. She has now been able to let it all go.

Emotional damage can never be successfully segregated from other parts of our lives. The impact of this man on his daughter was an emotional violation of her future hopes. But other relationships would also feel this man's damage and loss. Imagine the impact for harm if he had taught Sunday school or had been a deacon or house-group leader.

A Pastoral Response to Support Relationship Difficulties

We have sat with many couples, each partner perched at opposite ends of the sofa, as they have told us that they love each other, are committed to the Lord, but are killing each other. We have built up a whole range of ways to help such couples, but one principle stands out above all others: regardless of the years they have been married, a significant source of the problem is not what is currently happening in the relationship, but the emotional damage that both have brought into the marriage and have not dealt with. The couple's toxic histories, and what they have done about them, are the trouble. In order to be the person their partner needs them to be, each will have to let go of this damage and emotional baggage.

As we teach this, it is both a profound shock and also a great relief to the couple. It lifts from both of them the accusation that they are the only problem in their life together. Nevertheless, putting the marriage right is always a painful journey, and at first things will probably get worse for each of them. Both partners will need to see the sin and emotional debris that they are carrying before their marriage gets better and they are able to live in fullness of love toward themselves and each other. Only then will they be able to be a safe place.

How can pastoral care support this process? We would suggest that the first principle is to ask what is best for each individual. The challenge begins when their answers are incompatible. In Tomorrow's Church, both partners would feel supported. The Church would not take the careless route of labeling one more guilty than the other. As already noted, God's perspective is often radically different from ours. The more articulate are not necessarily the less guilty.

To offer pastoral care in the marriage, the support of two people is probably required. Each partner must know that they have someone they can talk to independently. This is invaluable while they are looking at historic baggage. However, it is important not to "separate" them, and give contradictory help. In some instances, six months spent living apart as they work through the baggage that they brought into the marriage can do wonders for them both. But if they take this step, it is essential that they make a prior affirmation of their intention to come back together and honor their marriage vows. Also, clear ground rules must be set down for their contact with each other.

Here the Church has an amazing resource. Can it offer hospitality to one of the couple? Can it give support with meals and friendship? Can it help with babysitting? Having one parent living away, but visiting often, is frequently more helpful for the children than having two parents who are fighting and permanently getting ready to separate.

When the husband and wife are both ready to begin the relationship again, they will go through a period of needing to change many habits, patterns, and coping mechanisms that have arisen over the years. If one or both has been through significant change as a result of the damage they have let go of, then there can even be a feeling of beginning again. We have watched such redemption on numerous occasions. They will need to court again, and re-introduce themselves to each other. This is often quite a traumatic time in the recovery process so there should be no reduction in the intensity of pastoral support. But now it is helpful for one person to be talking to the couple together, teaching them new ground rules as they learn how to be supportive of one another.

Guideline

- Inviting God's perspective on each pastoral situation we face is the safest way to Love. The obvious is rarely the most accurate.

Living Together outside of Marriage

We have already noted that many people in twenty-first-century society are choosing not to get married. Perhaps in a previous marriage they have been so deeply hurt that they can't face a repeat. Or perhaps the divorce of their parents led them to vow never to marry. How is the Church to respond pastorally when a couple want to join who have been living together in a committed but unmarried relationship?

Being together

> Rosemary came to Christ Church Deal in need, having had a very difficult previous relationship. When this relationship ended, she and her two sons began living with John. She had been with him for several years when she started coming to church. She was not married to him, and he could not marry her because he was not divorced. In time, he began talking to us as well. They both smoked, and they both had a drink problem. They went through good and bad times, but as they did the journey they began to realize that they were in love and wanted to marry.

What pastoral strategy would Tomorrow's Church want to adopt in such a situation? How would the principles we have been exploring throughout this book be applied? While being clear about what Scripture teaches, and the standards set down by Christ, Tomorrow's Church would not want to drive them away. So what is the balance?

We knew that if the couple felt judged, they would leave. We also knew that if they were asked to break up their newly-formed family, they would conclude that a God who required such extra damage for parents and children was not a God they would want to know. After carefully considering all the options, here is what we did in this instance and now do with others who come to us in a committed, faithful but unmarried relationship. In a non-judgmental way we supported first her, then him. We noted that there was a good prospect that they would get married if they could get through the baggage and legal complications. With this understanding on our side, we supported them. Though we hoped that they would get married in due course, at no time did we question their right to live together.

> **Redemption:** Rosemary went on to qualify professionally in her dream job. Following John's divorce, they married and the whole congregation wildly celebrated the event. They both dealt with their addictions. They are now both in leadership.

In Summary

In this chapter we have looked at a range of difficult pastoral situations, beginning with our duty to the needy, vulnerable and mentally ill. We then briefly noted the pastoral problems of the demonic, of self-abuse and difficult relationships that can be abusive. We concluded by suggesting a pastoral response, using as an example a couple living together who were not married but still wanted to join our community.

Questions to Ponder

1. What is your view of the idea that the most damaged in our society could also be the most gifted and naturally talented?
2. On what grounds could it be said that every congregation has a duty to help the sick, poor, and fatherless? Do you agree?
3. Do you believe that the demonic world exists? Do you have any evidence from your own life? How much power does the Enemy have to hurt us?
4. What is your experience of mental illness, and what do you think the Church should be doing about it?
5. Do you ever talk about your compulsions and addictions?
6. What, if any, are the Biblical reasons for saying that Rosemary and John should not be allowed to live together until they marry?

Notes

[1] Holmes, *Becoming More Human*, 329.

[2] Department of Health, *No Secrets: Guidance on developing and implementing multi-agency policies and procedures to protect vulnerable adults from abuse* (London: Department of Health Publications, 2003).

[3] Department for Education and Science, *A Legal Toolkit for Schools: Tackling abuse, threats and violence towards members of the school community* (Nottingham: DfES Publications, 2002).

[4] For a typical symposium of contemporary views on child abuse, see C. White (ed.), *Responding to Violence: A collection of papers relating to child sexual abuse and violence in intimate relationships* (Adelaide: Dulwich Centre Publications, 2003).

[5] <www.mentalhealth.org.uk/page.cfm?pagecode=PMMHST>

[6] Thank you to Prof. Mary Kate Morse for drawing my attention to the very helpful work by Torjesen—K.J. Torjesen, *When Women Were Priests: Women's leadership in the Early Church and the scandal of their subordination in the rise of Christianity* (San Francisco: Harper, 1993)—that outlines within Christ's own culture His different approaches to men and women.

[7] Holmes, *Becoming More Human*, 236.

[8] For a Biblical view of sexual abuse against children, see A. Michel, "Sexual violence against children in the Bible," in R. Ammicht Quinn, H. Haker and M. Junker-Kenny (eds.), *The Structural Betrayal of Trust* (London: SCM, 2004), 51–60.

13

A Safe Place for All?

Our definition of pastoral care is that it is Body life, through the Holy Spirit, that promotes Christ-likeness in us and in one another. This means that it is not just those who are sick, or very needy, who should benefit from pastoral care. It is everyone. Ironically, those who are least likely to receive pastoral care in most churches are often those who are most needy, who are trying to take responsibility for their lives. They will often be sent to professionals who are not part of the congregation. But if pastoral care is viewed as holistic—for the whole community—then the most "needy," who are possibly the most gifted, should be central. With the approach to pastoral care that we are suggesting, everybody's needs would be considered, especially those who may be considered beyond members' help.

Families

Family life in the twenty-first century is particularly demanding. There are few areas of church life that do not impact the family. It is said that most of us can only do three things well, and for most of us this is work, home, and personal friends. For the churchgoer a fourth, and maybe a fifth, raise their heads: relationship with God and the demands of church life. As well as trying to hold together marriages, bring up children, and follow careers, Christian families are also trying to meet the demands of church life. For many this is too much.

Although we all try very hard to balance family and congregational life, few of us seem to get it right. Likewise, we often find a real tension between having a social life with those we work with, and maintaining a social life with those we worship with. The "social dissonance" between our Christian life when we are doing church and our workaday life increases the conflict. As we move into postmodernism, more and more of us keep our various worlds in separate boxes and jump from the one to the other. Our observation is that some of those who appear to have achieved a balance are faking it, and few are successful. Even for the very best of us, bringing up children in the fear of the Lord while pursuing church life is sometimes one bridge too far. We had a small illustration of this recently. We have no Sunday church meeting at CCD on the last Sunday in every month. When we voted to bring it back, the majority said "No!" People enjoy their Sunday off.

Many of us living the tension of trying to hold all of these demands together tend to hurt one another. We get stressed by the number of commitments we have, and end up inflicting most abuse on those we love the most. Abuse follows pained effort. There seems to be a direct correlation between increasing church involvement and abuse in family life.

Within the complexity of pastoral relationships, the families of leaders can in numerous ways themselves be sources of abuse. Problems in the marriage can easily add to the loneliness and abusiveness of the job. Stories are legion of the children of Christian leaders and missionaries going off the rails. They sometimes even achieve the reputation for being the ringleaders of rebellion. Likewise, the children of Christian leaders and MKs (missionary kids) can and do walk away from the family's values. This is a deep source of pain to the parents and other siblings. Leaders must take the same responsibility for their family life as anyone else, and avoid the presumption that if they are serving God, then God will look after their family.

Though we live in an age when we all assume that we have the right to everything, most of us are unable to manage everything. But reducing our horizons often means that we lose something on the way. Once again, we have to find a balance. A number of books have been written to help us. Some even offer guidance on the management of time. For all of us, both as leaders and members, sensitivity and care are of paramount importance. It is also important to adopt some simple guide-lines. What can we delegate? Who can we train up to share the responsibility? When do we just say no? Will it really matter if we miss one of those weekly meetings?

Alongside the idea of being on a journey, and needing to adjust to lifelong learning, many of us need to relearn the basics of family life. Because if we cannot get family life right, congregational life will not be right. As authors, we believe there is such a thing in family life as "best practice," which helps create a safe place for us all. To cover this properly would take a book. "Best practice" is a principle borrowed from the business world, describing what is currently the best way of doing a thing. Perhaps it is an idea that should be explored?

Guidelines

+ None of us can do everything for everyone. What should we let go of?
+ Prioritizing our lives so that we first honor Christ and those we love is basic to our role as Christian leaders.
+ Loving God and loving people may be our calling, but we must be careful not to put service for Christ in the church ahead of the needs of our immediate family.

Children

Pastoral care of children is often forgotten or takes second place. Many Christians, especially those in full-time work, assume that if they can provide pastoral care for needy parents, then the children will be okay. To a certain degree this is true. Scripture is clear on the blessings that parents can pass on if they are living in righteousness, in contrast to the curses resulting from damaged lives (Ex. 20:5–6; Jer. 2:9, etc.). But in situations where the damage in parents' lives is clear, the needs of children bring a completely different dimension to pastoral care. Let us illustrate.

Church ignoring the evidence

The leaders of the church we belonged to knew that my father was being prosecuted for physical abuse. They knew what was happening in the family, but refused to look closely at the issues from the perspective of my brother, sister, and me. They said that if discipline was needed with my brother, an elder could discipline him as long as it was supervised by my mum. So the situation didn't necessarily have to go to social workers. But nobody ever said to me or my little sister, "How do you feel about what's happening with your dad?" It was more, "Let's try and keep this quiet and get your dad out of trouble."

People seemed to swing between assuming that I definitely knew what I wanted and was doing, and dismissing my views because I was only a child. A child can know what they believe, but adults will ignore this. So, for one reason or another, nobody ever asked me how I felt about my dad being abusive or came alongside so I could talk about it. People shouldn't assume that if children don't say anything, they are okay about what's happening. Finally, it was the staff at my sister's school who recognized the state she was in, and called social services. Not the church.

Redemption: The woman is now married and settled in a local church. She has learned to speak up, has completed her degree and is positive about her relationship with the Lord and her faith community.

Like so many others, this story illustrates that we are not trained to look at all aspects of a situation. Men especially will tend to make decisions on the basis of what is best for the congregation, themselves or one or two key people, thereby creating the possibility of unintentionally abusing others. What we are suggesting is that children are the ones who can get most abused by our attitudes, values, rules, and behavior. Let us illustrate further.

Christian insensitivity toward kids

I had been told that funerals were about saying goodbye to the people you loved. Saying this special goodbye happened in church, with family and friends. It was about leaving earth and going to heaven. That was good, for I wanted to say goodbye to Granddad properly; he was special, he had time for me. It was also good because he was going to heaven. Shock overtook loss when I was told that his funeral was an "adults only" privilege. Children were not allowed or expected to attend. Only adults had the right to say goodbye to him, express emotions and "celebrate" his going to heaven. The decision was endorsed by the school because that was where I would be going on the day of his funeral. It felt unfair and unjust. I wanted more than anything to say goodbye to him. He would want to hear my goodbyes and know I loved him. He would know I was missing.

Before the school bell rang, and against the rules, I slipped into the church with each step echoing throughout the empty building; empty, that is, apart from the bare coffin resting on two bare wooden supports. Granddad was in there. Kneeling in a nearby pew I told him and God how much I loved him and how sorry I was not to be part of his family on this special day. It felt lonely and unjust as I then turned around to live my day as if nothing extraordinary had happened.

Redemption: Some years later she was finally able to say goodbye to Granddad, and resolve a whole range of areas where she had been hurt by her family's and the church's rules.

Children's work in some churches is thought of in terms of activities and Bible stories, rather than spiritual formation. Tomorrow's Church would assume that children, like all adults, need to do a journey out of their baggage and their parents. Pastoral care would function rather as it does in an extended family so that children and young people in Tomorrow's Church would have a network of people they could talk to, homes that were safe, and friendships that were independent of family life.

Sociologically speaking, we are concerned that as Christian leaders we are not yet counting the cost of so many failed Christian and non-Christian marriages, and the toll taken on children who are brought up with several stepparents. We must also not forget that the coping mechanisms and denial that the children often adopt can have a devastating long-term impact on the parents.

Abuse by children . . .

> With two teenagers stretching my physical, emotional, and spiritual capacity, this period was interwoven with their mockery about my beliefs, a continuous mantra that I could not "cope" without these "props" called God and church. My Christian friends were viewed as "weird," and at one point I was being called a "Daughter of the Devil." Some days the sum of my prayer was "hope." Then I discovered Jeremiah 29:11, "'For I know the plans I have for you,' declares the Lord, 'plans to prosper you and not to harm you, plans to give you a hope and a future.'" This was to feed my spirit for six years. It became my daily prayer. My loneliness was excruciating. I hated the thought of being on my own for the rest of my life. At times I felt it was "my punishment" for being a divorcee.
>
> **Redemption:** This mother did happily remarry, but still struggles with her children, though her relationship with them is much better than it has been, and she is optimistic it will continue to improve.

We are only skimming the surface here of a very complex and damaging area of church life. What becomes apparent is that we are unable to do everything well: We all need to prioritize. Children are a gift from the Lord so need our special attention. Although we should not "worship" them, we should allow them to have a special call on our time and resources. Finding this balance may mean we do less of what we enjoy and more of what they enjoy.

Single People

Postmodernity values relationships while not enforcing commitment to those relationships. One of the results is that there are more single people.[1] The accommodation most in demand is now the single-bedroom dwelling and "living together apart" is the new way to live. Another result is that we are moving into the age of one-parent families and singles. On the whole, the Church has not caught up with this changing lifestyle phenomenon. It is easier to ignore or condemn it than confront what is happening and the opportunities it presents.

The Western Church as a whole lays a strong emphasis on the merits of family life. In some congregations the family in its two-parents-plus-kids form is almost given a divine status. There is almost a suggestion that to be part of a "family" is to be more holy. In such congregations, where the "family" is the building block of the congregation, where do the increasing numbers of single people fit? Do they need a new type of church where they go until they are able to marry? Or should traditional congregations welcome them?

Both of us believe in the idea of the traditional family, but I (Peter) am married to Mary and have an adult son, Christopher, whereas I (Susan) choose to be single. The same faith community should be able to offer a safe place to both of us. But in some Christian cultures single people are not honored in being single. Frequently they feel like second-class citizens, put into a sub-group with an implicit pressure to marry and have a family. Sometimes the position is even worse, as numerous single people have told us over the years. The single teenager, more often female, makes the perfect (cheap) babysitter, and the young single male the muscle for laboring in the garden or washing the car. (In the UK they are both often presumed upon, and are expected to work without remuneration.)

In Tomorrow's Church single people would be a key part of congregational life, every new person being encouraged to take a journey that allows them to become more like Christ (who was single). In time, as they let go of their pasts, they may want to begin to be the person who someone else would like to share their lives with. But there would be no pressure, and they would be able to enjoy being single if they chose, without feeling any pressure to marry. It's a way of life that Paul commended.

Choosing a Partner

There comes a time for many single people when being single is not their preferred choice. Because of the drift toward shorter-term relationships in an age that emphasizes relationality, loneliness is one of the curses of contemporary society. At one time or another we all experience it. From a Biblical standpoint, relationship commitment, whether to marriage, friendship or faith community, brings an end to loneliness. What is not so clear is what kind of pastoral strategy there should be to support the resolving of loneliness. In previous stories we have already seen how easy it is to be abused when trying to do relationships. In seeking to do relationships, for instance, damaged people can so easily give others power over them to hurt them. As already noted, where abuse can take place, it sometimes will. So how can we provide a safe place for those who are looking to learn how to do positive relationships?

As we noted in one of the earlier stories, in some churches there is a type of *anti-dating* mindset that jumps to conclusions when two singles go out for a first date: "When are they getting married? After all, they wouldn't go out, would they, if it wasn't the Lord's will?" This can make single people feel as though they are part of a containment culture that does little to help them find opportunities to let go of issues such as fear of people and of intimacy. Many postmodern people find traditional church culture far too stultifying and controlling. It is not the kind of environment that promotes learning relationships.

A typical Christian response would be to encourage people to ask the Lord to guide them regarding their future relationships. At times He does, in most spectacular ways, but at other times He does not seem to. It can then be very difficult to know what to do or even how to begin talking to someone as a friend. Such barriers can become too big for many to over-come. What is needed in many churches is a more relaxed, easy-going approach to friendship. We would suggest that it should be possible for two people to spend time together with-out their relationship being labeled "going out." What is so often overlooked is that to be able to learn to do relationships we all have to practice on one another. We cannot learn every-thing from TV soaps, romantic novels, and Christian books. Practicing relationships on one another can be real fun and very healthy.

Coupled to this is the often unspoken teaching of many churches that a single person needs to look for the "right per-son" prepared for them by God, if they are to have the ideal marriage that God (and the couple) want. Again, this can be a source of abuse. We know of a number of people who have spent years and years looking for this "ideal" person. They finally conclude that no such person exists, and that even if they were to find them they should probably not marry them as that would make them less than perfect! Cynically, they are forced to conclude that if it is too good to be true, then it prob-ably is, and that God is giving everyone but them a partner. As we have already noted, what is important is being the right person, not finding the right person.

Guidelines

+ Get real and get relational. Be willing to take risks in learn-ing how to do relationships. But do not let others abuse you.
+ Just because others believe someone is right for us, it does not mean they are. Our taking up personal responsibility is essential.

Gender Issues

Male and female approach most things in different ways. As Christians in the routines of daily life, we must not let society blur the edges, in seeking to make female more male, and male more female. Christianity celebrates the uniqueness of male and female. Together they reflect the diversity of the image of God. In accepting that male and female are different, we are more able to make a safe place for both men and women. But we do need to learn just how differently they do things! For instance, women's preferred ways of making decisions are normally relational, and this must be facilitated by, for example, allowing time to think and talk things through. Men will often want to make decisions *now*! Decision-making meetings are much less abusive where they allow for this diversity by including "consultation breaks."

It is important to remember that leadership is not just male. As authors, we welcome women into the responsibility of church governance, but no one should fall into the lie that women are as good as men at being men, just as men will never succeed at being effective women! At all levels, from their neural architecture to their biological framework, the two sexes are different. As Carol Gilligan so ably pointed out, they have different values and ways of looking at life.[2] So when women come to leadership, they bring a very different frame of reference and values. Women should not be expected to replace men but to bring some balance to them!

The comment was recently made to us that if you fill a church with men, it will quickly double in size as women are welcomed. But if you fill a church with women, this may help keep men away! In Europe, millions have left the Church, five hundred thousand in the last seven years. Today numerous men are leading congregations of women. We are watching the feminization of the Western Church.[3] Moreover, the smaller the number of men, the more concentrated the power those few men hold. Sadly, in some churches, men are subverting the goodwill of women. Abuse by male leaders of women by the imposition of unrealistic goals needs to be looked at very carefully. As churches become smaller, and more feminine, women's duties become more onerous. Pressure is laid on the remaining women to attend meetings, and they are told what they can and cannot do. Some (male) congregational leadership, women have told us, even tell you who you should and should not be friends with.

It is especially common for men to leave a congregation when there is a change of leadership (when they are over-looked?!). Abuse seems to be part of the leadership changeover process in some churches, with some male leaders stepping down and leaving under a cloud. Where a man either refuses or is unable to find other men to talk to about his problems, he may start to take his troubles out on his wife.

It is not surprising that ever-increasing numbers of women are seeking leadership for themselves. We believe that this should be encouraged, but both men and women need to be aware of how vulnerable the other is. We have found in our work that it is more common for men to be aware of how they might hurt women, than it is for women to be aware of how they might hurt men.[4] Creating a safe place for the opposite gender is a challenge that requires a careful understanding of gender distinctives. With their greater relational gifting, it's a blessing women can give in abundance or unwittingly with-hold.

One of the consequences of more women moving into min-istry is that a solitary woman will sometimes lead a church. Some men are not comfortable with this, and will take the opportunity to leave. This response varies between cultures. At present, it is probably more frequent in Europe, where gen-der roles are more distinct. Typically, the man will not talk about his decision with the (new) female leader or with women around him, but just quietly leave for "safer" places like the pub, club or golf links. We have heard this from many men as they have re-entered congregational life after a gap of many years. People need to be found who have the anointing for this "recovery" ministry.

Our experience suggests that, by contrast, if a woman is not happy with the male leader of a congregation, she will find it much harder to leave, being more attached to the rela-tional networks within the church, both for herself and for her children. If the male leadership feels abusive, or if she carries damage from her history with men in authority, she may repress the pain and anger, appearing more submissive;

or she may become more assertive. The trend may be changing, however. The latest English church statistics show that over the last seven years more women than men have left the Church.[5]

In a local pastoral setting, we have found it essential for men and women to receive experienced pastoral support from someone of their own sex. We are not suggesting complete gender exclusivity, but more acknowledgment that counseling and mentoring are often better done in a male–male and female–female setting. Same-sex mentoring and support is particularly appreciated by men. Sometimes it is clearly in the best interests of the person to meet with someone of the opposite sex, for example, when expertise or a gender perspective is needed. But even here we would ensure that there is a third person present of the same gender as the person receiving the pastoral support. Someone who is trained in pastoral counseling, who is being supervised, and who has prepared for their ministry by carefully addressing their own issues, may be more skilled at handling the complex gender dynamics than someone who has the academic training but has never done their own journey of personal positive change. Much pastoral care in Tomorrow's Church would be undertaken by church members, using their own experience and their growing spiritual gifting.

In the US in particular, the gender factor, as we call it, is a huge issue and could be an obstacle to making congregational life a safe place. In Tomorrow's Church we would expect gender distinctives to be celebrated without stereotyping or judging. Personal uniqueness accepts all. Women are different from men. Men should not assume that they understand the opposite gender, but would want to learn from women about women. Women in leadership would not need to be more male, just as men in leadership would not seek to be more female. They would find their own unique leadership anointing and be familiar with the ways in which each sex might feel threatened or hurt by the other. Adopting such value systems substantially reduces the possibility of abuse, and allows for more freedom for both men and women to become more unique as they become more like Christ.

Guidelines

+ Male and female are different so have different needs and perspectives.
+ Be gender exclusive when people want to be.
+ Welcome either your manhood or womanhood as a key contribution of your life in your faith community.

Christians in Business

Before moving on to the leadership of pastoral care, we would like to cover one final group of people with the potential to support or undermine the safety of the church. Many times over the years we have been introduced to Christians who are seeking to make a living as builders, tradesmen, retailers, financial consultants and in numerous other enterprises. It has become apparent to us is that anyone moving in these circles can become very cynical about Christians in business. Let me (Peter) give you a personal example.

Theft by a Christian leader

> Some 15 years ago a man stole 10,000 Swiss francs (about £6,500) from me while we were doing a business deal by asking for a loan but then not going ahead with the deal, and refusing to give the money back. Rather than going to court against this fellow Christian, I was required by the Lord to give both the man's actions and the lost money to Him, in order for God to judge the man in His way and in His time. I obeyed the Lord. I then wrote a very-matter-of-fact letter to the man telling him that I had left his theft of my money with God so God alone must now judge his actions. I was careful not to sound either revengeful or bitter. I left retribution with God so that I could get on with my life and not be eaten up by anger or revenge. It freed me.
>
> **Redemption:** The man died some years later, and I never did hear from him. I still have peace about this, as well as experi-

encing a deepening of my relationship with the Lord as a result
of taking this step of faith.

Anyone who has employed a Christian, rather than someone
outside the Church, may well have felt abused. Whatever the
trade or profession, whether you were employing a builder,
architect, contractor, lawyer or accountant, it is likely that your
high expectations were dashed. There are frequent complaints
of shoddy and unfinished work, carelessness and damage
done by Christians working in the office, factory or home.
Also, there is an unwillingness to respond professionally if the
client, perhaps another friend in church, complains. These
reports of mediocrity, or even sub-standard work, are a sad
comment on Christian integrity.

We have pondered long and hard on this issue. Why is this
the case? The reasons are not clear though in looking at the
matter more closely, we have both had to admit that at times
we ourselves have let people down when asked to deliver,
and failed to do so. The failure may be for a range of good
reasons, but it may still feel like abuse to those who have suffered or been disappointed. In such situations it is good to
say sorry.

One of the key factors seems to be the "God" issue, and the
presumption on the part of the people being employed of
"equality" because both employer and employee love the
same God. A person's reputation may have been built up over
many years, but the reality is that they must continue to deliver quality service or they will be out of work. Many Christians,
however, seem to rely for work as much on the God factor and
its buddy networks as on the consistent quality of their work-
manship or service. Even when a contractor does bad work,
Christians have a tendency not to speak the truth when someone else asks for a reference. This is surely false loyalty, and
even deceit.

Another reason for cynicism is the negligence of people who,
while claiming to bear the name of Christ, run businesses that
are illegal. This can range from being part of the black economy
(avoiding tax/cash-in-hand only), to evading sales tax and
other taxes.

Finance can also be an area of abuse. Lying about one's financial position is endemic in our culture and, sadly, Christians, and even congregations, are not exempt. A request to a "Christian" business for a set of its latest accounts is often met with a series of excuses or perhaps even lies. To ask people to speak honestly about their financial state is, in many cases, to cut to the heart of their problems. It exposes the fact that they do not know how to manage their lives, but have not had the grace to admit it. In business it is particularly bad when those retained to do the work will take the money and then go into liquidation or come and go on the job because, as you discover later, all the money you gave them went into a black hole of debt so they cannot then finance the work they are contracted to do.

Connected to this is the naive trust of some Christians who will hand over money on the basis of a conversation and prayer rather than through bankers or lawyers, supported by contracts, in the way most professional business is conducted. Over the years, we have had to support those who need to unravel numerous bad situations, sometimes involving large sums of money. In some church cultures, to insist on a legal agreement or contract—the way the "world" does—is thought to be akin to doubting God or distrusting the business representative. It is useful here to remember Jesus' words that the people of this world are more wise than the children of God, and we should learn from them (Lk. 16:8–12). We could share with you a dozen stories that focus on this area, but let us use one to illustrate how bad bad can get.

A woman being conned . . .

> I was approached by a man who was supporting a mission group in India. He said they were raising capital to build schools that would be partly financed by fees and partly by gifts. The whole program looked very attractive, with a promise of a modest return on my capital, as well as giving children an education. I took away some glossy brochures and even visited the website, which was modest but well presented. The fact that they had not built anything yet was not such a problem to

me, since this man said he had already put in money of his own, and was himself an accountant. So I gave him a check for £10,000, and he gave me a receipt. He said he would pass the money on to the lawyer who was acting on behalf of the mission.

I heard nothing for months, but finally contacted him to find out how things were proceeding. He was nervous and evasive, saying he had not heard himself, either.

Although I was still not suspicious, I was now annoyed. Another two months passed and I told him I was no longer comfortable, and wanted my money back if I could not see proof of progress. He then told me the truth—that there never had been a mission, and the whole program was a scam, sourced out of India, intended to steal money from Western Christians. He said that he had lost £5,000 of his own. Missionaries returning home from serving in that part of India confirmed that they already knew about this scam.

In talking it through with him, I found that he knew other Christians who had also been conned so we all met together. But this came to nothing when the lawyer who had received the money was found to have been barred from practice, and had himself vanished. When we counted up the cost to us it came to over £100,000. We had no hope of ever getting any of the money back.

(For reasons of confidentiality, this is compiled from two stories. Part of the money lost has now been repaid.)

Such stories can be repeated endlessly. They range from the "Christian" painter and decorator who takes an advance and is never seen again, to the high-stakes confidence trickster outlined above. For such abuse to occur, there usually has to be fault on both sides. Christians are often too trusting and vulnerable, while greed and arrogance so often drive such crime. Advice and guidance are readily available from organizations such as Christians in Business, and the Christian Chamber of Commerce, yet many Christians do not seek this or any other professional advice before moving ahead.

In Tomorrow's Church, it would not necessarily be the case that every Christian would offer work and service of the highest quality, although each would aspire to this. Those who wished to employ an expert would take full responsibility for obtaining references, getting several quotes and proper contracts. It would also be made clear whether the employer expected to pay a full price for the work or was asking for a discount or favored level of service from a fellow Christian—a misunderstanding that accounts for a lot of disappointment.

Guidelines

• God requires us all to be the very best we can be, for Him, ourselves, and others. This will sometimes mean moving out of our comfort zones.
• We should pay special attention to honesty, in both our work and conduct. We should not resent people when they want matters to be conducted in a more professional or different way.
• We should welcome the advice of others, especially avoiding being either arrogant or naive!

In Summary

In this chapter we have looked at a range of pastoral issues, from the abuse of people when they are serving the Lord to the impact this abuse can have on their children. We have also seen how single people can be second-class citizens in some congregations. We have looked at gender issues, and have noted the possible abuse inflicted upon both Christians in business, and those who employ Christians. These are all areas that can either promote a safe place or be a source of hurt and pain. But other issues also need to be considered, as the next chapter highlights.

Questions to Ponder

1. What would you say to someone who complained that modern church life was too demanding?

2. In what ways do the families of some Christian leaders suffer because they are serving the Lord?

3. What makes single people feel that they are second-class citizens in congregational life?

4. What is your view of the statement that loving God should be our priority, but serving Him comes after our responsibility to our family?

5. When, if ever, should Christians in business accept that serving the Lord means they will not get paid well?

6. What are some of the gender issues that make congregational life unsafe?

7. What are some of the problems of working with other Christians in businesses?

Notes

[1] <www.statistics.gov.uk>.

[2] C. Gilligan, *In a Different Voice* (Cambridge, Mass.: Harvard University Press, 1982/1993).

[3] L.J. Podles, *The Church Impotent: The feminization of Christianity* (Dallas, Tex.: Spence Publishing, 1999).

[4] One aspect of our ministry is teaching men and women how to lay down their unrighteous fear, mistrust, hate, and dislike of one another, which has often accumulated over many years.

[5] P. Brierley, *Pulling out of the Nosedive: A contemporary picture of church-going* (London: Christian Research, 2006)

14

Leadership of Pastoral Care

In Tomorrow's Church, as we have recognized, all members carry a responsibility to support one another in their journey of growing in Christ. Those in pastoral leadership, however, carry a special responsibility in this area. We are aware that though the idea of pastoral care as a shared responsibility is a goal to which churches might aspire, this is not the reality in many churches at present. So in this chapter we will explore the more traditional form of delegated responsibility for pastoral care. How can this be done in a way that is safe both for those in need and for the leader with this responsibility?

What Is a Leader Responsible for?

A theological qualification may lead to a church office, but it may not equip that leader to meet even the most basic of human needs. Confessional Christianity, with its emphasis on theology, is not well placed to meet postmodern need or to offer the framework for therapeutic personal change. Someone with gifting in preaching and teaching may not also be gifted in sensitive one-to-one relationships. In many organizations these two areas of responsibility would be the remit of separate departments, and require completely different training packages. But not so in much of the Church. Most church leaders are expected to excel in both (and much more besides!).

Trying to do something you are not equipped to do can create terrible stress and pressure. But there is a more subtle problem for many in pastoral leadership. Over the years, we have met a number of Christian leaders who have somehow taken on the duty of care for their flock in such a way that they believe they are responsible for the outcomes of their lives. If the person grows in their relationship with the Lord, the leader has done well. If the person doesn't, then the leader has failed. What is often not recognized is that the leader has virtually no control over another person's spiritual life, and the ultimate outcome will be down to the individual and circumstances, not to the leader. The pastor can take neither the credit nor the blame!

From God's perspective, it is not the responsibility of a leader to ensure the spiritual health, or any other aspect of the health, of the individual. Pastoral care suggests that leaders should be available as shepherds, when needed. But somehow many leaders allow a shift to take place in congregational life whereby they take on the responsibility of everyone. This is not a wise move. Sometimes it is arrogant. To take on responsibility for oneself is hard enough, and more than many can manage, as the apostle Paul has so powerfully illustrated (for example, Romans 7—8). Each of us must one day stand before the Lord, and the way we ourselves have lived will judge us, not the way our leaders conducted themselves.

When leaders begin to think they are responsible for others, this may quickly become self-abusive. We define stress as being in a situation that one cannot humanly change. And this is the position in which many Christian leaders find themselves when, having made themselves responsible for their congregation, they then find they are at the mercy of the whims of any member of their congregation who comes to them for help. We have both been in the place where intractable, intransigent pastoral problems lead to stress and frustration. This can be a very dangerous place for both the leader and the person seeking help.

The belief system of the leader will often dictate what should happen in pastoral situations. It is very easy for the leader to get angry with people who do not get well or sorted. The leader passionately believes that if only they had done just what they had been told to do, they would definitely have got well. Since they are not better, they are blamed. When members insist that they have done everything they have been told to do, but it has not helped, then the leader is tempted to say that they don't have enough faith or weren't sincere enough. Or some other justification will be found. This can be abusive, and in some ways is more abusive than most other things members may experience at the hands of the leader. What we are suggesting is that no one is more dangerous to others than self-righteous Christian leaders passionately driven by their beliefs, especially when in contact with the sick and fragile.

In Tomorrow's Church, when someone appears not to have changed, or not to have followed advice, the leadership would know that this was a matter between the person and their God, rather than something for the leader to carry personally. The stress and pressure of such situations is, of course, significantly reduced if the pastoral responsibility is shared. In Tomorrow's Church, others are encouraged to get involved, bringing fresh perspectives, a new word from the Lord or different spiritual gifting. Such flexibility can be very beneficial for the person, and is one of the strengths of a shared pastoral model.

It is of continuing concern to us that many leaders genuinely believe, first, that they have a correct view of the meaning of the words of Scripture, "Ask and you will receive," and, second, that such formulas should always work. In exceptional cases they may. But the exception does not make the rule. Sadly, most of the time human nature, spiritual reality, and God Himself are far too complex for such simple cause and effect beliefs to succeed. As already noted, it takes listening to God's voice and an ongoing personal journey with Christ, rather than the leader's opinions, to unpack the healing process. Christ spent three intensive years with the disciples, yet look at the mistakes they were still making as He went to the cross. In Tomorrow's Church, grace and love would always prevail to ensure that it remained a safe place for all.

What we are suggesting is that pastors have to go through their own metamorphosis, a life-changing shift in how they see their pastoral responsibility. As in business life, the 80–20 principle seems to apply: 80 per cent of problems will come from 20 per cent of members. Pastors need to know that when a congregation goes through bad times, as all do, the only ones a leader is often left with in membership are those who cannot leave, either because they have become dependent or they genuinely like the leader.

Either way, leaders who cannot help these folk to help themselves will be unable to go on indefinitely. They will find themselves in the soul-destroying position, Sunday after Sunday, of standing up in front of a group of damaged and dependent people who are constant reminders of the failure of their pastoral care. Such a situation inevitably creates an unsafe place for everyone. This is especially the case when there is a sole leader. Perhaps this is one of the reasons why a high proportion of pastors suffer burnout. It is said that only one in ten pastors ever reach retirement in service. Yet even the sickest and most fragile of groups can begin to love and support one another. A mutual model of pastoral care releases life to the congregation while helping to lift the yoke from the leader.

What we are suggesting is that the duty of seeing Christ formed in others does not include taking on spiritual responsibility for others. This must always remain with the individual, undergirded by a shared support structure within the community. The shepherd is there to provide safety, support, wise advice, and leadership. The leader should not take responsibility in the way the medical doctor, dentist, therapist or health-care worker does, nor try to take the place of God. Part of the leader's pastoral task is to live in such a way that this is clearly understood.

Guidelines

- Everyone is responsible before God for their own provision, health, and relationship with the Lord. Exceptions to this are incapacity for a season, for example, because of illness or disability.
- It is not helpful when leaders take responsibility for others in such a way that individuals abdicate responsibility for themselves.
- Church members should not abuse leaders by making such demands.

Avoiding Dependency

Adopting this new attitude of not taking responsibility for others will, for many Christian leaders, take some practice, but it is essential for their well-being. They will not otherwise be able to care pastorally for those in particular need. This is why we are uneasy in welcoming "professional" models into local congregational life. The suggestion with these models is that one person pays for another to sort them out. While recognizing a need for professional input, and, indeed, recommending it (see Chapter 10), we believe that new protocols need to be developed that clearly define what the pastor is responsible for, and what remains the responsibility of the individual. So, for instance, where a therapist is used in a local church setting, it is not always helpful merely to adopt non-Christian therapeutic best practice whereby the therapist is responsible for the client's well-being. Abuse on both sides can proliferate where an individual has no clear personal responsibility. All but the most disturbed of people can take some responsibility for themselves.

The Christ-being-formed-in-us process must always rest with the individual and the Lord. There will, however, always be those in the congregation who believe that they are paying the pastor to look after them spiritually. It seems that some members enjoy believing they are not responsible for their own spiritual well-being or their problems. In order to keep the church a safe place, and avoid unrealistic expectations, the leader will need to be clear where the boundaries are at every stage.

As part of the shift of responsibility, and as a fundamental practice in our work, we have found it helpful to send people away from a pastoral meeting with "homework," which must be done with a friend or mentor. Its purpose is to enable them to consider the spiritual guidance they have been given, and take responsibility for the next step. It is also very helpful if people understand from the start what the leader is and is not good at. A shepherd has overall responsibility for the sheep's protection and well-being, but sheep must feed themselves, avoid danger and do relationship in order to avoid failure in their lives.

The more hurt people are, the more vulnerable they will be. What needs to happen in most pastoral relationships is the increasing empowering of the person seeking help so that the leaders can be freed.[1] What can happen, instead, is that an unhealthy dependency develops, or, worse, an unrighteous emotional involvement that makes it unlikely that the person will find the help that is needed. As part of pastoral care, there is the hope and intention of personal change, of becoming more like Christ. Through this change, the individual can move from being a taker to being a giver in the wider faith community.

There are exceptions, of course, just as with any other guide-lines. People who are struggling with significant emotional trauma frequently need to develop a deep trust in another person, often in the form of dependence, if they are to dare to begin their journey. For a temporary period this can be remarkably healthy. Think of the person who has always lived in isolation, is committed to repeated acts of self-harm and carries deep trauma from past relationships. A close and trusting friendship built over a number of months as the person discovers healing is evidence of a miracle taking place. Involving a number of others in the pastoral care helps to ensure that the relationship remains healthy.

Ministering Alone

Working alone as a Christian leader can be a killer. From one week to the next the leader has few peers to talk to so it is very easy to lose perspective. Leaders who work alone get depressed and no one notices, or they begin to believe that they are better than they really are, and think more highly of themselves than they should. Many develop a range of disorders and find themselves unable to continue. And other traps lurk in the shadows.

In our own ministry, one of our golden rules is that we avoid seeing anyone alone in a pastoral setting. Socially, yes; pastorally, no. When we are doing ministry we always have a third person present who will write notes. It is a "bring-a-friend" philosophy, where the "friend" is often a mentor or an expert-by-experience. This automatically removes any possibility of what was said being twisted or any accusations of impropriety. Sometimes we will sit with a person of the same sex in an initial one-to-one session, but even this is unwise these days. We are disturbed by the cavalier lack of concern that Christian leaders show in this area, opening themselves up to all kinds of later accusation and abuse. We have never had objections, except from people who do not understand our reasons. The practice of having a third person present also promotes relationship, while the notes help the person to understand what needs to be thought through. The note-taking also benefits the leader, as the notes can be the basis of the person's homework (the next step).

Child sexual abuse

> Penny came from a Christian home, though the home was very dysfunctional. She was seven when she went to a children's evangelistic tent mission. She responded to an altar call at the end of the meeting, wanting to give her heart to Jesus. Two little boys also went forward. The evangelist told Penny to wait while he spoke to the boys. He talked to the lads and prayed with them, then sent them home. Only Penny was left. He took her on his knee, and began to put his hand up her skirt and explore her private parts, telling her that this was how Jesus came into her life.
>
> Although Penny stayed within the Christian community, her life was deeply damaged by this event. She has been unable to trust Christian men, and has a particular problem with those in authority.
>
> **Redemption:** None so far, but she is beginning to address some aspects of the experience.

This tragic and unredeemed event had a devastating impact on this woman's life and she has not yet recovered. But had the children's camp had a simple rule that no one sees a child alone, this would not have happened. In this case, the rule would have protected the child, but in other instances it would have protected the leader. We should not let issues of confidentiality and seniority stand in the way of the protection of a Christian leader or church member, no matter who they may be.

Guideline

+ It is inadvisable for a Christian leader to see anyone alone pastorally, especially someone of the opposite gender or a child. Have them bring a friend. Or the leader should seek the support of another member of the leadership team. Exceptions to this may include same-sex mentoring or friendships.

The Role of Professional Counseling and Support

One of the resources at the pastor's disposal is, of course, the professional specialist. Churches have a great deal to learn from voluntary and health-care organizations that specialize in helping the needy. You can invite speakers to provide training, liaise with local agencies, and get specialists to help provide supportive policies. This is all part of the process of "sharing the load" with the community, both inside and outside the Church.

Sadly, however, with the rise of public health-care services, the Church in many parts of the Western world has now largely had the responsibility of providing care for the long-term sick, the poor, and the mentally and emotionally ill taken away. The Body of Christ now finds itself with a very narrow range of responsibilities, having been left with "spiritual care," while the big brother, psychology, and its numerous therapies, look after all other needs.

Although this huge financial initiative and commitment by the government should have reduced the number of poor, sick, and vulnerable people in any local church, this is not always the case. Many people are still coming to our churches in deep need, with a range of relational and personality disorders, and numerous congregations find that these damaged people are the only ones who faithfully and regularly attend. The difficulty is that pastors can find them a constant drain. In looking at abuse, therefore, it is important that, along with children, young people and the elderly, we think in terms of these subgroups. Many are very keen to support others, but struggle with their own needs, too.

How does the Church respond to those who are in such need? One reaction is to rely on professional counseling and health services. Today some pastors would instinctively send a person to an unchurched medical professional rather than ask the Lord what He would do. Many Christian leaders enjoy public acclaim while sending away all the problem cases for others to deal with. Sometimes, given the complexity of modern life and illness, this may be a wise approach. To take on all human need would require messianic gifts. Whatever the justification, a distinction is emerging between the up-front teaching and preaching role, which traditionally is the responsibility of the senior pastor, and the more difficult end of pastoral care, which is increasingly carried by professionals, often outside the congregation.[2]

The difficulty with this approach is that the person's emotional health, which frequently has a very tangible spiritual dimension, becomes something that can't be discussed within the church. An additional difficulty is that many professional counseling models are one-to-one models, not group or family models. Some can be exclusive, a private matter between the client and counselor. This means that both parties are vulnerable and any therapeutic gain is at the initiative of the client. At times, such an arrangement may be essential, but it flies in the face of the model provided by social Trinity. For this reason it should not be the only help offered by the local congregation.

At the opposite extreme, some local churches react by affirming that they know better than the professional healthcare services. The person in need is discouraged from seeking help from outside agencies and instead is invited for prayer. Gratefully, they turn to God for instantaneous healing from deep trauma. Scripts and lies that have accrued will be deleted by prayer, they believe (and sometimes they are). But often the attempt to remove so many years of damage in this way is not successful. It may be of some help. God is always keen to bring whatever healing He can, and most people are encouraged by others praying for them. But where this fails to produce long-lasting healing, the person frequently feels ashamed, and perhaps even guilty for having failed God. At its most extreme, they are judged for having such need. Let us illustrate.

"You're not a Christian . . . !"

> A woman went to see a pastor to talk with him and his wife. She began by telling them about the amazing things she had experienced on her personal journey as she had worked through issues of emotional and relational damage that the Lord had brought to her attention. Such damage, she said, had been standing between her and Christ. She did have a remarkable testimony. But in response the pastor's wife suggested that if she were a Christian, she would not need to do all that. The pastor's wife was saying that the woman's experience was invalid because it did not fit in with her, the leader's, belief system. The pastor and his wife believed that when you come to Christ, all negative history and damage somehow vanish instantly so you never need to do a journey with Christ to sort such things out.
>
> **Redemption:** This woman was shocked by what had been suggested, but began to give the accusations to the Lord, allowing Him to take the hurt she had experienced.

We all come to other people's needs (and even our own) with a range of beliefs that guide our responses. People seeking help also bring their beliefs to the meeting. In some cases, our beliefs make us crass, insensitive, and abusive. Rather than seeing people from God's perspective, we challenge the "illness" in them by intimating that such sickness is their own fault. In a similar sad way, people seeking help can bring such doubt and self-loathing that the pastor has no hope of helping them. Christ, by contrast, wants to meet them at the place where they are, not from the perspective of where He thinks they should be. But then He leads them, through His teaching and example, to the place He wants them to reach.

Neither of these extreme reactions of sending people in need to professional therapists or refusing all outside help, supports the creation of a safe place for those struggling with disorder in their lives. If these are the people Christ told us to go to, surely there is an alternative? We would suggest that in Tomorrow's Church there would be a healthy combination of giving informed support from within the community, and of welcoming the expertise of external agencies.[3] People could receive prayer if they wanted it, but need not feel ashamed if they didn't or if it didn't bring immediate healing. They could also choose to be accompanied by a member of the church when attending appointments with specialists so that there would be no fragmentation between the different forms of help they were receiving. They would feel that their faith community was giving extra support that in no way undermined anything else that might be effective for them.

In the UK, organizations such as the Association of Therapeutic Communities have hundreds of communities in Britain and overseas seeking to help people in need. Our congregation is proud to be a member of this association. Sadly, we are one of the few churches in its ranks. In the USA, many prisons are designed and built along therapeutic community lines. Such work is a good investment as inmates are much less likely to reoffend after they have lived for a year or two in a therapeutic community. Likewise, people overcoming addictions are frequently offered the support of a therapeutic community. Each local church could seek out the links that best suit their own situation.

Caring for the Leaders

A chapter on leadership of pastoral care would not be complete without considering how to provide pastoral care for the leadership! Although it is important for the leader to have the support of a peer group, probably outside the congregation, this does not mean that the congregation should abdicate their own support of the minister.

Most Christian leaders will have in their congregations people they fear, who have abused them or who are abusing them now. It seems that many men and women leave leadership because members of the congregation are just too abusive and demanding. Let us illustrate.

Abuse of a minister

With my conversion in my forties came a call to Christian service. I decided that should my business ever fail, I would serve the Lord full time. It did, so I enrolled at a Bible college for three years and in November 1995 became a pastor.

The diaconate comprised one man, a woman who was the church secretary, and another woman. The elderly man stepped down at the first AGM, and since none of the other men in the church felt worthy, a third woman was elected. I had constant problems with the church secretary, who stood against any change. Also, a couple left during my "irreverent" worship. Also, the main church building was far too big. The place always looked empty. I proposed transferring services to the Sunday school, which held 100, ideally suited to the current congregation. This was opposed vehemently by the church secretary and was turned down at the church meeting.

Problem followed problem. The boiler broke so we transferred to the smaller hall anyway. This transformed the services, which became much more friendly and intimate. The congregation was actually growing, and more young people were coming along. I baptized one of the youth, who asked if the young people could join the main service for Communion. This was agreed by all the diaconate except one—the church secretary, who told them they were too noisy and could not take Communion because they were not baptized. Several never came back. She refused to apologize, and got very angry. This stunned and hurt enormously. The diaconate reluctantly allowed me to call a special church meeting.

At this meeting, the church secretary spoke of the unruliness and disrespectfulness of the young people. The youth workers walked out. Another woman accused me of not being reverent enough. Then the secretary started again, accusing me of being like my predecessor, who had also sought to change things. Every word hurt. Many who had seemed to support me either said nothing or got up and left. The meeting broke up early with matters unresolved.

Eighteen months into my ministry, I fell ill with pleurisy. A local doctor said she feared for me because she was aware of the church's treatment of the previous minister. This shocked and perturbed me. He had totally lost it mentally, abusing the congregation and having a breakdown. Also, his wife had become more and more ill. His predecessor, who had also tried to introduce change, had also become very ill and eventually resigned.

I sought help. I began a journey, and a man, Fred, stepped in to help with the services. My journey got worse before it got better, but it brought me closer to Christ in ways I had only glimpsed in the past. Also, Fred was elected as a deacon, and agreed to stand with me for a year. Many of the congregation were very suspicious of the positive change in me. Resistance continued, but I was getting stronger.

I encouraged another man, Kevin, to stand for the diaconate and persuaded one of the ladies to stand down. We had all worked closely to bring about changes and new ideas. Kevin was elected, but the church secretary launched into a tirade against me and my journey. She completely lost it, ranting while singing all the old hymns. Most were stunned, and some were embarrassed and left. I then suggested that the secretary stand down for a season, and this was seconded by Fred.

Fred and his wife Lydia told me they were leaving. My wife never attended another service or church meeting. Fred and Lydia's resignation was blamed on me. I also resigned and explained my reasons. I returned to the industry I had left nine years earlier, and this opened the opportunity to buy a home of our own again.

Redemption: He is now back in business and is in a senior position in his industry. He has worked through both his own illness and the abuse of the woman who made so much trouble for him. His wife has also found a fulfilling ministry on the leadership team of a local church.

We both feel that one of the most shocking aspects of this story is that at no time did the members of the church stop and ask what was the best way to support the minister. On the contrary, they quickly shifted to a "them and us" attitude that deeply hurt him. Although there were other factors not mentioned in this story, the sad reality was that he was allowed to be openly abused by a woman in the church. She was accountable to no one for her behavior. When he had another man to stand with him he began to recover, but not for long. Both ended up leaving. Sad.

Another observation is that several in the church were uneasy when it seemed that they might be getting close to the pastor. We both recall the shock on a person's face at home one day as we introduced one of the local Catholic priests, who is a regular diner at our lunch table. The idea that we could be his friend, and enjoy the pleasure of his company over a meal, seemed alien to our other guest.

In Tomorrow's Church, the humanness of the leaders would be more openly known: not just their gifting, but also their weaknesses and failings. They would be cared for and supported, and their needs would be considered. It is all too easy to blame leadership when something goes awry. In a safe place there would be shared responsibility, along with a desire to join in the task of finding solutions. The church member always finds it so much easier to blame the leader than to recognize that their being a member will always be part of the problem, and its solution.

Guideline

• Remember that our leaders have needs of their own. It is okay for them to be honest about their own mistakes and their own needs.

In Summary

We began this chapter by asking: What is the leader responsible for? In answering this question, we noted that many leaders take on responsibility for every member and friend; we stressed the need to avoid such an approach. We also noted some of the dangers and drawbacks of being a lone pastor, and discussed the different approaches that churches take to pastoral care. Finally, we looked at the importance of caring for the leaders. In the next section, we return to the idea of church as a safe place, and consider some of the Biblical issues.

Questions to Ponder

1. In what ways is traditional counseling psychology both a help and a hindrance to a congregation?
2. What are some of the ways we can avoid the dependency of members on the leaders?
3. To what extent is your pastor or Christian leadership responsible for your spiritual well-being?
4. When is it okay to speak in the name of the Lord?
5. What are some of the gender issues that make congregational life unsafe?
6. What are some of the ways in which we can care for our church leaders?

Notes

[1] R. Bucher, "Body of power and body power: the situation of the Church and God's defeat" in R. Ammicht Quinn, H. Haker and M. Junker-Kenny (eds.), *The Structural Betrayal of Trust* (London: SCM, 2004), 121–9.
[2] Holmes, *Trinity in Human Community*.
[3] We are aware that not all external agencies welcome the involvement of local churches in a person's care. It is important, therefore, to work at building mutually supportive relationships.

Part 6

What Christians Believe

We have explored individual relationships and leadership and pastoral care practices as part of creating a safe place. But what of the theology and belief systems of the congregation? How can these support the creation of a safe place?

15

Making Church Safer: Some "Bible" Problems

We started the book by acknowledging that there is considerable abuse in society and we suggested that churches are no exception. But in this chapter we explore the possibility that the problem is actually more serious and much deeper in the Church than in society. We will suggest that the Church not only mirrors abuse in the wider culture, but also includes additional areas of potential abuse not found in non-faith organizations. In simple terms, we call this the "God" factor. We will be noting that some theologies are more helpful than others in ensuring that the Church is a safe place, a sanctuary for all. Some churches, however, have the potential to lead more easily into abuse. In a similar way, some traditions tend more naturally to make congregational life safe, while others carry a greater risk of being harmful.

In this chapter we want to explore some of the theological ideas that could support the creation of a safe place. To be effective, they need to be embedded in the culture of the Church. But sometimes they are not. If the Body of Christ is called to be a safe place, especially for the needy and vulnerable, then there should be no difficulty in embracing a theology that supports this, and welcoming the necessary change. In writing this chapter, we have sought to avoid theological issues that are clearly denominationally specific.

An Isolated and Controlling Church—a Case Study

Let us start by describing a situation where the theology and practice of a congregation clearly prevented it from being a safe place for its members. We've deliberately chosen an extreme example in order to draw out a number of principles that will help highlight the guidelines we could adopt to make congregational life a safer place. As in Chapter 10, we have two stories, the first is the wife's, which looks more at the relational aspects, the second is the husband's, which comments on the theology and Bible teaching.

When church becomes cultish

I had been married for four years, and had a two-year-old son. I was living a very ordinary life when my husband became a Christian. I watched him change, and heard wonderful stories of the Holy Spirit meeting him in miraculous ways. I learned that there was forgiveness of sin and that God loved us; this impacted my life from a distance. Two years on I decided that I had nothing to lose and I prayed the sinner's prayer. My conversion was a non-event. Then I got bored with church.

I concluded that my husband was a first-class and I a second-class Christian. He had definitely arrived. I decided he must be special, a super saint. God did not seem to be interested in me. I could piggyback on my husband's popularity and relationship with God.

We then met a very zealous Christian woman offering us a whole new level of Christian experience. Just what I had been looking for. She introduced us to a small group of believers who met regularly to listen to teaching (tapes) from a church in America. Their emphasis was that "with God all things are possible." Here was my blockage. I needed to please God and gain His approval by placing complete faith in Him. He also wanted to heal His followers. I thought I had found a treasure that was so obvious, a system to access God's faithfulness.

I could not understand why Christian friends were so concerned about our joining this group of people as they were clearly believers who had found something very special. I also trusted my husband's discernment. About six months later we began to talk about the possibility of selling our house and moving in to rented accommodation to be nearer our meeting place and the people in the congregation. About this time I began to feel that something was wrong. I was told that Satan was ensnaring me. I so missed the lightness of my old church and Christian friends. Everything had become so heavy. Every corner of our lives was subject to scrutiny as we attempted to dig out any hindrances to our idealistic faith journey.

Then a baby in the congregation died and the couple who lost the child were accused of not having enough faith. I became afraid for my children and also for myself, as I had just discovered that I was pregnant with my third child. My husband still wanted to move to be nearer the meeting place. It was becoming exhausting driving back and forth, with meetings three nights a week, plus weekends. These meetings were very intense, lasting up to five hours. I privately now realized why our Christian friends had been concerned, but I was afraid to talk.

Then this woman who had introduced us to the group called with a message from the Lord. It required us to move and be part of this congregation. I developed an unrighteous fear of God. She questioned my allegiance. Was I going to stand between the Lord and my husband's calling? After this new injection of fear we moved.

The church's members were convinced that they were God's elect; to survive, I needed to fill my head with as much of this teaching as I could lay my hands on. I was eight months pregnant and very afraid. I must not get contaminated by anyone or anything outside the group of believers. It was only by God's mercy in the end that we delivered our son safely, alone in the bedroom of our house, with a little help from this woman. After delivering a healthy baby son, I found myself questioning this madness.

We were now a house church of 50 people. I started to question some of the teaching, though it meant being rejected and scorned by the other women. There was a huge distrust of one another, as we judged one another's lifestyles, actions, and the words we spoke. They said I was deceived by the Enemy, and was being used by Satan to tear down God's work.

I feel now that God had a rescue plan that began to unfold. Our leader had been very sick for about five months and no one knew what was wrong with him. The entire congregation believed the Lord would heal him, it was just a matter of time. He was being tested. He became sicker and sicker. We fasted, we prayed, we kept believing. His wife was now becoming quite agitated, wanting to take him away for a break with a few other members of the church. If they went away, they could be more focused and pray around the clock. It was the middle of winter, with thick snow everywhere. They became snowed in. Steve died.

I can remember receiving the phone call. This was not meant to happen. People don't just die when they are living a holy life in faith. But to my shock I was elated. I was free for the first time in three years. There was no fear. I was able to live again normally. Freed from a prison sentence.

Redemption: They are still married, with a grown family. Both are part of a local church, in leadership. This part of their Christian life has taken some years to unpack fully, but they are both the wiser for the experience.

Anyone coming into such a group would be quickly deceived and think that such chaos and conflict was normal. Over the last fifty years there have been many similar cults, such as the Jones-Town group, the Children of God and the Nine O'Clock Service.[1] What is common to all of these is that they are led by charismatic types, have compelling teaching, and convincing programs. Many similar groups and congregations exist in mainstream churches, especially in mission situations. Some lose their way and become exclusive or form new religious movements.[2] Increasing seclusion allows such groups to control the people in them.

Many congregations have some characteristics typical of this house church. Over the years numerous people have talked to us about being in congregations where they carried a fear when they missed meetings or were punished when they failed in duties they had been given. One example was a lady who talked about the paranoia she felt every Sunday: she was terrified of being accused from the pulpit of having put a foot wrong. Another sad example was a successful restaurant owner who left the church after being told from the pulpit that he had been turned down for leadership because he was unable to get to evening meetings.

Let us now hear the same story, but this time told by the husband.

Cultish teaching

The word of God was the only reliable reference point for a person to hear from God, especially when delivered by an anointed faith teacher. Only the King James Version was acceptable. To challenge what they said was challenging God: "Do not speak against God's anointed." To question could result in God's punishment or even death.

Hebrews 11:1: "Faith is the substance of things hoped for, the evidence of things not seen" (King James Version) was interpreted literally, and resulted in the most bizarre distortions of the truth. For example, somebody sick would confess that they were well. Completely ignoring the symptoms, they would declare that they were well until the health—or whatever else they were declaring—was manifested. This made it impossible to know where people really stood as there was always a positive confession on their lips, regardless of real circumstances. Where does truth begin and end?

For instance, my wife was encouraged to throw away her eye glasses. If, by faith, you have perfect sight, then why need glasses? By faith it has already happened. Many in our church remained in this condition for two or three years, with no improvement to their sight. There is no area in your life that is not open to this challenge to trust God for everything. So we burnt our medical records. If we did need them, it was either sin in our lives or an attack from the Enemy. One could never chat openly about feeling a bit unwell, tired or down. Where was your faith? Why were you letting the Enemy take ground in your life?

The teaching also put a great emphasis on the battle in the spiritual world, and the need for Christians to remain pure and continually vigilant as the devil was like a roaring lion continually on the prowl seeking whom he may devour. So in the name of spiritual discernment, anything that may have a hint of the occult was destroyed, including our collection of antiques and a comic book collection that turned out to be worth thousands of pounds.

The crucifix and any other religious symbols were considered an offence, a view based on the logic of the question: If Jesus had been executed by a firing squad, would we wear a revolver round our neck? Music was of the devil; the only music we listened to was the worship recording from the Sunday service and certain approved musicians. We are in the world, but not of it. Isolation and separation from others was normal. Conversations with anyone outside of the group were always very guarded in order to maintain a positive confession. We were required to maintain a positive confession at all times by avoiding the use of negative expressions. For instance, "I'm starving," was not an acceptable term because the Bible says, "I have never seen a righteous man starving or his children begging for bread."

We limited our children's after-school and social activities, including TV watching (a sewer pipe into the home). We should separate ourselves from anything that conflicted with the teaching. Christmas, Easter, and fireworks were rejected as these events were considered pagan, being derived from Roman and Greek paganism. (The church fasted on Christmas Day.)

Women were second-class citizens, serving the men. Seen and not heard. Their main uses were cooking, cleaning, and having faith babies. The ultimate goal was a "Mrs. far above rubies" (Prov. 31:10). God should be allowed to give us as many children as He chooses, resulting in a no-contraception policy. Some under this teaching in America had twelve and thirteen kids. Our small group was beginning to churn out five or six kids per couple, all delivered at home with no medical support. Having a midwife present meant not trusting God.

"Owe no man anything except love. Share everything." That meant not having a mortgage but renting property. We sold our house and went into rented, furnished accommodation. We gave the contents of our home to those less fortunate than ourselves, and gave our money to the ministry.

The worship leader in America died in his early thirties, refusing the regular use of medication. His worship material was withdrawn from the church library and previously recorded material edited. He was considered a failure because of his early death. Listening to his music could contaminate the listener. If you went to a doctor or a dentist, "Jesus will wait outside."

There was a very strong emphasis on end-time teaching, centered around God raising up an elite group of faithful believers who would be the remnant or the over-comers referred to in Revelation 2 and 3. They would be worthy to rule with Christ, and would be the ones raptured during the first period of the tribulation, returning with Christ to rule and reign with Him for a thousand years. The group's isolation from both the world and the mainstream Church allowed greater faith exploits and demands for holiness so fulfilling God's highest calling.

Redemption: The husband spent many years after this experience outside the Church, thinking all this through. How could he, a particularly intelligent man, have fallen for such teaching? He is now restored to the Lord, but with a wiser head on his shoulders. He has a beautiful home and successful business life.

This couple's tragic story has been repeated many times. We may think that it is so extreme that most of our churches would never fall into these areas of harm and self-deceit, yet numerous congregations have a tendency toward one or more of these types of damage, as does much teaching. Over the next two chapters we will contrast various aspects of this couple's story with what would happen in Tomorrow's Church.

Psychological Abuse

Numerous types of abuse are illustrated in this story but perhaps the most significant is the psychological abuse that the couple experienced. Psychological abuse is close to emotional abuse but is often more subtle, often more easily identified by its consequences than by intentional event or experience. We have noted that pastoral care involves empowering those seeking to grow in maturity on a spiritual journey. What becomes evident in cases of psychological abuse such as this is that it slowly wears the person down. They are either ground into submission so that they no longer think or act independently or they admit the damage and seek to change their circumstances. Let us share with you a further example of psychological abuse.

A friend with cancer

Most of the people my own age didn't want anything to do with me, which I felt was because I wasn't pretty, with my glasses and my goofy teeth. But I seemed to get on with people older than myself. There was this lady who was my best friend and the only person that really understood me and loved me. Let's call her Sally. She didn't care what I looked like, like other people did in church, and she didn't care that I was childish, which everyone else thought. She just loved me. She died from cancer at the age of 24 and the elders of the church handled this in a very hurtful way.

On the Sunday after she died they told the church that they felt that she hadn't wanted to come home so when she died they didn't pray for her to be raised from the dead. It was a useless piece of information. If they knew that, why did they need to tell everyone else? They didn't think of people's feelings; her friends' and her family's. I'm not even sure that all Sally's family were Christians. Anyway, not everyone's belief goes that far. She didn't want to come back so they didn't pray for her.

When she got ill, I know I was only young, but even though they must have known she was my friend, I don't remember one person asking me whether I'd like to visit her in hospital or spend time with her. I didn't even think I could ask so I was completely cut off from this person who loved me. I would have liked to have said goodbye.

Redemption: Although the ground could not be retaken, the woman did deal with the betrayal, and was able to write this note about what had happened.

Psychological abuse is very hard to define, and even harder to prove. It is often not until someone sits with a friend, mentor or counselor that they begin to define what actually happened to them. Just putting this into words is a huge challenge and can be a great release. Without sensitive support, however, the abused person will be unable to articulate the full extent of the problem. To someone who is listening with a sympathetic ear, it becomes obvious as people talk that they are "talking out" the answers to the questions they are asking. They realize what they already know of what has happened, and what they now need to do about it. But they needed to take the time, with a friend, to stop and admit that the abuse was as bad as it was.

With psychological abuse, there is often an apparent legitimacy to the behavior that can frequently confuse the mind. It can be justified and seem righteous, particularly when practiced by articulate leadership. The clue is to be found in the feelings of the individual. The woman in the story above clearly carried significant fear, feeling condemned and judged. That would not happen in the presence of Love.

Belief Systems and Dogmatism

The woman tells us that when she joined the house church, she already carried significant feelings of inadequacy, believing she was "second class." In Tomorrow' Church her needs would be put first and she would be deeply loved. What she actually encountered, however, was a belief system that said she wasn't good enough.

Such a belief system suggests a stockade under siege that nothing can enter, change or leave. Many denominations and even individual congregations require everyone to believe their view of "Truth." So a typical newcomer being welcomed into the congregation would be expected to quickly learn all that everyone else already believes. Until they do, they will always have to defer to the experience and understanding of others, which reinforces their feelings of inadequacy. Feeling safe, or an insider, becomes conditional on performance. Within most churches, the definitions and pronouncements of long-standing members carry an authority that can make new-comers feel uneasy, and vulnerable to abuse. Someone who is just learning to play the violin may feel shy in the presence of a master violinist. But if they are to learn well they must not be judged and condemned.

Many people see the Bible as a book of rules, a catalogue of dos and don'ts about which one has no choice: this is what one must believe to be a Christian, and this is the way one must live. So the Bible becomes a system of beliefs to be learned and lived. To some extent, this is true, but the learning and obedience should never be slavish. This can be a real danger, as learning with freedom of intellectual expression and debate is fundamental to human development. The privilege of learning is a key aspect of growing in Christ. The doctrinaire handing out of Biblical rules that one is expected to learn and live by constrains and endangers this learning process.

Frequently claiming, parrot-like, the authority of Scripture allows little room for either an admission of wrong exegesis or of being ill-informed. This group clearly had very fixed ideas, which they held on to in spite of the evidence. Their "faith" led them to deny the reality of what was happening—their leader was dying, and had been ill for a number of months. Reality did not fit with the belief system so reality was wrong. It led them to renounce the expertise of "outsiders" ("Go to the doctor and Jesus will stay outside"). There was no possibility of meeting together, having an open discussion about how people were feeling or considering a review of practices. The group's position was entrenched, and to disagree with their core beliefs was to disagree with God.

Another way of putting this is to say that belief becomes dogma, and dogma becomes dogmatism. It is intriguing to observe that all denominations have a system of belief, whether formally presented or not, about which they are dogmatic. Some observe that the newer denominations seem to lay greater emphasis upon the importance of their beliefs than do some of the traditional denominations. It is easy to see how such belief systems and their dogmatism can lead to abuse. If anyone should ever dare to question such a system, they may well be asked to keep silent or leave. One faces a "take it or leave it" choice. Along similar lines, where such teaching is overt, it is often presented in such a way that a "thus says the Lord" is behind every word. It is then very hard to tell the leaders that you have also read that passage, and have interpreted it differently, or that you feel uncomfortable about emphasizing a truth in the way they do. Behind such dogmatism is something much more sinister. The "we're right and you're wrong" attitude is frequently the hidden agenda. For those new to Christianity such an attitude can be very offensive.

In Tomorrow's Church, while accepting the basic guidance of Scripture, one would seek to put the person first. This does not mean allowing them to go unchecked in their behavior and lifestyle (we refer to this in Chapter 12), but that where the applying of rules could alienate them, we ought to be cautious, seeking to avoid this happening. Theologically, we note the example of Christ who, while acknowledging that we must live by His law, never allowed such rules to stand in the path either of relationship with Him or His ability to help.

What we are suggesting is that in some instances it is necessary to put the relationship ahead of the theology. This does not mean compromising the teachings of Scripture, but allowing the relationship to be established first. It is essential that we should be clear about the core Biblical teaching on what we should believe and how we should live, summed up in the early creeds of the Church, but other things should be left for each individual Christian to explore and decide. Called to Christ, none of us is called to conformity. But in practice, putting the other person first may grate on some of our own longheld ways of doing things.

Guidelines

* Avoid teaching dogmatism, especially with newcomers.
* Putting the other person first means that we do not impose lots of rules on them, but instead are willing to learn their perspective.

- With Scripture as your basis, be guided by the opportunity of relationships. Do not let your personal views separate you from those you may be being led to by the Lord.
- Be careful not to impose a way of life on others that not even you are able to live.

An Abundance of Rules

The issue of absolutes and rules is now in hot debate. Traditional Confessional Christianity asserts that it is our duty to live by them, especially the moral absolutes, while the emerging Church, responding to postmodern thought, now questions some of these beliefs and rules.[3] Many have left the Church because they were required to live in a certain way, and follow a range of dictates, without being given good reasons for keeping them or any help to achieve them. This left them with feelings of failure, inadequacy, and guilt. Some traditional Christianity uses its interpretation of "Biblical" absolutes and rules to require compliance. Though not necessarily wrong, it can be a yoke for some. Let us illustrate the problem.

Breaking the rules

> A pastor working for an American denomination found himself visiting friends in France. On arrival he was given a traditional French welcome, with a feast of French cuisine, including large jugs of local red wine. As part of His Evangelical upbringing, he had been required to sign the "pledge," promising that he would not drink alcohol. He was proud to have followed this rule. But after several days of saying no he could not deny that drinking wine was part of the French, and French Christian culture. On traveling to Germany for a short trip, he similarly found that a "beer break" was part of the German way of life, the giving of a bottle of Auslese wine a way of saying how much you valued a friendship. Eventually, he took a sip, and began to learn about wines and beer. With great unease, and to his own surprise, he admitted a particular partiality for English scrumpy (cider), but he was feeling very guilty.

Redemption: Is he now an alcoholic? No! It allowed him to begin the process of thinking through what was important and what was not.

This view of alcohol is binding upon Christians in some Church traditions and cultures. Clearly, some people need to be "dry" because of their pasts and relationships. And we understand how a reaction to the abuse of alcohol led to abolitionism. But feeling safe is being able to understand and accept the basic Biblical rules, such as the Ten Commandments and the Sermon on the Mount, while also being able to live the life of Love taught by Christ without experiencing social dissonance. Let us take this idea one step further. Let us illustrate.

You are sinning!

A man from a working-class background found Christ through a mission hall, and joined a large successful church that was supporting the mission. He would attend the local mission hall on the Sunday evenings, but in the mornings go to the "big" church. He never felt comfortable in the big church, but felt that he needed to go as a declaration of his new-found faith. Every third Sunday he had to work because he was an ambulance driver and medical attendant. One Sunday, on leaving the morning service in the big church, he was given a hearty handshake by one of the deacons, who said he had been missed the previous Sunday. The man apologized and explained that he had had to work. At this, the deacon's attitude changed, and with a dark face he told the man that he was sinning against the Lord by not keeping the Lord's Day holy. The deacon had not asked what the man's job was, but had made his judgment purely on the basis that no one should work on the Lord's Day. The man felt deeply hurt and never attended a service in that church again.

Redemption: There was none. He stopped going to the big church, and eventually the mission hall as well. He began to call Christians hypocrites. Although he later died well, having never let go of Christ, he never went back to church.

The spirit behind this deacon's judgment was arrogant and undermining. The outcome was tragic as it always is when the rules come before the person and any honor of them. Let us look at another example.

Not fitting . . .

He had never been to church in his life, but after months of internal torture he dressed in his best blue jeans and tee-shirt and walked across the road to his local church. He entered and sat down near the back, but was quickly given a warm handshake and moved to the second row. With only 30 people in a church seating 500, he felt conspicuous, but he stayed until the end, and on leaving was again warmly shaken by the hand.

He went back the following Sunday, and the Sunday after that. On the third Sunday he was approached by the minister, who asked to talk with him after the service. They went to his vestry where the minister began to tell him that theirs was not the church for someone like him, and he would be better served by going elsewhere. He was upset, and pressed to know the reason. So the minister told him that they were not sure that he would understand what they taught and believed. He would be better off finding a church that was more "modern." He left dejected and confused.

Redemption: He persisted, and is now a member of a more contemporary congregation where he is more than equal to the task, both spiritually and intellectually. He is currently writing songs expressing his new-found faith.

In this incident, internal rules shut out the newcomer. This was not the problem of finding oneself in a cultish-type community, but the struggle even to join a church. He did not dress right or have the right background. He was probably also the wrong age. This church was not a safe place for him because no one was willing to adapt to accommodate him. The church members had a very clear idea of the type of person they would welcome, and he did not appear to fit. Even if it had been right to suggest that an alternative congregation might be more suitable, this could have been communicated in ways that were far more supportive and full of Love.

Guidelines

• We need to distinguish between the Law of God in Scripture (for example, the Ten Commandments and the Sermon on the Mount), and the petty rules we are in danger of imposing on others that are not part of this code.
• Be open to change in the way you do things, and be especially vigilant where the suggestion may be coming from the Lord.
• Rules that have served well in one decade may not now be helpful. If rules make it difficult for people to be part of, or to join, your faith community, they may need reviewing.
• Although we must live by the guidance of Christ, and Scripture, in living this way it is important that we never show arrogance and seek control of others.
• Seeking to impose rules on others could dishonor them.

The Power of Leaders

As we are noting, some church cultures are more legalistic than others. Some seem to have no rules at all, except that you should come to church. Others make up a rule for every eventuality. On the whole, the older denominations are more relaxed about these matters, while the newer ones seem to feel the need to find an answer to everything. We are noting that the "do as you're told" culture can be abusive. Let us illustrate this.

Seeking help

I heard about this workshop from a friend of mine when we were talking in our discipleship group. She had clearly been helped and was now "on a journey," doing "homework." So I asked her for the details and contacted them. The information came and I decided to go to one of this group's weekend work-shops.

After church one day I was talking to the pastor's wife and with some excitement mentioned that I was off to this work-shop. Nothing was said at the time, but a few days later the pastor called and wanted to see me. At the meeting, he told me that they had the expertise to help anyone. He was forbidding me to go to such a "heretical" thing (even though he clearly knew nothing about it). The problem was that I had been asking for help from them for several years and they had only helped make me more sick.

Redemption: The woman did go to the workshop, but had to leave the congregation to do so. She is now settled in a new church and has successfully worked through the issues for which she needed the Lord's help.

Church and so-called para-church organizations do not always sit comfortably alongside each other. There can similarly sometimes be tension between denominations and independent missionary societies. Much work needs to be done in these areas to avoid the kind of abuse that this woman experienced. Her minister felt threatened and inadequate when he perceived her unspoken suggestion that he could not help her. Some church leaders also fear exposure to other ministries and ideas. They seem to feel that if someone does not live by what they believe, that person could get contaminated, suffer some spiritual disease, be deceived and even lose their faith. Sometimes leaders respond by laying down rules and telling people how they should conduct their lives. Some of this can be wise, but, sadly, not all the time. Individual learning growth curves will be more significant if people can think through the issues for themselves, and come to their own conclusions. Being told what to believe and do is not always helpful.

In Tomorrow's Church, as we have already seen, personal responsibility is the foundation of pastoral care, and the leaders are clear that they are not responsible for the spiritual health of all their members. People are offered choices, but are not judged if the "right" choice is not selected.

Speaking in the Name of God

A further issue, which applies to all who aspire to make a church a safe place but is particularly applicable to those in pastoral leadership, is the issue we raised in Chapter 8 concerning people who claim, directly or indirectly, to be speaking on behalf of God. Such "thus says the Lord . . ." talk has the possibility of being either uplifting and encouraging or extremely abusive. Sometimes it can be avoided simply by being more cautious and less directive, and by asking oneself, before speaking, how this will impact the person. We have suggested, for instance, that instead of saying, "I have a word from the Lord," one could present it in more modest language, such as, "I think the Lord may be saying . . . so please test it, and act if you feel it is appropriate." In Tomorrow's Church people will be taught to hear the voice of the Lord for themselves. When someone does hear from the Lord for someone else, they will be encouraged to write it down, and give it to the person to test. That allows the Holy Spirit to provide the witness of its authenticity as well as its interpretation.

Another, and related, cultural issue in congregational life is the question of "God's will." How often each of us has heard people say, "God told me to . . ." as a justification for a decision they have made! Typically, people say to us that they prayed about what to do, and the Lord told them to go ahead. We ask them whether they had already decided before they prayed, and although some say they had not, many will admit to having done so. We then point out how surprised they would have been if the Lord had said "no," when they were thinking "yes." Although the intention is sincere, making up one's mind often has more to do with personal conviction than with the will and purposes of God. We all have a tendency to live in denial, with the result that, having decided on a matter, it is all too easy to dismiss all contrary arguments.

How would these matters be handled in Tomorrow's Church? A growing emphasis on personal responsibility would allow people to say, "I want to do this . . . " instead of hiding it in, "God wants me to do . . ." They would resist imposing their own actions on God's will. In an attitude of mutually supportive dialogue, a member would feel free to discuss such choices more openly. Then, when God did speak, it would be significant.

Knowing God's purpose can take on a special significance with the teaching that at conversion one is a new creation (2 Cor. 5:17). This is good Biblical exegesis. But some then go on to argue that as new creations, people do not need to live with all the baggage and sin of their pasts but should have faith to believe that it has gone. For those who find this teaching true in their own experience, we are very pleased. But not everyone experiences life this way after they have committed to Christ. Where such teaching is taught in an exclusive way, it can suggest that someone who is not able to live "victoriously" is under some kind of judgment. For some, this teaching is authentic, but for others, especially those who are vulnerable or quite ill, such a view of conversion and the atonement of Christ can be devastating when it does not prove "true." It can make congregational life very unsafe.

Guidelines

- Be cautious when speaking in the name of the Lord. Couch any such statement as a question or write it down for the person to test rather than presenting it in the first person.
- When seeking the Lord's will, do not pretend to know it when you do not. Maybe the Lord is silent because He is waiting to hear from you what you want.
- New creations we all are, but always leave room for the journey of conviction of sin. Sanctification is a journey for all of us in Christ.

A Culture where Diverse Learning Is Encouraged

Another type of abuse that is demonstrated in the story at the beginning of this chapter is intellectual abuse, seen in a reluctance to allow people to ask questions. In some quarters of the Church, asking questions is thought to indicate a lack of faith or trust rather than a healthy curiosity. Behind this attitude can be a prejudice against learning and enquiry, with intellectual journeying often frowned on. It is a culture that requires levels of intellectual conformity and sameness at the expense of the celebration of diversity. In our own ministry we emphasize the uniqueness of the individual and particularity rather than conformity.

The inevitable consequence of such thinking is a suspicion of "un-Christian" learning. Especially suspect is anything that is considered anti-Christian, such as psychology, the biological sciences (with the exception of medicine), anything deemed to be "New Age," and even the use of New Age terminology. We are expected to learn, but only what is "Biblical" or related to the Scriptures. The argument goes that if it fails to equip us to win people for Christ, then it is irrelevant. Sometimes it is almost as if nothing is important outside "Christ and the Church." Such a culture can be abusive. Hobbies, for instance, may not be winning the world for Christ so can be frowned upon, as can academic study and research that does not "build the Kingdom." Many of us feel a deep conflict between wanting to be fully ourselves in all areas of our lives, in some ways being like everyone else, more part of the wider world, while also being totally sold out on the Great Commission. It has taken us years to find a balance. Each of us has to find a balance, a balance that is uniquely our own.

In Tomorrow's Church, people will be able to follow their hearts and their minds. Evangelism will be the most natural thing in the world as a person experiencing more and more wholeness in Christ begins to share this with others. Such success will be contagious and natural. When two people have differing opinions, they will remain in fellowship, celebrating the difference. They will not need to judge each other. Each will know that they do not have the whole counsel of God, and avoid being dogmatic, unless it is a core doctrine that cannot be compromised. They will avoid arrogant and high-handed attitudes. Church members will welcome the honesty of leaders saying they do not know or have not yet decided on an issue. Pretence will not be needed. Where there is unhelpful disagreement, both will say "sorry," resisting the temptation to decide which view is "correct," since this can be judgmental and result in one getting hurt, and so no longer being safe, while the other feels vindicated. Instead, the discussion will run on, for the honoring of the relationship will come first.

Guideline

- Celebrate and encourage diversity of ideas, godly lifestyle, education, and all forms of learning, taking seriously the mandate of God (Gen. 1:31).

In Summary

We began with the story of a couple caught up in a subtle type of cult, then moved on to defining psychological abuse. We noted the belief systems behind such thinking, and the abundance of rules. The power of leaders was our next concern, and the danger of abuse when speaking in the name of the Lord. In the final part of the chapter, we considered our need to celebrate diversity of gifting and learning, and the enrichment this brings to the Church. In the next chapter, we will be looking at several other areas that can prevent congregational life being a safe place.

Questions to Ponder

1. Belief systems are essential as an intellectual framework for what we believe, but when are they not helpful?
2. If you yourself have ever felt abused by a Christian leader, discuss the effect this had on you.
3. Why is believing good, but dogmatism bad?
4. When is it unrighteous to use Biblical truth?
5. What change is needed in us before we can be a team that stays together while welcoming differing opinions?
6. When is it okay to speak in the name of the Lord?

Notes

[1] R. Howard, *The Rise and Fall of the Nine O'Clock Service: A cult within the Church* (London: Mowbray, 1996).

[2] S. Wookey, *When a Church Becomes a Cult* (London: Hodder & Stoughton, 1996).

[3] Carson, *Emergent Church*, 125ff.

16

Views of Church, Society, and Satan

In this chapter we will be looking at the need for balance in some of the contentious areas of church life. For instance: How do we find a balance in being a niche congregation with a unique role while also being part of the wider Church? How do we find our place in wider non-Christian society? How much can we realistically blame on the Enemy?

Another range of issues is evident in the stories that began the previous chapter. As well as the abusive ways in which the group managed itself internally, their relationships with other churches seems to have been non-existent. In what way would Tomorrow's Church differ?

The clash between being unique and being able to integrate into the global Church is still one of the most divisive issues that most Christians have to face. It is sometimes a struggle for members of a local congregation to see themselves as part of the global Bride of Christ. This can be especially true when you have been taught that other churches or denominations are all wrong! So although our local congregation may be a safe place for us, the reality is that we are always in danger of teaching others that anywhere else is unsafe. This teaching can be a plunderer of safety from us all.

"Us and Them"

If you are the leader of a congregation there is a certain cachet in telling your members that they are part of something unique, be it an experiment in emerging church or a sense of destiny and purpose in one's local community. It is a mindset that we ourselves have both been "guilty" of slipping into. The difficult balance is that people do need to believe in the significance of the congregation they are part of, they do need to feel that they are a significant part of a bigger picture. But the danger of having such a sense of destiny can create an "us and them" mentality that can be very unhelpful. It can be exclusive, and, in its worst form, dangerous and cultish. Believing we are part of something significant for the Lord is wonderful, and will no doubt be the experience of those in Tomorrow's Church. But this has to be balanced with an acceptance that other congregations and even denominations are likely to have equally significant ministries and anointing. In Christ none of us has an exclusive on anything. This is the prerogative of the Bride.

We need to find mature and honorable ways of celebrating the distinctives of other followers of Christ, as well as other congregations—ways that are seen by them to be significant expressions of Kingdom life. This means seeking commonality and fellowship rather than engaging in pitched battles that focus on who is right and who is wrong. We are suggesting that we study to know what we believe while accepting that not everyone will believe as we do   and we do not have a duty to impose our views on others. They have an equal right with us to believe what they believe.

It is a sign of insecurity to feel threatened by others' views. In Tomorrow's Church people would accept the commonality of Christ, but would not think that it is their duty in Christ to clone followers of Christ. Each Christian community would be part of a group of very distinct local churches and would help new and existing members to move from one church to the next as it became helpful. If we do not learn to live this way, the next 20 to 30 years are going to see a great deal of bitterness and abuse between churches and leaders, abuse that can only end in greater division, and bring shame on the Lord and His Bride.

Guidelines

- Avoid emphasizing either your personal or your faith community's uniqueness in Christ at the expense of being part of the wider Church.
- Do not allow your attitude to other Christians, congregations or denominations to divide you from the wider Church.
- Be willing to encourage the establishing and growth of other local churches, as well as your own.
- When you hear rumors about other churches, check them out before passing judgment. It is always easier to be negative than it is to be supportive, since being supportive will cost you something.
- Always strive to remain part of the wider body of Christ, and help others do the same. Isolation can lead to error and cultishness.

Traditional and Emerging Churches

In the West we are seeing the emergence of many new, independent churches with ways of worship and structures that are markedly different from those of traditional congregations. As leaders in a congregation that enjoys both the old and the new, we have already made peace with the fact that sometimes the new needs to take root and prosper in a new wineskin (Mk. 2:22). But at times it is necessary to seek change in an existing organization where some will be content not to change. During this period of transition it is essential that both groups honor one another. The old and the new should be able to live and learn alongside each other in mutual honor.

Becoming exclusive

In CCD, one of the early mistakes we made in planting our community was that of ignoring the reservations of other Christians in town. By not immediately addressing the questions that were asked, we appeared to be saying that we were not interested in what others thought. Although this was far from true, some local church leaders and members did harden their attitudes because of what they heard. We naively thought that we should wait and let the fruit of the Lord's work speak for itself. That proved unhelpful. The situation was further complicated by some who left our community, and said hurtful things about us.

Redemption: As a faith community, we are now a member of the Evangelical Alliance, and part of the Association of Therapeutic Communities. We are also enjoying much better relationships with the local churches that want to be in fellowship with us.

As a community, we made numerous mistakes in our relationships with other local congregations. In order for there to be positive change it helps for all parties to admit their mistakes. We have sought to say sorry for the mistakes we have made. We are now nearly a decade old, and are prospering in the Lord. We count it a privilege to be part of the wider Body of Christ alongside other congregations and denominations with differing significance from us.

Guidelines

* Encourage new growth and ideas in local congregational life, and where problems arise, talk together openly.
* For the sake of the Lord, be willing to say sorry to allow restoration of relationships.
* Unless Church leaders can live honorably with one another, none of us will ever be capable of creating a safe place for members. Criticism makes everyone feel insecure.
* Know your own personal prejudices, and don't allow the grapevine to reinforce them. Question wisely all that you hear, and do not jump to conclusions.
* Respect viewpoints that are different from your own.
* Never think that you know it all.
* Stay abreast of developments in the wider Church, and allow them to teach you about your own needs and those of your faith community.

Writing an Exit Strategy for Those Leaving a Congregation

Knowing that we are part of the wider Body of Christ is likely to reduce significantly the potential for abuse when someone leaves a congregation to join or form another. Surely it should be possible for us to support people who move from one congregation to another or even take "time out" for a while? Protocols of good practice seem to be seriously lacking in this area. Let us illustrate.

"This is not God's will . . ."

I had decided over several months to move to another church. My wife had died and I was finding it increasingly difficult to sustain relationships with this small group of people. Also, as I began to see that I had very few friends in the church, and no deep relationships, I had realized that she was the one who had kept us there. I knew of another church that ran workshops for people like me, and I had already been helped by one so thought it was time to make a move. I went to see the pastor to tell him that I had decided to sell up and move to this new church.

In his study we talked for a while, then, with all guns blazing, he laid into me, saying that this was not God's will because God had not told him this. He said that I was being disobedient and would suffer by even trying to leave. What right did I have to leave a sinking ship when everyone else was still standing? I left the meeting feeling assaulted and in profound shock. I was also disturbed by his final prayer that asked the Lord to show me my sin, and do something to stop me. I felt like he had laid a curse on me.

As the days passed, I became increasingly disturbed by what had happened so I met with some of the leadership of the church I was thinking of joining and told them about my meeting with this pastor. They said sorry to me and prayed with me that I would be able to make a clear decision for myself. After I told them I definitely wanted to change churches, they even came and prayed through my house to make sure it sold. I only went back to the church another couple of times, and it was obvious that the pastor had already told everyone that I was leaving as they treated me as if I had a disease. On my last Sunday I walked away without anyone saying goodbye. My wife and I had been part of that church for over twenty years.

Redemption: In the new congregation he found new hope and even a new wife, and is now part of the leadership team of this church.
(Some of the facts have been changed to avoid embarrassment.)

We have chosen this story from a large number of similar stories. Here, the most shocking thing for us is that the pastor placed no value on this couple's long and faithful support of the church. In Tomorrow's Church, the man's ministry would have been celebrated, and he and his wife would have been honored for their many years of faithful service. On his last Sunday he would have been allowed to stand up and say a genuine goodbye and thank the church for their honoring of him and his late wife. The church would then have prayed for the blessing of Christ in his new bold venture and have commended him to his new congregation. The pastor would also write a letter of commendation to the new church.

Where the person or couple leaving have agreed, we have sought to do this in our own community. But on several occasions we have been rebuffed. Do not beat yourself up when this happens.

What we are suggesting is that we celebrate ongoing change as part of people's maturing in Christ. It can be very liberating for everyone when a church is not possessive, and allows an honoring of their moving on. If someone should later change their mind, as once happened with us, it would be difficult to welcome them back if they had they left under a cloud. But of course, there are times when this approach is not possible. People leave because they have been hurt, because that church does not feel so relevant for them, because their private circumstances have changed but they do not feel able to talk about what has happened. These are sad situations that can end up adding more damage to their lives. If those who are leaving do not wish to be publicly honored and to say good-bye, nothing stops you from praying and blessing them in their absence so that the congregation at least has a way of saying goodbye.

Some kind of guidance note or practice could very easily be adopted by a local congregation or even denomination to ensure that folk leaving are honored, and not just allowed to slip out quietly, shamefully, by the back door. Such honor takes very little effort and could do a great amount of good. One wonders whether in at least some instances one of the reasons why this is not done is because of the anger or even jealousy of remaining members who can't believe that someone has had the boldness to leave. Many churches have a superb celebratory joining strategy, literature, pre-arranged meetings and a range of support. But very few congregations have an exit strategy where a person can leave with dignity. This is not good. It seems that some churches do not even notice when people are no longer attending.

Very few of us stay in a congregation for a lifetime so an exit strategy would be very helpful. People should be celebrated as much when they move on as when they first arrive. They can be given support in joining a new church, if that would be helpful to them. Those who move to other parts of the world can be made associate members of the community. If we all viewed ourselves as part of the global Body of Christ, there would be no need for local bad feeling.

An Unrighteous Fear of the "World"

Suspicion between churches is often matched by suspicion within the Church of the outside world. In some churches there is even a fear of talking to people outside the Church. Some of this fear can be instilled by the leaders themselves as a way of manipulating members. A cynical view would be that the attempt to separate members from other Christians or the unchurched, ostensibly for their safety or well-being, is really a way of manipulating them. We noted this in earlier case studies. Some guidance, such as not having sex before marriage, makes huge sense. But laying down rules leaves people with little personal responsibility beyond choosing whether or not to submit. A much more helpful and empowering approach might be to require them to choose their own carefully-thought-through pathways.

Some leaders will seek to instill into others a fear of the "evilness" of society. They suggest that only continual obedience to God can save a person from the "evil" world. It is an attitude toward life, society, and even the natural world that sometimes resembles a tightrope—anyone can fall off at any time if they have not been careful to follow the rules. The argument goes as follows: What one believes influences what one does. Therefore, wrong beliefs can open a person to wrong and sinful actions. If you do not believe the right things, then you will believe the wrong things, and if you believe the wrong things, then you are vulnerable to the evils of the world and the Enemy himself, after all, is he not a predatory, prowling lion waiting to pounce on you when you do something wrong?

On the basis of this view, Christians should only buy certain "Christian" books, a certain type of "worship" music or only go to certain places. That is, do things that are "Christian," and avoid dancing, movies, clubbing, hobbies, secular pursuits, and education, etc. All of these are not allowed as they are "sinful." It is interesting to compare this with Christ, mixing as He did with the tax collectors, the Samaritans, the lepers and outcasts of society, yet without sin, while avoiding the religious leaders, who considered themselves holy.

Since, according to this teaching, the world is contaminated with "mammon," putting the Kingdom of God first means that Christians should stay away from certain careers or some types of success. To have their calling accepted by their church, they need to prove that it is "from God." This fear-of-the-world attitude steals from individuals the ability to grow in what they are interested in, or in what they want to explore, either professionally or personally.

The outcome of such attitudes has been devastating for the wider Church here in the West. In the 1950s, on both sides of the Atlantic there was a huge reluctance by Christians in some denominations to work in areas such as the arts and media.

Contemporary music was largely shunned by some sections of the Church, along with politics and social moral issues (for example, abortion and euthanasia). The results now speak for themselves. The Church has suffered a loss of credibility and has no answer to the valid accusation that Christianity is no longer relevant in our Western culture.

Such a view of reality is fundamentally flawed. It was a massive attempt at social control. It does not teach people that life can be safe, but instead that certain parts of life can be dangerous and should be avoided. We would question the wisdom of the claims that are made: for example, that only Christian leaders are qualified to teach people what is beautiful and good about, say, the business world; or that the arts and the media can be labeled "sinful" because they do not directly promote Christian values. This is a type of Christianity that promotes segregationalism, a dividing of life and society into what is good and what is not, what is holy and what is secular. It denies a Biblical holism of the created world. Such exclusivism or separatism can be very costly in terms of both winning others and being transparent to a watching world. Having said this, however, we are not challenging the importance of a "Christian" education, which is a different issue.

As Christians, we all need to be more wise and mature in discerning how to avoid involvement in any appearance of evil. In Tomorrow's Church, it would be clearly taught that we all have a dark side that the Enemy can exploit. But the choices we make would not be based on rules derived from what we think is righteous and unrighteous. Rather, Tomorrow's Church would see it as important to discover what does and does not make us more human, more whole, and more Christ-like. Enjoying fully and righteously the world God has given us to live in is preferable to fear and withdrawal from it. Postmodern people are confused and offended by such behavior.

Guidelines

• It is essential that we encourage people to follow their hearts and abilities in finding things that suit their natural skill set.

• We should encourage people to excel in all areas of their lives. The Lord and they together know best.
• Are you able to let others be better than yourself?
• Love the unchurched before judging or seeking to "convert" them.

Between Christ and Satan

Connected to "fear of the world" is a more general fear that characterizes some types of Christianity. Here, instead of a fear of the Lord, one develops a fear of Satan, darkness, and the spiritual world, as well as sin and difficulties such as sickness. The suggestion is that all these are dangerous and out to "get us." It is almost as though we believe that the Enemy is more able to deceive and harm us than the Lord is able to teach, protect, and keep us.

We are not suggesting that there is a deliberate intent to teach such fear, but it seems to be implicit in the way that some of us live as Christians. It is common, for example, to hear people say "between Christ and Satan," linking together Christ and Satan almost as if they were equal and were it not for our knowledge of the atonement and Christ's resurrection, Satan would be more powerful. The whole matter always seems to be just in the balance. Alongside this is the compulsive need to use the name of the Lord, as if otherwise we would be taken out by the Enemy. We attribute to the Enemy a whole range of powers. We credit him with bringing about misfortune, disaster and sickness that he has probably had nothing to do with. For some of us this is so serious that we fear doing anything wrong lest either a vindictive God or the Enemy then exploit it. Part of the problem is our naive trust in a simplistic idea of cause and effect whereby either God or Satan is behind everything good or bad that happens to us.

Biblically speaking, this idea of an almost equal balance of power between Christ and Satan is far from the reality. Satan is merely an angel, not God (2 Cor. 11:14). It would appear from Scripture that Lucifer's equals are perhaps Gabriel or the archangel Michael (Dan. 10:13,21; Jude 9). In the hierarchies of the spiritual world, the Enemy may even be below these. But this is a more authentic comparison, and one we should not forget. Satan answers directly to Christ as Lord. All power is given to Christ (Col. 1:15–20; Rev. 12:7–12; 20:7–10). There is no cause for fear, just caution. We should show deference to the Enemy of God, but we should not unrighteously fear him or give him more power than Christ has given him.

Also connected to this fear of the Enemy is the fear many of us have of the spiritual world, by which we mean that reality that is spiritual, though not necessarily outside material reality. The two co-mingle within one another. The spiritual world is that realm where God directly dwells, and where all spiritual creatures, except human beings, primarily exist. Some Christians are clearly afraid of what might happen if they were to move into this "spiritual" realm. Many believers see Satan as waiting to pounce on them the moment they venture into spiritual reality. What is missed is the simple truth that this is where God dwells, and that one day He will rule the earth as He already rules in heaven. This truth of God ruling in heaven is central to the Lord's Prayer (Mt. 6:10).

What we are suggesting is that a culture of fear of the Enemy and of spiritual reality is unbiblical. Such unbiblical teaching can be very abusive in its outcomes. Most of us know what it is to live in fear from time to time, but to have a life of fear, where the root is fed by a wrong view of God, the Enemy and spiritual reality, is very sad. What is even more sad is that as Christians some of us have not been able to promote a type of culture where people can feel safe, but allow an unrighteous fear to dominate. We need a contemporary theology of the sovereignty of God and the all-sufficiency of Christ.[1]

Guidelines

+ We must always be seen to put Christ first.
+ Christ is God, Satan merely a fallen angel.
+ Be careful not to focus on the Enemy's attempts to harm or deceive us.

In Summary

In this chapter we began by considering the problem in some churches of an "us and them" mentality. We suggested that helping people to leave well, is as important as helping them to join. We also looked at an unrighteous fear of the world and an unrighteous fear of Satan, a fallen angel. In this next chapter we will be looking at what we should do when things go wrong or when we are abused.

Questions to Ponder

1. How would you describe Satan?
2. How much power has Satan really got?
3. Why is it that so many of us in theory believe in the supreme power of Christ, but in practice act as though we think the Enemy is equally powerful?
4. Do you suffer from an "us and them" attitude problem?
5. What are some of the problems between traditional and emerging churches?
6. What problems, if any, do you have with seeing yourself as part of the wider Body of Christ?
7. What do we mean by an "exit strategy" when referring to someone leaving a local congregation? Why can it be a good thing?
8. When could exclusivity ever be good or helpful?
9. What should we fear in the world around us?
10. How is it possible to enjoy being part of contemporary society, but without sin?

Notes

[1] E. Kolini and P.R. Holmes, *Christ Walks Where Evil Reigned: Responding to the Rwandan genocide* (Colorado Springs: Paternoster, 2008).

Part 7

When Things Go Wrong

We all believe that we have the right to justice, but such a demand can have a dark side: we can create a blame culture. This is a particular problem in the Church. This chapter looks at this problem, and makes a number of suggestions on how to prevent such a blame culture turning community life into an unsafe place.

17

A Blame Culture?

One of the key themes of this book is that in congregational life things will go wrong, people will get hurt, places will become unsafe, because we are all human. If we are to offer sanctuary to needy people, a safe place for all, we must not pretend we are perfect and that there is no risk. We have to find a different way, a counter-cultural alternative, for managing the potential of abuse. In this chapter we will explore how a safe place can stay safe after thingshave happened that make people feel unsafe.

It is very helpful and necessary for all of us to remind ourselves that we are only human, and that we will make numerous mistakes, some of which will result in harm to others. One of the most healing aspects of authentic relationship is being able to talk openly about the mistakes we have made, and how we intend to resolve them if we need to or can.

In Tomorrow's Church, mistakes would be recognized, and talked about openly. Although the task of creating a safe place involves reducing the possibilities of risks, mistakes, and harm, it also entails having the correct responses when things do go wrong. In Tomorrow's Church, there would be constructive procedures in place to deal with breakdown in relationships, and a forgiving culture so that as a mistake is remedied, Love is also restored. Creating a safe place can only happen when people begin to believe in the procedures that are in place to deal with abuse. They need to see that something is being done, that people are being honored, that the matter is being acted upon.

Guidelines

+ We are all human so we will get things wrong.
+ In making mistakes, we may be unsafe for others from time to time.

The Response of the Church

The Church seems to have few structures or policies that make it able to resist the abuse that is so frequently found in the surrounding culture. This is probably also true of other religions.[1] Because faith communities do not see abuse as a major problem, they have taken few steps to reduce or exclude its occurrence. They are more likely to deny abuse, or go for a cover-up, than follow a policy of open admission.

The Church, like most institutions and businesses, is all too often obsessed with secrecy and, indeed, has a culture of secrecy. None of us wishes to give God a bad press. As already noted, we all seem to feel the need to protect Him. Many of us will therefore instinctively become co-conspirators, a party to cover-ups. The extent of this deceit is shocking, and is only now surfacing as people are brave enough, often after many years, to speak out about what has happened to them. Such abuse and its deceit are unacceptable. Many are now writing about this.[2]

We have seen this abuse of people in both the institutional Church and independent congregations. An extreme example is the thousands of court cases now pending in the United States against Catholic priests and Christian leaders who were running Christian institutions. These cases focus on the abuse of children who have now grown up and are turning on their abusers. The pattern seems to be that when abuse initially came to the attention of those in leadership positions, they chose to cover it up, simply moving the perpetrators on. So the abuse would often continue.

Denial may be forced on the Church because we are in a litigious age and admitting negligence makes matters worse. This is something the North American Catholic Church knows only too well. Court damages against the Catholic Church in North America are now estimated to be up to $1 billion dollars and insurance companies are refusing to cover this risk.[3]

These court cases would seem to be a specific affront to God were they not also the trend in businesses and institutions, witnessed to by the growth of employees' tribunals and litigation claims against practices such as unfair dismissal and personal injury while at work. It may be that businesses and religious institutions are no more abusive now than they were in the past. Maybe even the opposite is true. But increased accessibility to the media and fee-free legal process have opened up to most people the benefit of justice and the opportunity for financial gain. Greed has been behind some false accusations, sometimes with tragic consequences to those accused.

Institutional denial, cover-ups, hostility, and judicial self-protection are not unusual. This happens simply because the institution is more committed to self-preservation than to open dialogue and positive personal change. The victim may make complaints in writing, even through a legal process, but much of the time will be met by a wall of denial or limp promises. Our observation is that many abused people either do try to tell someone, or attempt to seek justice, but are shunned or stonewalled by the system.

There are some situations where protection from abuse is now required by law (for example, police checks for those working with children and vulnerable adults). But many congregations have been slow to implement these changes. And even where matters have been addressed internally within denominational hierarchies, ecclesiastical courts have not always been just.[4] Some Christian leaders seem to believe that they have a spiritual and moral duty to defend the Lord's name. So when accusations of abuse surface in a congregation, they feel they need to gloss over them somehow or deny them. One wonders whose name is really being protected. The result is that the abuse does not surface in the helpful way that it needs to, and learning and positive change never occur. Moreover, the example of one person's abuse being dealt with in a less than honorable way discourages others from speaking out, and both the memory and its toxic emotion fester until they turn to a desire for revenge. Let us look at more helpful ways of ensuring that the Church sets a good example in these areas.

Accepting the Reality that Abuse Will Happen

Some of us have buttressed ourselves into never thinking the unthinkable. So even where abuse is threatened, or does actually happen, we have a tendency either to ignore it or to seek to control the outcome. Many of us, as committed Christians, think so highly of those who lead us that we resist the idea that there could be anything in them other than pure righteousness. After all, isn't God using them in our lives? Surely the mistake must be ours? But our observation from both Scripture and clinical pastoral experience is that God will use all means available to Him to talk to us, to glorify His Son and to achieve His purposes—a burning bush, a mule, the natural world, and even television—He is not limited to "holy" Christian leaders or whatever we deem to be "pure vessels." Nor does His use of leaders endorse them, any more than His use of a mule, a television soap or a movie endorses them.

We are suggesting that even the most godly will make mistakes. Even in the most anointed environments it is possible for abuse to occur. This seems obvious, yet many of us are reluctant to accept it. Why? Perhaps because we want to be able to trust absolutely in a leader or a church, without having to take responsibility for ourselves. In Tomorrow's Church, leaders would be taught to acknowledge openly their mistakes (even the minor ones), to say sorry, and remind people publicly of their need to form their own opinions. They would teach each member how to become confident that they can hear God's voice for themselves, and trust the witness of the Holy Spirit through their spirit.

Without these practices, it is very likely that we will all have a tendency toward cognitive dissonance. Cognitive dissonance is Festinger's observation that when we have more than one perception of what is happening, a dissonance occurs.[5] This dissonance is a driving force that compels us to acquire or invent new thoughts or beliefs, or to modify existing beliefs, so as to reduce the amount of dissonance (conflict) between cognitions. One of our coping mechanisms could be that we ignore any and all evidence that contradicts our chosen view.

The implication of such behavior is disturbing since it means that we can be closed to the idea that there might be a different view from the one we have formed. No doubt our negative scripts will support us in this. If others come to us to suggest a different view, we will be quick to dismiss it. Alternately, we do explore it, but are soon reassured by finding the evidence that we wanted, and we dismiss all the contrary evidence. This creates a culture of denial that is incapable of admitting that things are what they actually are. The result is that damage continues to accrue. Our situation remains hopeless until we are prepared to admit that we may be wrong.

Guidelines

- Christian leaders are only human, even if they are unwilling to admit it.
- Practice getting God's perspective yourself. Do not always depend on others.
- Listen to the consensus around you, it may be right and you wrong.

When Abuse Is Recognized

Once abuse has occurred, a sequence of events may be put in motion that can lead to accumulating damage and the ongoing involvement of other damaged people. Alternately, the incident and its resulting pain may be dealt with thoroughly and speedily to create the maximum opportunity for redemption in the church and in the lives of those caught up in the events.

When someone has been harmed, their initial response is usually one of shock, then anger, a righteous anger, at the injustice. How the shock and anger are handled is critical to the maintenance of a safe place. Anger needs to be expressed rather than buried. If you are a leader, be prepared on occasions to be the lightening rod for such anger, even though you may have had nothing to do with the matter. A lack of anger can indicate denial—that someone is already beginning to bury the problem rather than honestly facing it. It is important that they begin to see the abuse remedied and redeemed. Ideally, the most helpful thing is for them to go straight to the other person involved to talk the matter through and make peace. If there is a solid relationship of trust, and both have maturity, this is often the end of the matter.

But where someone is feeling very angry and hurt, it is rarely constructive for them to express it spontaneously and directly to the other person or people involved as this can lead to additional harm being caused to one or both parties. A pastoral-care strategy that involves every member of the congregation is invaluable here. There should always be someone for the hurt person to go to—a listener who will respond supportively through this first wave of anger, helping them to the next stage. In some instances, we encourage the hurt person to "let off a head of steam" by speaking out their anger and pain to an empty chair. In this way, the guilty party will not get the full blast, but the matter is "defused" so that there can be reconciliation without the toxic emotion. Where the hurt person is seeking revenge that they feel is their just right, an extended time frame needs to be put in place to allow the dust to settle. Most people are unable to forgive unless the matter of just revenge is first settled for them with the Lord.

What happens next is usually up to the listener. Listeners have a choice. They can get angry, too, and fire up their friends, planting seeds of bitterness; they can take sides, and begin making judgments, without having heard any other perspective; they can start telling the person who has been hurt of the seven other occasions they know of over the last six months when the same thing has happened in the congregation. It is clear that any of these reactions is going to make the damage even worse as the anger quickly turns to a shared vindictiveness.

Another choice is for the listener or mentor to refuse to take the complaint seriously. We are all in danger of accusing the person's "baggage" of talking. The reason they are feeling hurt, so this argument goes, is because damage has been stirred up from their past. A hard lesson for us both has been the importance of recognizing that whether or not the person is being influenced by their toxic history, they are still trying to communicate that they are hurt, and this should always be heard.

A third response open to the listener is to invite the Lord to give wisdom to see how the matter should be remedied. While supporting the person who has been hurt (and without judging them), a listener can begin to seek justice and healing. Here the guidelines and policies of the local church will be very relevant, and will direct the outcome. Some situations might require legal action, especially where children or vulnerable adults are at risk. At the other extreme, some situations might naturally resolve themselves over the following two to three days as the individuals involved talk about it, say sorry and find reconciliation. In Tomorrow's Church, there would be a number of people who the listener could turn to for advice about the way forward. What is guaranteed is that they would do everything they could to seek justice while also ensuring that the hurt person is honored.

Our own experience is that not everyone who has been abused has the integrity or maturity to want to settle the matter. Over many years we have had to make peace with the fact that some people are not willing to be reconciled. The hope of reconciliation must always be extended to them, but it becomes clear that holding on to the bitterness, anger, revenge or their prejudices is more important to them than becoming one in Christ. This is how enemies are made. Just be sure you have done all you can by saying sorry where this is appropriate.

Guidelines

- If you have a criticism or concern, first go to the person directly, not to third parties.
- But if you are very angry, go to a listener first before talking to the person you are upset with.

Resisting the Blame Culture

When a mistake is admitted, our natural fallen reaction is to look for someone to blame. Local congregational life can be the most vindictive and abusive place on earth. Strong language, but, sadly, true. Everyone can slip into a blame mentality. We all believe we have the right to take revenge so we seek to blame someone. Every day in the media we hear about people wanting to blame someone, or we hear of others "getting their just deserts."

We do agree that on many occasions it is clear who has been responsible for a mistake that has led to another being hurt. Recognition of this is essential in order to see a resolution. However, it is the spirit in which the conversations occur that is most relevant to the outcome. Is there a righteous desire for justice and remedy or a revengeful desire to blame? Sadly, when we are feeling hurt, blame is the most natural course of action, especially when what has occurred has exacerbated historic toxic pain and its wounds. It is unfortunate that in the heat of the moment most people will not be aware that much of the anger and bitterness they feel will probably be historic, having little to do with the incident in question, which has merely become the immediate lightening rod or whipping post for the past abuse to rise and cry out for revenge.

We often read reports in the press about the need for people to get justice in the courts, or we hear of those who are calling for the removal of a person in public life because of their actions or inaction. As we have already said, there is a significant rise in the number of court cases involving abuse in both the US and Europe. Everywhere, from employment tribunals to High Court appeals, claimants focus on issues of what is abusive and what is not. Damages are now much easier to claim, as the regular advertising by legal businesses touting for trade illustrates. There are now a range of agreed sums for different types of accident, as well as recognized degrees of carelessness or abuse by employers.

So often the only course open to many victims, apart from doing nothing, is to enter the courts, either by persuading the Crown Prosecution Service (UK) that they should prosecute or by taking out a private (expensive) court action. This is not entirely satisfactory since it means that the victim has to continue to carry the pain up to the time of the court hearing, and then relive the events several times in open court before recompense, if any, is awarded. But unfortunately all of this pales into insignificance compared to the way someone can be treated in congregational life. When people believe that God is on their side, the outcome can be toxic. Carrying the blame for something for the rest of your life can be debilitating and must be prevented wherever possible. It is helpful to avoid legal processes where this can be done without injustice. Let us use an extreme example from our own experience.

Taking confidentiality too far

A woman visited our church and was welcomed. She had had no previous contact with us and did not live in the area, but came along for three Sundays. We did what we usually do. We offered to meet with her and invited her for lunch should she wish to come. She took us up on the offer and lunched with members of the community. She shared very little, only remarking that she had some needs that she was hoping we could meet. She said she would share these if she decided to settle. We did not see her again, but learned some months later that she had taken her own life, and in her note she said that no one was able to help her.

This was devastating, as many had come in the past with a background of self-harm, and we had seen them helped. But what was worse was that we also heard that she had been a member of a congregation in another part of the country, and this church was now openly blaming us for her death. Apparently one of the leaders had read one of our books and sent her to us but because of his view on client confidentiality had not felt able to tell us she was coming, or that she was liable to self-harm, having threatened to take her life on several recent occasions. Had he told us this, we would have been able to approach her in a very different way, and maybe even have helped her. As it was, we could not. And on her side, she had clearly already made up her mind about her next move. Yet he and his congregation were now blaming us for her death.

Redemption: We talked with the pastor, who heard us graciously. We told him how sad we were because of what had happened and because we had not been able to be part of the solution. We also conveyed our sympathy to the family as best we were able.

(Compiled from more than one incident).

When someone takes their own life, it is rarely spontaneous. Although we all know of sudden and surprising exception, it is usually premeditated and, as in this case, has been attempted before. In fact, there will often be a history of such behavior in a person's life. So no one person can or should be blamed. But refusing to apportion blame is not easy. At first people are hurt, shocked. Then shock gives way to anger and anger to the need to blame someone. When this happens in congregational life, the community instantly becomes a very unsafe place. Everyone begins to talk about the last time they saw or spoke to the person. As a community we have been through this and could write a book on it. When blame begins to raise its ugly head it must be dealt with swiftly, openly, and in love. Where matters are left to linger, or are unresolved, fragmentation of a community is inevitable. Some congregations never survive such events, especially where blame is allowed to rest.

Leaders and members have a clear responsibility not to blame themselves or one another. A faith community, like any institution, society or club, will, in the natural course of events, become a blame culture if this is not actively avoided. When something goes wrong, as it inevitably will at some point, the instinct is to say, "Heads must roll." Scapegoating in congregations and even at a denominational level, is a terrible practice, and has caused the ruin of many good people. In part, this will stem from a natural sense of justice, but it can clearly be caused by something much more toxic.

As an alternative, in Tomorrow's Church, if someone had made a serious mistake, the first principle would be to take steps to ensure that the mistake could not be repeated. It would be discussed clearly and supportively with the individual. Perhaps they would recognize it straight away and be horrified and ready to say sorry. But on some occasions it might take them some time to grasp what had happened. Care would be taken to manage the situation wisely, offering support to all parties while minimizing the potential for future harm. No matter what the facts may be, a blame attitude is very likely to emerge if the matter is not dealt with in this way. It is the responsibility of everyone involved to prevent the emergence of a blame culture.

It takes great maturity for a leader to steer a congregation or organization through a period when it has an instinct to blame. Nothing is gained by laying blame on one another. Congregational life should be a blame-free culture where forgiveness prevails. None of us is ever blame free, but grace should prevail. It is always so much easier to blame someone, and let them be driven from the camp, than to seek forgiveness and reconciliation. In Christ we are never called to take the easy path. He takes all our guilt and blame (1 Cor. 1:8; 1 Tim. 5:7, etc.). When people are in pain, they are often vindictive, so the anger has to go somewhere. It is helpful to teach them to give it cathartically to the Lord. It is best left at the cross. It is essential that all parties come through the events stronger and wiser, not scarred, embittered, and feeling that no justice was offered.

Forgiveness Is Not Enough

When we talk of forgiving someone, we so often do this as a head exercise. This rarely works, even when we try to forgive every day, because within us is an age-old need for justice. So our head says forgive, but our heart cries out for justice. The answer is that we need to make peace with our emotional need for justice. Instead of going into the courts or creating a vindictive blame culture in our faith community, we can be supported to engage the anger and pain, and then choose to lay down at the cross our right to revenge, giving this right for justice to God: *Lord God, I know that I feel hurt, angry, and revengeful, but I surrender at your feet my right for revenge. I give this person(s) to you, to do with as you see fit. I leave him/her/them with you so I can get on with my life.*[6]

Guidelines

- Never become part of a blame culture, regardless of how justified you may feel. Either leave the matter with the law or with the Lord.
- Remember that to blame others can be an abdicating of (partial) responsibility.
- Do not let bitterness take hold of you because if it does, you will be unable to love or hear the Lord's voice.
- Give to Christ your right to revenge, but also remember to leave it with Him.

In Summary

We have looked at one of the biggest areas of damage in modern church life—the blame culture with its demand, "Someone's head should roll!" The Church has an opportunity here to be different from our prevailing culture. It can acknowledge that mistakes will happen and put in practice guidelines to minimize damage when they do. Without being soft or unjust, it can allow people to let go of the need for justice by giving the revenge to Christ, allowing a no-blame culture to prevail. Where there is the need for discipline, this should be done with justice and grace. May God give us grace in these areas.

Questions to Ponder

1. What are your church's procedures for when things go wrong?
2. What do we mean by the "blame culture?"
3. What is most challenging about the role of a listener?
4. How would you feel if you had been abused and it was covered up by the leadership?
5. How would you approach the opportunity to blame someone publicly for what they had done to you?
6. To get justice: What does this mean to you?

Notes

1. E. Puttick, *Women in New Religions: In search of community, sexuality and spiritual power* (London: Macmillan, 1997).
2. A recent example is Martha Beck's book, *Leaving the Saints: One child's story of survival and hope* (London: Portrait, 2006), which tells of her father's abuse of her when he was a professor of ancient languages at Brigham Young University. A similar story is Bernard Cornwell's account of his adoptive childhood in "Peculiar People" reported in the *Telegraph Magazine*, "Most peculiar," (25 June 2005), 44–50.
3. See<http://news.bbc.co.uk/1/hi/world/americas/1923484.stm>. The UK based CCPAS warns that some insurance companies are now making exclusions to their public liability cover where abuse occurs. Contact them for details on <info@ccpas.co.uk>.
4. P. Hammond, et al., *Character Assassins: Dealing with ecclesiastical tyrants and terrorists* (Cape Town: Christian Liberty Books, 2004).
5. L. Festinger, et al., *When Prophesy Fails* (New York: Harper Torchbooks, 1956).
6. See our website for a Bible Note on this subject: <www.lifegivingtrust.org>.

18

How to Put Things Right

In this chapter we will be looking at ways in which we can pour oil on troubled waters. Whether you have offended someone, or need help saying sorry, this chapter will help this process. We look at breach of trust, what to do when you have been abused, dealing with complaints, being alert to the threat of sexual abuse, what to do when people leave your congregation, and how to be proactive.

We have recognized that things will go wrong, even in Tomorrow's Church. We can choose to avoid blaming someone, but that will not be enough. What steps will we take together to create an ongoing culture of reconciliation and healing?

Scripture reminds us that we each have a responsibility to avoid being a stumbling block to one another, especially to those who are "weaker." This injunction lays on all of us the requirement to actively support the restoration of relationship, even if we feel that the other person has taken offence unreasonably. And support must be at all levels, from dealing with the crises to helping with mundane, everyday details. When restoring a broken relationship, nothing is too big or too small for our attention. As someone put it to me (Susan) this week as we talked about a very painful situation, "Is it enough for me just to forgive or do I have to go all the way and become their friend again?" We can't judge one another, but each of us must decide for ourselves what we believe God is requiring of us in our relationships with others. In this chapter we explore some ideas about how to support one another through these painful times.

When We Have Been Abusive

As you read this book, it may be that you begin to sense the conviction of the Lord, or guilt over the way you may have treated someone. You may recall a friend who you broke off with in a huff. Or maybe you are out of relationship with family or close friends over a stupid thing. Or perhaps you are unwilling to forgive someone for what they did. Regardless of the circumstances, it is more healthful for you to seek reconciliation than to let the matter fester. Frequently in our ministry, we have to help or support people who have lost their way in relationships. We have seen sons meeting fathers after thirty years, mothers reconciled to daughters, brothers to sisters. And we have seen pastors restored to members and vice versa. We have even seen marriages reconciled.

When someone comes to us seeking help in restoring a relationship, we begin by asking: What would be best for the person you have hurt. How would it be most easy to contact them?

The normal answer is by sending a card or a letter. When you first make contact, begin gently. Say that you would like to meet to talk. Add that it is nothing sinister. If it is someone in your immediate circle, then do the same. You have a responsibility to give the other person the opportunity of finding a way back to you. If there is no reply after, say, a month, then write again and say sorry. Let the matter then rest with the other person. Leave it to them to make the next move. Do not take it further unless they want to.

But if you do get to meet, it is okay to suggest that they bring a friend if they wish. Expect them to be angry with you, but be meek, saying sorry. Do not under any circumstances get defensive. Nothing is gained by raising your rights or your perspective. You are there for reconciliation, not to score points. Do not let your baggage have its way.

Before the meeting, it is very good to imagine saying sorry as if the person were sitting in front of you. This helps you to prepare. It is also good to be clear in your mind about what you would like the meeting to accomplish. It may not all happen the first time, but you should be able to prepare the ground, at the very least. In most cases, you hope to come out of the meeting with a newly recovered friend, a redeemed relationship. When that does not happen, you may both choose to invite in a mediator. If there is no reconciliation, yet you have done all you can, then you can at least know that you have made a start and fulfilled your responsibility to cover the sin.

Mediation

When a person has been very hurt, mediation will at times be necessary. Someone impartial will need to step into the situation to listen to what is being said by both people or parties and identify what is going on. A way through the problem must be found. The ultimate goal is to help make peace and ensure that the matter does not become more divisive. If the conflict or dispute is between two people or groups in the same congregation, it is easier to resolve, providing impartiality prevails and both want reconciliation. If one side is not ready, then the mediation will probably not be successful. Where the conflict is between people both inside and outside the community, then achieving reconciliation gets more complicated.

But regardless of who is involved, the golden rule is that the mediator must listen to both sides, and never go into a situation having already decided what the outcome must be. The second essential rule is that the mediator must be in a good relationship with both parties or be completely unknown to both parties, and so be able to love and support both.

It can also be wise to have two people do the mediation. We have both observed that in mediation situations men tend to believe and understand men, and women tend to believe and understand women. Therefore, if an inexperienced man is seeking to mediate between male and female, he is likely to side with the man. If a woman is mediating, the man may feel threatened or judged by her even when this is not the case. Likewise, a woman may feel intimidated if the mediator is a man and she has been hurt by a man. Mediation, when seen and done openly, restores a safe place for everyone. But effective mediation is a gift that has a significant accountability with it. When dealing with damaged and hurting people, biased, prejudiced or unloving mediation can make things much worse.

History often demonstrates that the majority are more likely to be wrong than right. Although it is good to have the counsel of friends, to involve too many can be chaotic. In congregational life, what the majority believe may turn out to be true, but not necessarily. For instance, most communities will have one or two lateral thinkers, those who look at situations in a way the majority do not. When choosing new leaders or adopting new policies, most people would support the democratic principle of asking everyone to vote. But members will always have a tendency to vote for popular people rather than those who might be more spiritually gifted or anointed, who they might not even know. We must be careful not to listen only to the majority view. The lone voice can sometimes be the Lord's voice. Our calling is to reconciliation.[1]

Guidelines

* Choose to honor all parties who are involved, seeking reconciliation.
* Listen to all parties impartially, and do not ignore the lone voice.
* Be quick to listen, slow to speak, and never judge.

Deal Quickly with a Breach of Trust

At times, we all tend to forget the essential binding nature of trust between community members. Trust is an essential element in community life. Without trust we cannot build authentic faith or create safe places. When there are ruptures in relationships it is therefore essential that where possible they be attended to and repaired. If we allow the emotional debris to remain in people's lives, it will fester or they will carry it into the next church situation in which they find themselves. Perhaps they will leave the Church altogether. In pastoral care, if a breach of trust is not dealt with at the time, the next leader will inherit all the mistakes of both the individual people and the leadership they were under—an onerous gift. The damage will also continue to build up in the congregation. If it is not confronted and dealt with, it will never go away.

Being a young leader

I had been king of my world. I succeeded in all I attempted, as abuse had trained me well. Success was birthed from survival, and rather than bowing my head, I trained in isolation against the world, and felt I had it beaten.

Then I read my Bible and saw myself in every page. All that was on offer I gladly received. I loved learning and learned to love as I painfully laid down my isolation. The church rejoiced in the heathen saved. I was the answer to their prayers and also their religious success. In those early days, like a breath of fresh air, I was welcomed. My hunger knew no satisfaction. All teaching and courses were eagerly devoured. The light I carried attracted others, and spiritual gifting and anointing soon followed. Lives were changed, many were healed, particularly those outside of the church.

My church's response was to accuse me, later, of having had "too many girlfriends." This conclusion was reached because I had brought into the meetings a "strange woman," whose family were involved in the occult. I found it necessary to pray continually with my arm around her to alleviate the migraine headache she experienced in church. I admit I was young in the faith, naive. But I continued learning and giving. However, I was misunderstood, overlooked, and abused. I continually asked myself quietly, "What are they going to do with me?" By the church leaders I was viewed as eccentric, risky, and uncontrollable. I merely thought I was imitating Christ.

Ten years of committed service had now passed. I had become lonely, on the fringes, and yet, because of my church involvement and commitment, I still desired more. I began to ask the question openly, "What are you going to do with me now?" I hungered for a leadership role so that I could give more, but I slowly realized that I had been merely tolerated, and the leadership of my church did not love me. I was told I must be tested, that that was what the Bible required them to do. I never knew the test results, in fact, I never knew what the tests were, only that by my fruit I had not been known or honored. I fought for the church, for the gifts of God that lay in otherness, but I lost out to tradition and fear. My heart eventually broke.

Six months I waited for an appointment to see the pastor to discuss my leaving. The meeting never happened. I came to the conclusion that it was felt that I was no longer a part of the church, and therefore not worth bothering with. I was somebody else's problem. I took this from the Lord that it was time to depart. I had been battered into isolation, but I still loved God in the wilderness . . .

Redemption: Some years later, following a failed marriage, he was able to begin to rebuild his life in a local faith community.

What is evident in this story is the sad but inevitable outcome. Both sides were to blame, and for the young man the result was tragic. He was no doubt a difficult man to manage, but clearly carried anointing. When we look at Scripture, it is full of such characters—wild bucks who the Lord called and used though they would not have fitted in to any congregation. Behind this situation was a breakdown in trust. Neither side was able to express enough maturity and Love, with its trust, to build the bridges between them.

Inexperienced, immature disciples and leaders with enthusiasm and gifting, hearing from God clearly, can cause chaos! There is no doubt that Tomorrow's Church would face similar messy situations, probably even more. How would they be dealt with? Training from people who knew their job would release the new leader or member into more gifting than they themselves had experienced! Feedback would be prompt and open. A range of people would be involved in developing gifting in a range of others—a shared load. Mistakes would be made—but trust and Love would be quickly restored.

Guidelines

◆ Behind most problems between people there is a breakdown
  of trust.
◆ Restore trust, if you can, so that when you stand before the
  Lord you will never be guilty of not having sought restoration.

What You Can Do When You Realize You Have Been Abused

We are very aware that in this book we are outlining what is
and is not abusive, and some of you will find yourselves
described here. Seeing this, sometimes for the first time, may
leave you very upset and angry. Many of us have accepted that
being abused is part of our Christian walk, and we no longer
see it as abusive. But first we are giving you permission to call
abuse abuse. You are allowed to say, "That is what happened
to me!" So what do you do when you begin to feel this anger
or pain rising up in you?

The first thing to do is to talk to someone about it, someone
who is able to listen to your perspective rather than maybe
continue to defend the other person(s). If you desire healing,
find someone who you trust who is not a gossip who will be
able to help you to welcome your feelings. Admit that you
were hurt or abused. Write it out, and engage the pain of the
events. Let the feelings flood you. Invite the Lord to be with
you in this. Have a box of tissues available as you allow the
emotion and its pain to rise in you. Perhaps you need to raise
your voice as you let the anger out. Give the pain to the Lord,
and say to Him that you do not wish to carry it any longer. If
the emotion does not come easily, then put your friend or
friends on a chair in front of you and speak to them.

Do not blame God for what people have done to you in His
Church. This will cut you off from His restorative Love. Let
Him be on your side in resolving the problems. Own the
shame of the events, giving it to Christ. You will probably need
to do this several times. It is healing to be able to admit that

you have been wronged and now want a way to let it go. You must let Christ teach you how to live as though it had never happened.[2] When you do this, only the fading memories will remain.

Dealing with Complaints

We believe that there could be a case for an alternative way to seek and receive justice. At present many victims in small, independent faith communities do not have access to an "appeals" procedure that is able to circumnavigate the stonewalling of controlling leaders, large congregations, denominations, and institutions. Some of the larger institutions do have a process for such complaints, but these are usually self-managed, which means that their impartiality will always be questioned, especially where doubt is expressed about the accusations. If an independent complaints authority were set up within denominations, or even outside them, then people would be able to seek some form of recompense. Such an authority would be similar to those already established in some areas, such as the media and the travel industry.

What first needs to be recognized is that where there is the power to do great good, there is also the power to do great evil.[3] Boundary issues are therefore very important.[4] Normally, the boundaries are initially set up by the institutional Church so that it is not always easy to get its thick-skinned attention without either a media campaign or litigation. Moreover, many victims are timid and broken, either by nature or events, so are hardly in a place to withstand the might of the institution. Some of their pain might be alleviated were an independent body available that was able to take up their cause. Such an appeal body would not look for the support of institutions or denominations as this would compromise its integrity. Instead, its reputation would be established by its power to question these bodies. It would also be in a unique place to screen out pranksters, deceivers, and those seeking unrighteous revenge, of whom there are many.

It would be essential to a successful appeals process that such a tribunal should be seen to be an independent voice. It must not have people on it who are also part of the leadership of a church since in many cases someone in leadership could be part of the problem and there would be a conflict of interest. Those hearing the appeal should also be representative of both genders, and have direct access to the most powerful people in the Church or denomination so that action could be taken where appropriate.

At present, the tragedy is that the people who feel most hurt are those who are often least able to help themselves. They slip away by the back exit, leaving the complaint unresolved, and the victimizers still in control and able to continue to abuse. These hurt people will need help in healing. This is the calling of Christ to a broken and damaged world. We must let the Lord heal where He is invited to, otherwise we remain guilty, and will have to give account to the Lord for our negligence (Mt. 18:5–7). This is particularly true where sexual abuse is concerned. In such cases, the person must find healing from the damage, and will maybe then move on to reconciliation and/or retribution. This second stage is not essential for the healing to occur, though a "sorry" can be very healing.

Guideline

* Do not be afraid to speak up when abused or when you believe others have been abused.

Be Alert to the Risk of Sexual Abuse

Positive change in the Church has in some areas been driven by government policy rather than internal complaints procedures. For instance, all local congregations in the UK now need to go through police checks before adults can work with children and young people. Not all congregations have taken kindly to this, as the following comment illustrates. This is followed by a complex sexual abuse story that illustrates several issues that will often need to be addressed.

Police checks

Some people in our church were offended because they needed to undergo a police check before they could continue to work with children. They argued that they had worked with children for many years so why should they need to? If only they knew what can happen within the church when an outsider comes in with a hidden record of abuse against children.

Love or abuse?

In 1960, at the age of 7, I, Michael, was sent to a boarding school in the west country for boys aged from 5 to 11. Four or five nuns looked after about forty of us in three classes. The Sisters were covered from head to foot, mainly in black, with bits of white. They were mostly old, austere, and difficult. Their height helped me identify them.

Other younger novice nuns visited the convent and helped out. They wore white, and were more fun, singing and playing with us. One of them was called Sister Martha. I met her during my first year at the convent. Three years later she returned to the convent dressed in black.

She seemed to favor me ahead of the other boys. I was a bit like a teacher's pet. She gave me sweets and cakes secretly (a real treat in that place) and always chose me to run errands for her. After a trip away for a couple of months she returned with gifts, like a cross and chain and an autograph book (with a message in it from her). I was of course sworn to secrecy and kept her presents in the one private place I had (a suitcase under my bed). Along the way I learnt her proper name and that she was from Ireland. Her brothers were priests.

I caught a bad cold and was confined to the infirmary—one evening she appeared at my bedside with some medicine. She spooned it into my mouth and then kissed me on the lips for several seconds. I cannot really remember my reaction other than actually feeling really special. Over the next few months we kissed on several occasions, always when she arranged we would be alone. At this stage there was no real touching, although I still cannot really remember.

After the summer holidays I received some photos and a letter from a girl I had become friendly with. I left them in my desk. They disappeared. She started to ignore me, and deliberately laugh and joke with other boys. I had to go to the dentist in town, and she accompanied me. She had taken the letter and photos. She cried as we walked into the town. On the way back we stopped by a field and kissed in a much more passionate way than before. I was mortified at getting an erection. She just giggled.

The rest is confused memories of what is real and what I may have imagined. Certainly I have caressed her hair and neck and breasts under her habit. I have seen her legs and knickers and long black socks. She touched me. I had orgasms, although I didn't know what was happening—the real confusion was that she seemed so happy. But although feeling really special, I was worried sick. I remember on one occasion after a passionate clinch we were late for chapel. She didn't seem to care, just talked about our running away together. It didn't seem to bother her, whilst I felt condemned, the most evil a man could get.

I finally confided in a friend who of course didn't believe me. I took from my suitcase some notes she had written, and showed him, leaving them in my desk afterwards. That afternoon I was sent to the chapel—alone. I returned to find my desk had been emptied—I never saw her again or heard anything about her. Nobody said anything to me. At the end of term my father collected me from the school and told me I was going to another school. He didn't say why, and I didn't ask. I ended up in a military school—three hundred boys—my punishment.

Redemption: This man, who is now in his fifties, had to work through addictive disorders before he could begin to be free. He is a full member of a local faith community, and still thinks about this time in his early adolescence.

What stands out in this story is the confusion and guilt of the boy. The novice sister who is out to explore relationships with the adolescent is clearly someone who has very little experience of the world. It is abuse, but for him it is also a sexual awakening. Unfortunately, it is typical of the kind of behavior that can go on between members of a community. It sits in a grey area of subtle abuse of people. What surprises us is the number of similar stories we have heard. They can happen in even the smallest of congregations without any awareness from the leadership.

The next story is of abuse by a leader against a church member who, from her perspective, was just needing the love of other members. This story also highlights what can so easily happen when another member is given some power. In this case the power rests with the youth leader, who is able, as a predatory male, to take advantage of the young woman's vulnerability.

Sexual abuse

> I was being abused sexually by my youth minister when I was 18, though I didn't see it as abuse at the time. I was just wanting "love" and affirmation. I was vulnerable because of being abused as a child, and because of the history of secrecy in my family. This meant that I didn't feel like I could tell anyone what was happening, and didn't know whether they would believe me anyway. I also didn't want to cause a fuss and get him into trouble. But I now see that he used both his position and my vulnerability to play out his own insecurities and desires.

> **Redemption:** This was just one of a number of occasions on which this woman, with an institutional background had experienced abuse at the hands of others. She came to us as one of the most disturbed women we had met. Had it not been for a Christian couple who took her in, she would probably have ended up on the streets. She has now completed her education and is a full member of a local congregation.

What was particularly bad in this situation was that on top of her guilt and fear, the woman felt she could not tell anyone, both because she was afraid she would not be believed, and also because it would put the abuser in a bad light! Such behavior from an abuser is reprehensible, and should be exposed. The leadership must develop a culture in which members know that if they come with stories of abuse, they will be treated with honor and justice.

These leadership skills have to be learned. They come to few of us naturally. What the Lord has required of us in our own ministry is illustrated in Jesus' conversation with the woman at the well (Jn. 4:4–26). He met the woman relationally where she could begin to connect with Him, and He then gently led her to the place He wanted her to reach, where she was able to accept the truth about herself, as well as His Messiahship. This allowed a relationship of trust to begin that no doubt continued. But not everyone finds this level of compassion and acceptance. Some just want to escape and when you meet such a person just say sorry.

Guidelines

* When you hear rumors of abuse, always check them out.
* When people talk to you about abuse, do not be tempted just to dismiss it as baggage or prejudice. Always be open to the possibility that it could be true.

Being Proactive

The best way to respond when something goes wrong is, of course, to anticipate it! There have been many occasions when, if we had all carried a shared responsibility, any one of us could have quickly acted to prevent a situation becoming abusive. Our final suggestion in this chapter is that any local congregation should have a program of review, an awareness and sensitivity to potential hurt, and a deep commitment to doing everything possible to minimize hurt. People are, of course, responsible for themselves, and if they choose to put themselves into situations where they are likely to be harmed, then one cannot prevent them. But there are many situations in which people would welcome having an alternative course of action.

Being proactive also means thinking carefully about what is best for the individual from their perspective, rather than slipping into default mode and choosing whatever course of action is easiest. Here is an unusual example of abuse.

A hole-and-corner baptism

Although I came from a non-churchgoing family, when I was in my late teens I met and fell in love with a church organist. Gradually, through attending services at the churches for which he played, I reached the decision that I wanted to be part of "all this." So I joined the next series of confirmation classes being run by the local pastor. There was one slight snag, however: I had never been baptized and therefore couldn't be confirmed. My parents had decided that I could make up my own mind when I was old enough, which up to that moment had seemed quite reasonable. But when the vicar realized this, suddenly my lack of baptism became shameful, something that must be concealed.

So one dark November afternoon about a week before the confirmation service was due to take place, he baptized me hurriedly, secretly, and without witnesses, at the back of his dimly-lit Victorian church. It was a ceremony without ceremony. Afterwards I cycled home and got tea ready. The confirmation service went off without a hitch, and meant nothing to me.

A lifetime later I still feel ashamed, but also cheated. I am so much more of a Christian now than I was then and I have experienced many dazzling moments of discovery over the years, but those two moments, my baptism and my confirmation, are lost for ever, and it breaks my heart.

Redemption: She is now a full member of a local faith community, and has been learning that the Lord can go back to these moments with her and help her redeem them.

This story says to us that even traditional rituals can be a negative experience for people if they are not shared and witnessed by others who see redemption in them. The joy and celebration of her baptism and confirmation were stolen from this lady. The rules got in the way of her best interests. What should have been times of great celebration became instead moments of shame.

We are suggesting that it may be necessary for some of our traditional practices to be reviewed. We need to ask people what they feel is best for them, not decide this ourselves as though we know best. Had the minister sat down with this lady and explained the problem, asking her how they should manage it, there would no doubt have been a very different outcome. We often hear the cry, "It's always been done this way, and it worked in the past so why should we change now? Why should others tell us what to do?" The answer is simple.

The world is waiting for the Church to offer a radical and relevant Christianity that takes postmodern life and values into account. Many people are looking for more than a life without Christ. So we need to look at our well-established traditions to see what we may need to change to honor those who are unchurched. We need to ask: What is more important, the practice or the person? What is more important, the survival of the faith lived out or the survival of the ritual and its rules? Interpreting the rules in new ways, brainstorming alternatives, can help to guard against the danger of putting the practice before the person. This also helps us to offer the best opportunity or perspective to people, especially if both men and women are involved in the decision-making process, so giving a balance.

In Summary

It is not your duty to suffer abuse as a member of any local faith community or para-church organization. Any form of abuse is a violation of your personal God-given rights and is unacceptable. All of us need a safe place where we can meet Jesus and begin practicing living eternally with both Christ and all those who stand with Christ. We must all learn how to be people who can make an unsafe place into a safe place.

Questions to Ponder

1. How would you describe a "breach of trust?"
2. What principles would you put forward to help two people who disagree over something, but want to remain in fellowship?
3. What do you understand by a "complaints procedure?"
4. Was what happened to Michael sexual abuse or his sexual awakening?
5. Do you know someone who is being abused? What are you going to do about it?
6. Do you agree that secrecy can be a problem in local church life? How would you seek to avoid it?

Notes

[1] See the final chapter of Holmes, *Trinity in Human Community*.
[2] What we are suggesting here is just a very brief outline of what we teach people they can do to let go of damage in their pasts. See our website.
[3] Dowding, *Power*, 88.
[4] T. Augusta-Scott, "Dichotomies in the power and control story: exploring multiple stories about men who choose to abuse in intimate relationships" in C. White (ed.), *Responding to Violence: A collection of papers relating to child sexual abuse and violence in intimate relationships* (Adelaide: Dulwich Centre Publications, 2003), 203–4.

19

Church as a Safe Place

None of us is born Christ-like. None of us automatically becomes like Christ when we get converted. We all need to change to be like Jesus. So as we change, let us make for one another a safe place.

I (Peter) began my learning journey with Christ around 1960, and as I moved into my twenties I believed I could influence anyone to remain in fellowship with me. In my thirties, I began to learn that this was not the case as people fell out of fellowship with me and did not want to resolve it. I found myself deeply hurt, but could do nothing about it. Sadly, this experience has repeated itself several times since, and I have had to let go of the ideal of being friends with everyone. Some people will just not allow this to happen. The result has continued to be deep personal hurt, especially when people with whom I have walked the road for many years have chosen to turn against me. I understand what Christ felt like when He wanted to go after the one lost or stray sheep (Mt. 18:10–14).

I (Susan) was a consummate people-pleaser. Early in my life I abandoned my own sense of self, preferring to be who others wanted me to be. I slipped (accidentally) into manipulation and control, desperately seeking to be liked and using every opportunity to serve others in order to achieve this end. I naively thought this slavery made me the ideal safe person. But it denied my gifting and my uniqueness. The safety was illusory, my own creation, rather than Christ-centered reality. As a result, abuse was perpetuated.

As noted several times in this book, in hurtful and abusive situations there will always be mistakes on both sides. It is never just a simple case of a victim and an abuser. It is always far more complicated than that. Both of us, as fallen, damaged human beings, have had to live with this reality. For a place to be safe for any of us, we need to share with those around us the values that help make us safe people. For most of us, these values and their learning journey will come from a common purpose: our desire to know Christ better, to become more like Him and to live together at peace as the Body of Christ. For many with an unchurched background, their initial purpose will be the need to find help, to find community or to find God. The ongoing change needed to achieve this is the journey we share together, the journey of becoming more safe.

Most of us assume that safety means somewhere familiar, comfortable, with plenty of stability. But the message of this book, and of Tomorrow's Church, is that safety requires flexibility, sensitivity, and a dynamic responsiveness to individual need. Somewhat counter-intuitively, a safe place is a place where ongoing personal and corporate change is the norm, a place where the "common purpose" is our desire to change to be more like Jesus because we are not satisfied to stay as we are. The journey we are on together is a journey to become more Christ-like, which is also to become more human and more safe for ourselves and others.

What we have been describing is a place into which we can give life, and from which we can all draw life. In a fast-moving world where abuse and anonymity are common, it is an oasis. In my research I (Susan) have identified this safe place not as a geographic location, but as a relational network that creates a form of social structure with a spirituality and interconnected relationality of its own. I am calling this network "a salugenic Place," a relationality that is wholeness-inducing and "Change-enabling."[1]

This is a goal in Tomorrow's Church. When someone belongs to this salugenic Place, they become aware of its importance. It becomes part of them. It is a womb of life. More than just "attending" meetings, there is a participation that grows, a giving and taking that is at the heart of the perichoretic nature of the social Trinity. Perichoresis is the inter-mingling of all the persons of the Trinity in the life of one another, wholly cohabiting, pouring Love into one another. This is the safe place we, too, are called to be. The person is changed by being in such a place. One of our community described it as getting on a moving train. Even if you are not yet ready to change, you are changed by being caught up in the journey that everyone is sharing. My research suggests that a synergy is created by interdependent core characteristics, such as acceptance, choice, and openness, combined with change-enabling resources and journeying together. This synergy produces a harmony of safety and freedom that creates the change-enabling dimensions of a salugenic Place.

In such a healthy change environment there is also trust in ourselves and others. This trust is not a tenacious determination to have things remain the same, as we see in some churches, but rather it is trust in the process of change that we are experiencing together. It is trust in our capacity to live in an environment that is changing all the time as we ourselves change to be more like Christ. As one of our members so aptly put it, "If you are having a problem with someone, don't worry. By next week they will have changed and so will you!"

One final, obvious outcome of allowing such a change environment to emerge in a faith community is that looking at personal faults, mistakes, and bad practice is so much easier where the culture of the community is the desire to change. In an environment where we spend much of the time seeking to keep things the same, owning up to mistakes that hurt others is very hard. But in an environment where one expects things to be changing all the time, admitting mistakes and wanting to change are part of the culture.

Contrary to this, as we have noted, in some churches, bad practice is tenaciously defended as sacred, regardless of how much it hurts and offends people. In a more fluid change-enabling culture, where the individual is more important than the tradition, people naturally change in order to honor themselves and others. What we have been noting is that insisting on keeping things the way they are can in itself create an abusive culture. Deep change in any organization begins with us, but must continue and be "caught" by others, not just taught.

If we can begin to appropriate some of this "wholeness," this Christ-likeness, then we can move into new ways of living that allow us to be safe for others. One of the qualities most valued by the people we help is consistency, especially in the truthful and open way we respond to abuse, pain, and inconsistency. It is a paradox to many of us that a safe place is where we can be most vulnerable. We need to be transparent, open, spontaneous, and real, and yet be able to temper our actions with a lightness, joy and sometimes a salty mix of reactions. Christ taught us to bring peace into any home that we enter (Mt. 10:13). The same must surely apply to our churches.

The Church does not have an exclusive on safe places. Yet it should be the exception to society's unsafe norms. For as we have already noted, the Church is called by Christ to be a safe place, a sanctuary. It should be capable of offering refuge, reflecting social Trinity and the divine harmony within the Godhead. It should be a place where we can admit and let go of the darkness in us, a place where we can change and learn to live righteously in relationship with ourselves, becoming Christ-like in our capacity to Love. This means that the Church must be able to resist the negative trends of the society we are all part of. It is not just individual choices that can lead us into abusive situations, it is the social milieu as well. The natural momentum of our society will take us to the lowest point unless we purposefully resist. Where there is power, there is always the possibility of abusing power. The Church's greatest power to resist such hierarchical and personal abuse lies in Christians living Christ and His values, by the Holy Spirit, in all of their relationships, creatively implementing the Christ-centered mutuality that is central to Body life.

It should be no surprise to us that our congregations have become environments where some members experience abuse. As we have observed, where the surrounding culture is abusive, this is almost inevitable. The good news is that they don't need to stay that way. We can adopt a counter-cultural way of life in our relationships together. But this will require a significant commitment to change both ourselves and our faith communities.

Notes

[1] My research suggests that in addition to a salugenic Place, there are other forms of relational network that are not devoted to Change-enabling. These I have termed "social Place." I expect the results of this research to become more widely available during 2007.

Review of the Guidelines

Chapter 5. The Five Main Types of Abuse

+ If you need to raise a sensitive issue, consider carefully the most supportive way of doing this. For instance, first talk it through with those you trust personally (but without gossiping), as their perspective will help bring balance to your views. 61
+ If you need to shout or raise your voice against another person, you are not yet ready to speak with them about the matter! Never speak out of unrighteous anger, that is, an anger that is intended to hurt the other person. We must never let anger be vindictive. 61
+ Never speak publicly about personal issues unless you have the direct consent of the person or they have already talked openly about the same subject. The exception is when under supervision in a therapeutic context or as a mentor seeking advice about how to deal with a situation. 61
+ Take careful note of a person's emotional state, especially during times of suffering. Do nothing to make them more vulnerable, for instance, by telling them they are wrong, orby being directive with them. 64
+ Never allow your own sin and negative views of God to be a judgment you lay on other people. It is so much easier to be negative than to seek out the facts and say sorry. Christ should always be our sorry. 65
+ Words can all too easily hurt those who are frail or vulnerable so we must speak honorable, loving words that help bring healing. We are called to build up one another, not to

be negative and dismantle what the Lord and others are seeking to do.   65

- Physical abuse can leave many hidden scars. Accusations should always be treated very seriously. For instance, we should not let our loyalties or prejudices stop us from hearing the person's perspective.   67

- We should be open and vigilant regarding physical assault by either men or women.   67

- Never ignore any rumors of sexual abuse in any form. Always ensure that the appropriate person checks out such suspicions, regardless of who the alleged perpetrator may be. But be careful, because a person's reputation can take years to establish but be destroyed in an instant by careless negative comment, even when it is not true.   71

- When anyone comes to you to talk about being abused, treat what is said seriously and listen carefully. Talk it through with others you trust. Your actions must either be those required in law or have the victim's consent.   71

- Be aware of revengeful or vindictive human nature. Sometimes things are not as they seem!   71

- Build up effective relationships with local agencies who can be supportive in giving advice when you are unsure of how to handle an issue. For instance, in the UK, the police and the Public Protection Unit; in the USA, Christian legal professionals.   71

- Listen carefully and transparently to all sides when it seems someone might be being harmed. But do not jump to conclusions without talking to others.   74

- Do not use the name of God when giving your opinion. Do not seek to impose your view of reality on others. Respect diversity of opinions and practices in the Body of Christ. Seek to honor, and encourage honor amongst others. The way we treat others is the way we will be treated by God (Mt. 6:14–15).   74

- Remember that authority and standing in the Church are to build others up, not to abuse them in any way. Always be alert t the fact that it is much easier to be negative than positive, to believe bad things than defend or create good things.   74

6. Group Dynamics and Creating a Safe Place

+ Practice living and teaching by the example of Christ.   92
+ Learn to write Christ-like scripts and social rules that honor and build up people. Learn Love, not revenge.   92
+ Celebrate diversity, not a bland conformity. Maintaining relationships with others in the Body of Christ is more important than lecturing, judging, controlling them or laying blame on them. They could be right and you wrong. 92

7. Relationships of Honor

+ Let's remember that none of us has any more than a small fraction of knowledge of Christ or Scripture. So none of us has the competence to judge.   104
+ Defending Constantinian Christianity is fine, but never cross the line into forcing personal views on others.   104
+ Judging other people dishonors them and makes us less human. Judging is the domain of God.   104
+ Better to Love than to judge, but remember that loving is much harder than judging.   104
+ Our prejudices are usually based on our baggage rather than God's objectivity. Instead of judging, be careful to practice Love, because the way we judge is the way in which we will be judged. None of us is ever right all the time.   107
+ It is not our place to judge whether or not what happens to others is from the Lord. We must all seek wisdom in our relationships with others, but honor must come before judgment.   110
+ We do not have a duty to correct other people's beliefs when we think they are wrong. Instead, we should encourage others to read Scripture for themselves, and mature in their own views, even where these are different from ours.   110

8. Your Unique Contribution

+ Remember that leaders should point us to Christ, not themselves. Be careful if a leader begins to expect an unrighteous loyalty.   115
+ It is each member's responsibility to look to Christ, not the leader or anyone else.   115
+ Passivity is a sickness that any of us can catch, and it makes all of us vulnerable to abuse.   115
+ No leader is "god."   115
+ Christ liberates us from our sinful damaged pasts, allowing us to be more of who He created us to be. 116
+ Empowering people to possess the person God created them to be is fundamental to the gospel of Christ. He is our "Yes!"—intellectually, emotionally, and spiritually empowering us.   116
+ Encourage one another to hear from God for themselves. This also builds greater discernment in hearing from the Lord through others.   121
+ Live as the Body of Christ, not as a group of isolated, private individuals.   122
+ If we are to invite the adventure of hearing God's voice, we have to be willing to be honest, and act on what we hear from Him, especially about how He might see us. 125
+ In learning to hear the Lord for ourselves, we should be careful not to believe we are always right in what we hear or what we say.   125
+ Speaking in the name of Christ is a deep privilege that should never be abused, especially in a way that exalts us.   125
+ All of us must learn that we will be accountable to the Lord for every word we say. It is helpful to treat others in the honorable way in which we would like to be treated.   125
+ Beware of carrying responsibility in a possessive way that excludes others. Practicing a "light touch" is a good discipline.   126

9. Professional Leadership in a Safe Church

10. Shared Leadership Responsibilities

- Be honest at all times, but be careful that your honesty or "speaking the truth" does not come across as abusive to others.　　156
- None of us needs to defend the Lord's actions or inaction.　　156
- Hold steady in what is true, but be open to correction from the Lord and others.　　156
- People must be honored financially if they are serving the Lord.　　156
- As Christians, we have the duty to create wealth, but it should never be at the expense of relationships or integrity.　　157
- There should be transparency in the church's management of its finances.　　158

11. Looking Again at Pastoral Care

- Welcome diversity of interests and beliefs among your friends and fellowship. You have Christ in common.　　169
- Be personally willing to change in positive ways in order to become both more unique and more like Christ. Your positive change makes you safe to be around.　　169

12. A Safe Place for Those Needing Help

- Seeing potential in even the most clumsy and awkward of people helps them to believe in themselves, too.　　177
- Those who are fragile or emotionally ill need extra pastoral support, often in conjunction with specialist professional services.　　177
- Let's remember that self-abuse is still abuse, and as such it makes us unsafe. Becoming safe people will mean inviting the Lord to help us undo these areas so we can help others, too.　　183
- Inviting God's perspective on each pastoral situation we face is the safest way to Love. The obvious is rarely the most accurate.　　188

13. A Safe Place for All?

- None of us can do everything for everyone. What should we let go of? 194
- Prioritizing our lives so that we first honor Christ and those we love is basic to our role as Christian leaders. 194
- Loving God and loving people may be our calling, but we must be careful not to put service for Christ in the church ahead of the needs of our immediate family. 194
- Get real and get relational. Be willing to take risks in learning how to do relationships. But do not let others abuse you. 200
- Just because others believe someone is right for us, it does not mean they are. Our taking up personal responsibility is essential. 200
- Male and female are different so have different needs and perspectives. 204
- Be gender exclusive when people want to be. 204
- Welcome either your manhood or womanhood as a key contribution of your life in your faith community. 204
- God requires us all to be the very best we can be, for Him, ourselves, and others. This will sometimes mean moving out of our comfort zones. 208
- We should pay special attention to honesty, in both our work and conduct. We should not resent people when they want matters to be conducted in a more professional or different way. 208
- We should welcome the advice of others, especially avoiding being either arrogant or naive! 208

14. Leadership of Pastoral Care

- Everyone is responsible before God for their own provision, health, and relationship with the Lord. Exceptions to this are incapacity for a season, for example, because of illness or disability. 213
- It is not helpful when leaders take responsibility for others in such a way that individuals abdicate responsibility for themselves. 213

15. Making Church Safer: Some "Bible" Problems

- Be cautious when speaking in the name of the Lord. Couch any such statement as a question or write it down for the person to test rather than presenting it in the first person. 244
- When seeking the Lord's will, do not pretend to know it when you do not. Maybe the Lord is silent because He is waiting to hear from you what you want. 244
- New creation we all are, but always leave room for the journey of conviction of sin. Sanctification is a journey for all of us in Christ. 244
- Celebrate and encourage diversity of ideas, godly lifestyle, education, and all forms of learning, taking seriously the mandate of God (Gen. 1:31). 246

16. Views of Church, Society, and Satan

- Avoid emphasizing either your personal or faith community's uniqueness in Christ at the expense of being part of the wider Church. 250
- Do not allow your attitude to other Christians, congregations or denominations to divide you from the wider Church. 250
- Be willing to encourage the establishing and growth of other local churches, as well as your own. 250
- When you hear rumors about other churches, check them out before passing judgment. It is always easier to be negative than it is to be supportive, since being supportive will cost you something. 250
- Always strive to remain part of the wider body of Christ, and help others do the same. Isolation can lead to error and cultishness. 250
- Encourage new growth and ideas in local congregational life, and where problems arise, talk together openly. 251
- For the sake of the Lord, be willing to say sorry to allow restoration of relationships. 251
- Unless Church leaders can live honorably with one another, none of us will ever be capable of creating a safe place for members. Criticism makes everyone feel insecure. 251

17. A Blame Culture?

18. How to Put Things Right

Bibliography

Ammicht Quinn, R., et al., "Postscript" in Ammicht Quinn, R., H. Haker and M. Junker-Kenny (eds.), *The Structural Betrayal of Trust* (London: SCM, 2004), 130–5

Augusta-Scott, T., "Dichotomies in the power and control story: exploring multiple stories about men who choose to abuse in intimate relationships" in White, C. (ed.), *Responding to Violence: A collection of papers relating to child sexual abuse and violence in intimate relationships* (Adelaide: Dulwich Centre Publications, 2003), 203–4

Bebbington, D.W., *The Dominance of Evangelicalism: The age of Spurgeon and Moody* (Nottingham: Inter-Varsity Press, 2006)

Beck, M., *Leaving the Saints: One child's story of survival and hope* (London: Portrait, 2006)

Bondareff, D., "Numbers," *Time Magazine* (28 August 2006), 12

Brearley, J., "Working as an organizational consultant with abuse encountered in the workplace" in McCluskey, U. and C.A. Hooper (eds.), *Psychodynamic Perspectives on Abuse: The cost of fear* (London: Jessica Kingsley, 2000), 223–39

Brierley, P., *The Tide is Running Out: What the English church attendance survey reveals* (London: Christian Research, 2000)

—, *Pulling out of the Nosedive: A contemporary picture of church-going* (London: Christian Research, 2006)

Bucher, R., "Body of power and body power: the situation of the Church and God's defeat" in Ammicht Quinn, R., H. Haker and M. Junker-Kenny (eds.), *The Structural Betrayal of Trust* (London: SCM, 2004), 121–9

Carson, D., *Becoming Conversant with the Emerging Church* (Grand Rapids: Zondervan, 2005)

Cherlin, A., *Marriage, Divorce and Remarriage* (Cambridge, Mass.: Harvard University Press, 1992)

Chevous, J., *From Silence to Sanctuary: A guide to understanding, preventing and responding to abuse* (London: SPCK, 2004)

Davies, G., *Genius, Grief and Grace: A doctor looks at suffering and success* (Fearn, Ross-shire: Christian Focus Publications, 2001)

Department for Education and Science, *A Legal Toolkit for Schools: Tackling abuse, threats and violence towards members of the school community* (Nottingham: DfES Publications, 2002)

Department of Health, *No Secrets: Guidance on developing and implementing multi-agency policies and procedures to protect vulnerable adults from abuse* (London: Department of Health Publications, 2003)

Dowding, K., *Power* (Buckingham: Open University Press, 1996)

Duck, S.W., *Human Relationships* (London: Sage, 1986/1998)

Etzioni-Halevy, E., *Fragile Democracy: The use and abuse of power in Western societies* (London: Transaction Publishers, 1989)

Ferguson, N., *The War of the World* (London: Allen Lane, 2006)

Festinger, L., et al., *When Prophesy Fails* (New York: Harper Torchbooks, 1956)

Field, A., *From Darkness to Light: How one became a Christian in the Early Church* (Ben Lomond, Calif.: Conciliar Press, 1978/1997)

Finke, R. and R. Stark, "How the Upstart Sects Won America: 1776–1850," *Journal of the Scientific Study of Religion* 28 (1989), 1:27–44

Gilligan, C., *In a Different Voice* (Cambridge, Mass.: Harvard University Press, 1982/1993)

Gladwell, M., *The Tipping Point: How little things can make a big difference* (London: Little, Brown, 2000)

Goleman, D., *The New Leaders: Transforming the art of leadership into the science of results* (London: Little, Brown, 2002)

Gottman, J.K. and J. de Claire, *The Relationship Cure: A 5 step guide to strengthening your marraige, family and friendships* (New York: Three Rivers Press, 2002)

Grudem W., *Bible Doctrine: Essential teachings of the Christian faith* (Nottingham: Inter-Varsity Press, 1999)

Hammond, P., et al., *Character Assassins: Dealing with ecclesiastical tyrants and terrorists* (Cape Town: Christian Liberty Books, 2004)

Hickin, M., *Uncomfortable Reality: Abuse, the Bible and the Church* (Swanley: CCPAS, 2004)

Holmes, P.R., *Becoming More Human: Exploring the interface of spirituality, discipleship and therapeutic faith community* (Milton Keynes: Paternoster, 2005)

—, "Spirituality: some disciplinary perspectives" in Flanagan, K. and P.C. Jupp (eds.), *The Sociology of Spirituality* (to be published)

—, *Trinity in Human Community: Exploring congregational life in the image of the social Trinity* (Milton Keynes: Paternoster, 2006)

Holmes, P.R. and S.B. Williams, *Changed Lives: Extraordinary stories of ordinary people* (Milton Keynes: Authentic Media, 2005)

Hooper, C.A. and U. McCluskey, "Introduction: Abuse, the individual and the social" in McCluskey, U. and C.A. Hooper (eds.), *Psychodynamic Perspectives on Abuse: The cost of fear* (London: Jessica Kingsley, 2000), 7–24

Howard, R., *The Rise and Fall of the Nine O'Clock Service: A cult within the Church* (London: Mowbray, 1996)

Hunter, T., *Beyond Foundationalism: Shaping theology in a postmodern context* (Louisville, Ky.: Westminster John Knox Press, 2000)

Johnson, D. and J. Van Vonderen, *The Subtle Power of Spiritual Abuse: Recognizing and escaping spiritual manipulation and false spiritual authority within the Church* (Minneapolis: Bethany House, 1991)

Kolini, E. and P.R. Holmes, *Christ Walks Where Evil Reigned: Responding to the Rwandan genocide* (Colorado Springs: Paternoster, 2008).

Krug, E., et al., *World Report on Violence and Health* (Geneva: World Health Organization, 2002)

Lynch, G., *After Religion: "Generation X" and the search for meaning* (London: Darton, Longman & Todd, 2002)

Macpherson, W., et al., *The Stephen Lawrence Enquiry* (London: The Stationery Office, 1999)

Martin, P., *The Sickening Mind: Brain, behaviour, immunity disease* (London: Flamingo, 1998)

McLaren, B., *A New Kind of Christian: A tale of two friends on a spiritual journey* (San Francisco: Jossey-Bass, 2001)

—, *The Story We Find Ourselves In: Further adventures of a new kind of Christian* (San Francisco: Jossey-Bass, 2003)

Michel, A., "Sexual violence against children in the Bible," in Ammicht Quinn, R., H. Haker and M. Junker-Kenny (eds.), *The Structural Betrayal of Trust* (London: SCM, 2004), 51–60.

Milan, A. and A. Peters, "Couples living apart," *Canadian Social Trends* (Summer 2003)

Mollon, P., *The Fragile Self: The structure of narcissistic disturbances* (London: Whurr Publishers, 1993)

—, "Is human nature intrinsically abusive? Reflections on the psychodynamics of evil" in McCluskey, U. and C.A. Hooper (eds.), *Psychodynamic Perspectives on Abuse: The cost of fear* (London: Jessica Kingsley, 2000), 67–78

Murray, J.P., "TV Violence and Brainmapping in Children," *Psychiatric Times* 18 (2001), 10

Office for National Statistics, "First estimates of the number of people 'Living Apart Together' in Britain," (2005, online). Available from <www.statistics.gov.uk/pdfdir/pop-trends1205.pdf> (accessed 10 June 2006)

Pease, A. and B. Pease, *The Definitive Book of Body Language* (London: Orion, 2004)

Peels, E., *Shadow Sides: The Revelation of God in the Old Testament*, Lalleman, H. (tr.) (Milton Keynes: Paternoster, 2003)

Podles, L. J., *The Church Impotent: The feminization of Christianity* (Dallas, Tex.: Spence Publishing, 1999)

Puttick, E., *Women in New Religions: In search of community, sexuality and spiritual power* (London: Macmillan, 1997)

Quinn, R.E., *Deep Change: Discovering the leader within* (San Francisco, Calif.: Jossey-Bass, 1996)

Randall, P., *Adult Bullying: Perpetrators and victims* (London: Routledge, 1997)

Rawe, J., "Why your boss might start sweating the small stuff: New sensitivity training at the office focuses on all the little ways a tone-deaf manager can demoralize staff," *Time Magazine* (20 March 2006), 42

Staniforth, M. (trans.), Louth, A., (ed.), *Early Christian Writings: Apostolic Fathers* (London: Penguin, 1968)

Stanko, B., et al., *Taking Stock: What do we know about interpersonal violence?* (Egham, Surrey: ESRC Violence Research Programme, 2002)

Tombs, S., "Death and work in Britain," *The Sociological Review* 47 (1999), 2:345–67

Tombs, S. and D. Whyte, *Unmasking the Crimes of the Powerful: Scrutinizing states and corporations* (Oxford: Peter Lang, 2003)

Torjesen, K.J., *When Women Were Priests: Women's leadership in the Early Church and the scandal of their subordination in the rise of Christianity* (San Francisco: Harper, 1993)

Vanzetti, N. and S.W. Duck (eds.), *A Lifetime of Relationships* (Pacific Grove, Calif.: Brooks/Cole, 1996)

Webber, R.E. and P.C. Kenyon, "A Call to an Ancient Evangelical Future," *Christianity Today* 50 (2006), 9:57

White, C. (ed.), *Responding to Violence: A collection of papers relating to child sexual abuse and violence in intimate relationships* (Adelaide: Dulwich Centre Publications, 2003)

Williams, S.B. and P.R. Holmes, *Letting God Heal: From emotional illness to wholeness* (Milton Keynes: Authentic Media, 2004)

—, *Therapeutic Community as a Salugenic Place: Four stages of insider status in a synergistic model of community* (Association of Therapeutic Communities Windsor Conference, 2006), available at <www.lifegivingtrust.org>

Wookey, S., *When a Church Becomes a Cult* (London: Hodder & Stoughton, 1996)

Yaconelli, M. (ed.), *Stories of Emergence: Moving from absolute to authentic* (Grand Rapids: Zondervan, 2003)

Young-Eisendrath, P. and M.E. Miller, "Beyond enlightened self-interest: the psychology of mature spirituality in the 21st century" in Young-Eisendrath, P. and M.E. Miller (eds.), *The Psychology of Mature Spirituality: Integrity, wisdom, transcendence* (London: Routledge, 2000), 1–7

Scripture Index

313

Author Index

Subject Index

For more information or further resources to support the ideas in this book, look at our website

www/lifegivingtrust.org

And see our other books

Trinity In Human Community

Exploring congregatinal life in the image of the social Trinity

Peter R. Holmes

(Milton Keynes: Paternoster, 2006)

Becoming More Like Christ

Introducing a Biblical contemporary journey

Peter R. Holmes

(Milton Keynes: Paternoster, 2007)

Autobiographies of healing and wholeness

Letting God Heal

From emotional illness to wholeness

Peter R. Holmes and Susan B. Williams

(Milton Keynes: Authentic, 2004)

Changed Lives

Extraordinary stories of ordinary people

Peter R. Holmes and Susan B. Williams

(Milton Keynes: Authentic, 2005)

Mission and Social Theology

Christ Walks Where Evil Reigned

Responding to the Rwandan genocide – writing a social theology in a Rwandan setting

Peter R. Holmes and E.M. Kolini

(Colorado Springs: Paternoster, 2008)

Academic articles/texts

Becoming More Human

Exploring the interface of spirituality, discipleship and therapeutic faith community

Peter R. Holmes

(Milton Keynes: Authentic, 2005))

Academic articles/texts

Spirituality

Some disciplinary perspectives

in K. Flanagan and P.C. Jupp (eds.)

The Sociology of Spirituality

(Ashgate, 2007))

Forthcoming

Fasting: A Handbook

Peter R. Holmes

(Colorado Springs: Paternoster)